The Green Investing Handbook

Harriman House

Harriman House is one of the UK's leading independent publishers of financial and business books. Our catalogue covers personal finance, stock market investing and trading, current affairs, business and economics. For more details go to: www.harriman-house.com

The Green Investing Handbook

A detailed investment guide to the technologies and companies involved in the sustainability revolution

by Nick Hanna

HARRIMAN HOUSE LTD

3A Penns Road
Petersfield
Hampshire
GU32 2EW
GREAT BRITAIN

Tel: +44 (0)1730 233870
Fax: +44 (0)1730 233880
Email: enquiries@harriman-house.com
Website: www.harriman-house.com

First published in Great Britain in 2010
Copyright © Harriman House Ltd

The right of Nick Hanna to be identified as Author has been asserted in accordance with the
Copyright, Design and Patents Act 1988.

Set in Palatino 10pt/8.5pt and Rockwell

ISBN: 978-1906659-67-7

British Library Cataloguing in Publication Data
A CIP catalogue record for this book can be obtained from the British Library.

Printed in the United States of America

THIS BOOK IS DEDICATED TO MY LATE FATHER CHRIS HANNA
AND MY UNCLE PIP HANNA, BOTH CITY GENTS IN THEIR TIME.

Contents

Risk warning

No responsibility for loss incurred by any person or corporate body acting or refraining to act as a result of reading material in this book can be accepted by the Publisher or the Author.

The information provided by the Author is not offered as, nor should it be inferred to be, advice or recommendation to readers, since the financial circumstances of readers will vary greatly and investment or trading behaviour which may be appropriate for one reader is unlikely to be appropriate for others.

Every effort has been made to ensure that any company information provided in this book is correct at the time of going to print. The nature of the green sector is that it is fast moving, however, and so company information can change quickly.

PREFACE

About this book

Many analysts and commentators believe that there is a huge, generational change taking place as the world moves inexorably towards a low-carbon economy. This book is aimed at the serious, experienced investor who wants to learn how to profit from this global transition. The book provides a detailed perspective on the opportunities in environmental technologies and services that are being created, as well as an indication of the direction of these trends. Significant attention is also given to the companies operating within the various 'green' technology sectors. The goal is to help the investor make better-informed investment decisions when engaging with a range of complex, innovative and rapidly growing renewables industries. Opportunities as well as pitfalls are marked out, and every layer of the new technologies – and those companies responsible for each part – is looked at in turn from an investment perspective.

A couple of caveats should be mentioned:

1. It would be impossible to cover *all* of the companies operating in these sectors – the numerous firms covered here are by and large intended as a representative cross-section rather than a comprehensive list.

2. This is an extremely fast-moving field. In that respect, it is incredibly exciting: new innovations and solutions to environmental problems are constantly springing out of research labs and business incubators. Because of the speed of technological change which is taking place, there will inevitably be instances where the information presented here has been superseded by events. Although every effort has been made

to ensure that the contents are reliable, accuracy cannot be guaranteed. Readers are advised to undertake their own research and to seek assistance from a professional advisor before making investment decisions. Opinions expressed here are provided on a general basis and should not be considered as a recommendation to buy equities or other financial instruments.

How this book is organised

This book is divided into four parts, which are organised as follows:

Part I: How to Invest

This brief introductory section covers the background of green funds, indices and shares.

Starting with the history of green funds and the issue of just how green some can be, it then looks at whether they can carry more risk than other funds. Green indices and green private equity funds are introduced after this, before looking at the unique challenges that exist when building a green portfolio.

Part II: Where to Invest

This section is divided into chapters covering the ten main areas of environmental services and technology, which are:

- Solar power
- Wind power
- Marine energy
- Geothermal
- Power storage
- Smart grids
- Hydrogen and fuel cells
- Green transport
- Green buildings
- Waste and energy resources

Each chapter outlines current trends within these industries, including an investment overview that provides advice and opinions on where these sectors – and the numerous technologies within them – are heading. This is followed by a round up of some of the individual companies in this sector. Pure-play companies (those that are quoted on accessible stock exchanges) are highlighted in **bold**, and these companies will also have a listing in the Directory (Part III). Companies that are at the development stage and/or privately held are highlighted in *italics*, and these companies are listed under 'Companies to watch' at the end of each chapter. Those companies that are listed on stock exchanges but which are not pure-play investments will have their ticker symbol next to their name at their first mention.

At the end of each chapter a glossary is included for abbreviations and terms specific to that green energy area.

Part III: Directory

The directory is divided into four sections.

1. *Listed companies*: this covers mostly pure-play companies involved in environmental technologies and services that have listings on recognised stock exchanges. The purpose of these profiles is to provide some history and background to the individual companies and their products – they aren't intended to provide detailed financial information or analysis. Instead, you are advised to research individual companies through external sources or through our companion Green Investor website (www.thegreeninvestor.co.uk), which provides links to financial data.

2. *Green funds*: this provides background details on a cross-section of green funds, including comment from fund managers.

3. *Green indices and exchange traded funds*: this covers exchange traded funds (ETFs) and their underlying indices.

4. *Green private equity funds*: this section provides full details on private equity funds.

Part IV: Resources

Additional resources on green finance and investment in general can be found in Part IV. These include:

- subscription services specialising in cleantech finance

- useful news websites and RSS feeds

- green and ethical banking services

- green microfinance

- green and ethical financial advisors.

INTRODUCTION

"There is no doubt that the shift to a low carbon world is now underway. The implications of this for the global economy are immense and the opportunities that this is creating for investors from global institutional pension funds, fund management organisations and individual retail investors are becoming increasingly clear."

Investment Opportunities for a Low Carbon World[1]

Time has now been called on the old-world economy, which is depleting global resources at an unsustainable rate. The scale and complexity of the challenges involved in transforming the economy to make it more sustainable will require the development of solutions spanning a multitude of technologies and processes. This will in turn create huge opportunities for investors in the energy and environmental sectors, as companies and countries all over the globe compete with each other in the transition to a low-carbon economy.

Among other factors, the threat of peak oil (the point when the maximum rate of global oil extraction is reached), the lurking menace of climate change, and the accumulation of environmental problems such as a shortage of basic natural resources (including food and water) have combined to alert the world's governments, businesses and communities to the seriousness of the problem.

The world has switched remarkably rapidly in the space of just a few years from a position where climate change was seen as an unbearable (and unmentionable) burden to one where countries are competing with each other to provide solutions. No one wants to be left behind in the race to win market share in the technologies of the future, whether this will be electric cars or smart appliances which reduce home energy usage. Companies which prioritise climate change will be the ones to profit in the long term.

The global nature of this transformation to a low-carbon economy is presenting investment opportunities spanning almost every sector of society as innovation drives sustainable development forward.

Even the well-documented failure of the Copenhagen climate summit in December 2009 won't stall the momentum. Although Copenhagen failed to produce legally binding emissions targets, it was the first time that 193 countries from around the world endorsed the science that says we must if possible prevent warming of more than two degrees centigrade, and engaged in discussion on the actions that needed to be taken. This marked a distinct shift from the positions held previously by the Chinese and Indian governments, for instance, who had maintained that it was their right to pursue economic growth at any cost. Both of these countries are now making massive investments in renewable sources of energy.

So, what about the performance and development of green companies?

Although green technology shares had a patchy year in 2009 with some sectors (energy efficiency and power performance) gaining strongly whilst others (solar, wind, and biomass) languished, the overall trend was upwards, with crucial indices such as the Wilderhill New Energy Global Energy Innovation Index (NEX) performing well. "We happen to think this is a sign of investor optimism when it comes to how cleantech will perform throughout the new decade as a whole," says Jon Mainwaring, editor of *Quoted Cleantech*. "It's our belief that 2010-2019 will be notable as the decade when big business gets serious about cleantech."[2] Indeed, many large corporations are already moving in this direction (see 'Jolly green giants?' on p.21).

"If low-carbon thinking has become a normalised component of political and corporate thinking over the past three or four years," writes James Murray at BusinessGreen, "2010 is the year when it really begins the long journey towards changing both the way businesses operate and people live." Murray says he thinks 2010 will be the year when "the concept of a green business become meaningless," because all business will need to be green.[3]

It is worth bearing in mind, also, that none of the developments outlined in this book are taking place in isolation. On the contrary, they are all feeding off one another, developing a matrix of opportunities in different business areas. Renewable power, smart grids, green transport, new battery technologies, zero carbon buildings and numerous other sectors of the economy are just some of the more notable places where synergies are becoming apparent and investment opportunities developing in perhaps unexpected ways. It is a very exciting and dynamic time to be a green investor.

"Investment provides the bridge between an unsustainable present and a sustainable future. Investors have a unique role to play in shifting the engine of commerce into sustainability gear [and] are capable of creating a sustainability revolution."

Sustainable Investing: The Art of Long-Term Performance[4]

Support of governments in the development of green business

The trends towards green business will be bolstered by support from government policies globally. Analysts at Bloomberg New Energy Finance estimate that 700 new pieces of legislation have recently been passed around the world promoting clean energy – partly thanks to the spotlight thrown on these issues by the Copenhagen process.[5] Renewable energy policy targets now exist in 73 countries, with stiff renewable energy standards in place in 49 countries, according to the Paris-based Renewable Energy Policy Network for the 21st Century.[6]

In Britain the Climate Change Act of 2008 created a legally binding framework to achieve a mandatory 80% cut in the UK's carbon emissions by 2050 (compared to 1990 levels), with an intermediate target of 34% by 2020. A Carbon Reduction Commitment for large business has also been introduced, alongside other energy efficiency initiatives. In April 2010 the UK introduced its first feed-in-tariff (FIT), a mechanism to stimulate the development of the domestic renewables sector.

In May 2010, the new Con/Lib coalition government announced various green measures including promoting smart meters, a network of charging stations for electric cars, promoting energy from waste, the development of the underwater grid in the North Sea, and the creation of a Green Investment Bank, along with new products such as green bonds and green ISAs to encourage investment in green infrastructure.

Elsewhere in the world, it is a similar story. The European Union (EU) has set a target to cut at least 20% of greenhouse gas emissions from all primary energy sources by 2020 (compared to 1990 levels) and cuts of 50% by 2050. In the US, stimulus funding from the American Recovery and Reinvestment Act (ARRA) has already provided around $100bn of investment into the cleantech sector, with more yet to come. The US government is also expected to beef up funding for renewables in the wake of BP's Gulf of Mexico oil spill, with President Obama making a renewed call in June 2010 for the US to embark on a future of clean energy.

Major economies have pledged a total of $177bn towards the development of clean energy technologies and the developed world has also agreed to provide $30bn over the next three years to help mitigate the cost of slowing emissions growth in the developing world.[7] A figure of $100bn a year has also been mooted to aid the transition to clean energy globally, although where this is going to come from and who is going to administer it are unclear. The International Energy Agency estimates that $10.5trn needs to be spent on clean energy between 2010 and 2030 to prevent a potentially catastrophic rise in temperatures.[8]

Even if the ambitious targets for renewable energy set by Britain, the EU and other countries globally are not met in full, attaining even a proportion of this growth represents a massive opportunity for environmental services and technologies. Of course there will be blips on this roadmap but there will also be many surprising moves forward, as the best and brightest entrepreneurial talents in the world apply their skills and knowledge to climate change solutions.

As evidence of the expanding investment opportunities, the number of investment funds targeting this sector has grown from around ten in 2004 to more than 30 in 2009, many of them managed by high street names such as Barclays, HSBC and Deutsche Bank. According to Mark Dampier of independent financial advisor Hargreaves Lansdown "the theme of industrial revolution will be what drives the investment market for the next 20 years."[9]

Dampier's comments point to the fact that, taking a long-term perspective, the environmental investment theme is in its infancy and will continue to play out over the next couple of decades and more. This view is supported by Mark Hoskin from investment advisor Holden & Partners, who noted that "climate change will continue to be one of the principal drivers behind world politics and economics in the 21st century."[10]

The aim of this book is to provide committed investors with a thorough and authoritative reference work for understanding and engaging profitably with these opportunities. *The Green Investing Handbook* should prove essential reading for anyone interested in making money in this very diverse sector, whether an institutional investor, financial advisor, venture capitalist, or any other serious financial actor. It may also prove of interest to dedicated private investors hoping to gain a stronger understanding of the technology and outlook behind the biggest growth story of the 21st century.

NICK HANNA
JUNE 2010

HOW TO INVEST I

T his section covers:

- the background to green funds; how green they can be; and the risk they contain

- green indices and private equity funds

- the challenges unique to building up a green portfolio.

Both actively managed funds (such as units trusts, investment trusts, etc) and passive funds (such as trackers or ETFs) can have a part to play in a well-balanced green portfolio. Some of the pertinent issues and other considerations you will need to take on board when making green investment decisions are outlined below.

Ethical vs Green Funds

There is a lot of confusion around different kinds of funds in this sector, with considerable overlap between what are variously known as ethical, green, sustainable, cleantech or climate change funds.

Ethical investing started over 100 years ago with the Quakers and Methodists screening out companies involved in alcohol and gambling when they decided to put money in the stock market. This became known as socially responsible investing (SRI) and it grew steadily through the 20th century as more and more investors demanded that social and environmental criteria were taken into account when considering which shares to buy. The first UK ethical fund was launched by Friends Provident in 1984 and today there are over 100 green and ethical funds to choose from.

Traditional ethical funds are involved with a positive and negative selection process, where money is invested in companies they judge to be making a positive contribution to the world and withheld from companies they judge not to be.

The three main approaches for traditional ethical funds are:

1. **Negative screening**: avoids 'sin stocks' such as tobacco, arms manufacturers, alcohol, pornography and so on. Also avoids environmentally polluting industries, or those with a poor human rights record.

2. **Positive screening**: bias towards socially useful or community-oriented companies, as well as those with good environmental policies, equal opportunities and management transparency.

3. **Engagement**: this 'third leg' of ethical investing seeks to influence a company's policies or corporate behaviour for the better by applying pressure as shareholders for positive change.

Ethical funds have also traditionally been classified into light green and dark green funds, depending on how strict they are at applying social and environmental criteria. However, although the green label is often applied to ethical funds, and the terms 'socially responsible', 'ethical', 'green' and 'sustainable' are often used interchangeably, this is not always appropriate. For instance, many ethical funds have holdings in mainstream stocks such as banks, telecoms providers, outsourcing companies, supermarkets or media conglomerates – and there is nothing intrinsically sustainable or green about these companies. Conversely, green thinking is also deeply embedded in ethical ideals so that ethical funds have a tendency to be very forward-thinking and progressive – hence open to green investment trends.

The rise of the green fund

Whilst traditional ethical funds have continued to grow on the back of green concerns, a new phenomenon has been the arrival of a different breed of *green* funds that are specifically geared towards profiting from the transition to a low-carbon economy. The first properly targeted green fund, the Jupiter Ecology Fund, was launched in 1988, but over the last few years many more have been launched and to some extent they are beginning to eclipse run-of-the-mill ethical funds. In *Green Money*, Sarah Pennells notes that:

> "Today, some ethical finance experts predict that our current appetite for funds that take climate change and environmental factors into account could overtake our enthusiasm for ones that invest ethically. As oil reserves decline and problems caused by climate change become more evident, we are likely to see an even bigger number of green money products on offer."[11]

The big year for green funds was 2007, when numbers were swelled by the addition of funds from Schroders, Calvert, Pictet, Bank Sarasin, HSBC and others.

Are all green funds as green as they say they are?

Whilst many green funds carry 'climate change' in the title, it pays to look beneath the label to see what they are actually investing in. This is true of any mutual fund of course, but it is particularly the case with green investing since the definition can be very broad. There is also an element of having to beware of 'greenwash': old economy companies slapping on a veneer of green responsibility to cash in on the trend, when in fact they have not changed their carbon-intensive ways at all.

'Clean energy' and 'alternative energy' are other labels which deserve some scrutiny, since these can often include nuclear power. Some investors may feel more nuclear power is essential to a low-carbon future, but others may have objections and prefer not to invest in nuclear companies.

More positively, some funds have chosen to extend the boundaries of what is meant by 'sustainable' into perfectly legitimate areas. The IM WHEB Sustainability fund, for instance, is divided equally between what the managers believe are the three main growth areas of the 21st century: climate change, water and demographics. Similarly, the Henderson Industries of the Future fund revolves around ten separate themes, which include knowledge industries and health services alongside more traditional green threads such as energy efficiency and sustainable transport.

Those who wish to invest in green companies should research a fund before selecting it, to find out what types of companies and industries the fund has holdings in; most funds are clear enough about their investment principles and how they are diversifying within the green / sustainable / climate change market.

While ethical funds may be predisposed to consider green investments, many of the new green funds do not have any ethical criteria. This has its advantages though – as Brigid Benson of the Gaeia Partnership says:

"I think that greener environmental funds that do not have any specific ethical remit have a strong place in the market because it means that the fund managers will probably have good quality scientific knowledge and will be encouraging and putting money into companies, large and small, that are going to be focusing on either energy conservation or renewable energy, and they do not want to be constrained by an ethical remit."

However, it is also notable that green funds with an ethical background seem to do better than those that do not. In their third annual *Climate Change Investment Guide*, Holden & Partners noted that three of the top five general climate change funds came from investment houses with ethical research teams based in the UK (Henderson, F&C and Jupiter: see box for the full list). "We're always keen to point out that ethically screened funds do not implicitly invest in climate change, but the extra resources these investment houses have is undoubtedly giving them a lead in the climate change market," they comment.[12]

Top performing funds

The five best performing climate change funds in 2009 were:

1. Impax Environmental Markets

2. Henderson Industries of the Future

3. Schroders Global Climate Change Fund

4. F&C Climate Opportunities

5. Jupiter Ecology

Holden & Partners, who compiled this table, comment that the best performing fund over one and two years was the Schroders Global Climate Change fund. Over three years the Impax Environmental Markets fund excelled and outperformed the MSCI World Index by a multiple of four, while Henderson Industries of the Future was the top performing climate change fund with an ethical screen. All of the five funds shown outperformed the MSCI World over different periods.

Specialised green funds

Within climate change funds, you can also choose smaller, speciality funds targeting particular areas. For instance, both First State and Impax run funds aimed at companies tackling environmental problems in Asia. First State launched their Asia Pacific Sustainability fund in 2005, whereas Impax's Asian Environmental Markets has been going since October 2009.

Do green funds carry more risk than other funds?

Whilst socially responsible investing was formerly driven by morality, now it is driven by the rising price of carbon – and this has given managers with an SRI background a head start on their mainstream counterparts in being able to spot the commercial opportunities and reduce the risks of environmental investing.

However, some experts maintain that green funds are intrinsically more risky than their mainstream (non-green) counterparts for several reasons: firstly, they tend to invest in small and mid-cap firms, which suffered in the recession, and secondly they tend to be reliant on government policy to drive growth in green industries – and often this goes astray. Ethical funds were also badly hit by being overweight in financials in 2008/2009.

Other advisors maintain that the transition to a low-carbon economy is a massive structural change and that the drivers behind green funds are not going away; investors looking at this sector need to be thinking in the medium to long term.

What to look for in a green investment fund

- Quality of management and the period of time the management has been in place

- the fund's ranking against its peers (see Resources)

- cost, as expressed in the total expense ratio (TER)

- fund description, to confirm the fund fits with your ethical/green criteria.

More information on funds

For detailed information on funds, the Ethical Investment Research and Information Service (www.eiris.org) has a database of around 90 ethical/green funds with a handy checklist so you can see at a glance what criteria each fund uses.

➡ Financial information services, p.333

➡ Green and ethical information services, p.334

Green and ethical indices

There are a growing number of specialised indices tracking the performance of companies in environmental technologies. The WilderHill New Energy Global Innovation Index, or NEX, which tracks the performance of 88 clean energy stocks worldwide, is one such benchmark. There are also sector-specific indices such as the ISE Global Wind Energy Index and the MAC Global Solar Energy Index. Indices are used extensively by researchers, fund managers and brokers for analysis, the measurement of performance, asset allocation, portfolio hedging and so forth. For investors they can be useful for researching specific sectors or companies in particular countries. More pertinently, indices are used for the creation of passively-managed finds such as trackers and ETFs.

➡ Green and ethical indices, p.317

Green ETFs

There has been an enormous growth in the value of funds invested in ETFs in recent years. One of the largest ETF providers, iShares, claims that more than £38bn was invested in 800 ETFs available in 2009.

The general consensus is that it makes more sense to buy ETFs in large, efficient markets such as the UK or US, where it is more difficult for the fund manager to outperform an index. In specialised (and possibly more volatile) areas such as green and ethical investments, it may be better to have a fund manager who is able to react to trends and get in and out of certain themes where appropriate; there is a sense that with markets that require specialist knowledge careful stock-picking is more likely to turn up a winner. This may well be the case with, say, Asian environmental stocks, or high-concept green technology companies which the general market will be a long way from understanding. Also, wild fluctuations in solar stocks over the past year or two have demanded considerable skill from fund managers in their timings.

However, ETFs in the green arena do still have something to offer investors. They present the option to choose between funds that track the whole green sector or just specific sub-sectors such as wind, solar or smart grids. Therefore, an investor in green ETFs can play these themes as and when appropriate. If you think that it is time the sun shone on solar stocks it is very easy to buy into a solar ETF without having to go through the detailed analysis required for individual stock-picking. Of course, it is still important to check the constituents of ETFs yourself to make sure that they have got the right mix of technologies.

➡ Green ETFs, p.320

Green private equity funds

Venture capital (VC) finance is traditionally thought of as the province of wealthy philanthropists or bold entrepreneurs who can afford to gamble millions on futuristic and risky start-up ventures.

The good news is that these opportunities need not be confined solely to Californian billionaires – some of the opportunities are as easy as trading an AIM (Alternative Investment Market)-listed stock, though others are private equity funds which require minimum investments of £25,000 or more. Any investments you make should of course be considered as part of a balanced portfolio, taking into account your own risk profile.

A fascinating glimpse into what the future holds for green technology is provided by the example of Khosla Ventures, the VC outfit created by Vinod Khosla, originally a co-founder of Sun Microsystems (www.khoslaventures.com). Khosla's portfolio contains an eclectic mix of hi-tech companies involved in everything from enhanced geothermal to future fuels, and low-carbon cements to electrochromic glass technologies. One of the world's top venture capital investors in green technologies, Khosla announced he was forming a new fund in 2009 which would invest a further $1.1bn in high-risk cleantech innovation and science experiments.

Other high profile green venture capitalists are less forthcoming about their investments. Al Gore's Generation Investment Management, for instance, has strong statements of principle but declines to provide details of its investments.

The Quercus Trust, another major VC player in the green arena, is notoriously secretive. Founded by David Gelbaum, a teenage maths prodigy who later made his fortune in hedge funds, the Quercus Trust has investments in around 50 cleantech companies which range from quoted stocks such as Ascent Solar, Beacon Power and Axion Power International to cutting-edge technology firms such as Nanoptek (solar thermal to produce hydrogen), Cyrium Technologies (quantum dots), and Octillion (PV windows). A dedicated environmentalist, Gelbaum maintains a low profile and neither he nor his company even has a website: details of where Quercus is invested have been unearthed by journalists at Greentech Media and on renewable energy blogs such as UN (Unlimited Natural) Energy (www.unernergy.org).

The general principle of most of these funds is to develop and manage small firms that can eventually be floated, with the majority aiming for an exit in the form of an initial public offering (IPO) within about three to five years. Some are simply taking stakes in early-stage companies which are already listed, others are aiming to incubate companies which are developing intellectual property arising from university research centres. Imperial Innovations, originally a wholly owned subsidiary of London's Imperial College, is one of these. Today it is one of the largest incubators in the UK, with stakes in around 80 companies involved in cleantech, software, information technology and engineering. It is traded on AIM, so it is easy to access.

Other AIM-traded funds include the Ludgate Environmental Fund, Low Carbon Accelerator and the Specialist Energy Group. These companies either invest in directly owned subsidiaries or a mix of private and public companies.

Moving up a stage in complexity, after this there are venture capital companies offering specialist funds, some of which have tax advantages. These include the Ventus funds from Climate Change Capital, which are venture capital trusts, and the Oxford Gateway funds from Oxford Capital, which are classified as Enterprise Investment Schemes (EIS). However, the tax regulations around this are being reviewed in 2010: check with your financial advisor or HM Revenue and Customs.

Finally, there are private share issues from Triodos, the ethical bank. Their Triodos Renewable Energy Funds are mostly invested in on-shore wind farms in the UK.

➤ Green private equity funds, p.323

HMRC information

Enterprise Investment Schemes: www.hmrc.gov.uk/eis

Venture Capital Trusts:
www.hmrc.gov.uk/manuals/vcmmanual/VCM60020.htm

Building a Green Portfolio

"Clean tech's rising tide won't necessarily lift all of its boats: individual technology niches, companies and investors will no doubt see some stormy times."

The Cleantech Revolution[13]

One of the first rules of investing is, of course, that different investments suit different people or institutions at different stages of their lives. This applies to green investments as much as it does any other kind, so when starting to build a green portfolio you need to be clear about your investment aims and how long you are planning to invest for.

You might need to be prepared to see some loss in the value of your investments in the short term in exchange for medium to long-term gains. Brigid Benson of the Gaeia Partnership says:

> "If you choose a good fund, or good companies, then be prepared to stick with them in the medium term at least. Do not look for short-term results – it could be typically three years before that company is moving into positive territory. Evaluations may well dip in the early years as they invest more or ramp up production but if they really are responding to a need – for energy conservation or renewable energy, for instance – then hopefully that company will come right in the end."

Overall, it is the companies that can provide solutions to environmental issues – not just climate change – that will add real value. And identifying these businesses now will give investors the possibility of handsome profits in the long term. The global nature of these markets means that there is huge potential for big rewards, which is why the world's largest economies are battling it out to gain market share.

"Climate change investments are not necessarily about being ethical, although that's a nice, warm feeling which you may get as a result of it – it is actually about making money," says Mark Hoskins of Holden & Partners. "The people who get this first will make the money, because the market will eventually get there."

Investing Tips

Know yourself: as usual, identify your investment aims, what you can afford to invest (and possibly lose) and the level of risk you are comfortable with.

Take a long view of this sector: only invest money you do not expect to need for the next five or ten years. You should be prepared to ride out short-term volatility and a possible fall in the value of your investments in exchange for long-term gains.

Do not put all your eggs in one basket: as with any investments, diversification is important. This is even more the case with green investment; positions should be across sectors, asset classes or geographical areas.

Decide what proportion of your portfolio is going to be green. Some people are committed 100% and green is the be all and end all. For others, green is just part of the picture. A sensible approach is to balance your green equity investments with solid holdings in bonds, treasury stocks, etc.

Investing in green companies

"Do not use sustainability research in isolation: always combine it with more traditional fundamental and/or quantitative investment research. Being a sustainability leader does not mean that a company is worth investing in at any price, at any particular time."

Investing in a Sustainable World: Why Green is the New Color of Money on Wall Street[14]

When researching green companies, as well as consulting the usual media sources of investment information, it is worth considering specialised green finance services that will keep you up to date with company news, profiles, prospective stock market floatations and so forth. One of the most reasonably priced subscription services is *Cleantech Investor* (www.cleantechinvestor.com) and the most comprehensive news service is Bloomberg New Energy Finance, which also issues a free weekly newsletter by email. There are many more industry and green business-oriented RSS, email or web-based services to help keep you up to date.

➡ Green technologies news sources, p. 331

➡ Green business information services, p.332

The universe of green stocks

The majority of listed companies featured in this book are small to medium-sized companies. There is a good reason for this, in that it is more likely a smaller company is going to be able to innovate rapidly and introduce new technologies. This is not always the case (see 'Jolly green giants?' on p.21), but they are often able to move more quickly in response to events – in this case, the challenges of climate change.

There are caveats of course: these stocks tend to be inherently more volatile, with lower liquidity levels and a much higher risk profile. They have often borrowed heavily to start the business, and might be dependent on a single product or technology working and being successful. Larger companies can afford to have failed enterprises, but if a smaller company is completely dependent on just one technology or new product that fails, then it might go under.

However, it is far easier to grow from a small base and the potential rewards are greater: it takes an awful lot to shift the share price of a £20bn company but a £100m company might well double its share price within a couple of years (or even months).

Further, ground-breaking discoveries or disruptive technologies are more likely to be manifest in this kind of fast-moving sector than traditional investment areas, usually with dramatic consequences on companies' market capitalisations. Smaller companies are also less well researched by brokers, increasing your chances of finding a gem, and they are more likely to be the subject of a takeover bid – which can create significant added value for you, the shareholder.

In his classic book *The Zulu Principle*, Jim Slater elaborated on his preference for investing in smaller companies with above average growth prospects, largely based on the dictum that "elephants do not gallop". In other words, the share prices of larger companies are less likely to take off at a trot and surprise the market. There is far more to it than this, of course, and Slater also advises being extremely careful when dealing with smaller companies. Slater wrote:

> "The principles for selecting [small companies'] shares remain exactly the same as for larger companies, but the differences between being right or wrong is much more extreme … proceed gingerly and with the utmost caution."[15]

However, it is no longer the case that just smaller companies are involved in green technologies. The 'investment universe' of green stocks has changed considerably in the last few years as the sector has matured.

The rising number of companies in the green area

A decade or so ago, investment managers were limited to around 200 companies operating in this sector – now that number has multiplied many times. Of course this depends on what criteria are being applied. Clare Brook, co-manager of WHEB Asset Management's Sustainability Fund, imposed a bottom limit of $200m on their investment universe and still found that there were 400 companies to choose from. If their lower limit was $50m, she estimates that the number would be "a couple of thousand or more," which would be overwhelming, so the fund took the decision that 400 stocks was plenty of companies to look at.

Charlie Thomas, director of Jupiter Asset Management, sets no lower limit on their investment choices within the green themes determined by their funds. The Jupiter Ecology Fund is global, with a bias towards smaller and medium-sized companies. "This universe is about 1000 companies today", he says. "We have greater diversity by style, by size, by geography and that is ever-increasing. We are continually getting new floats coming to the market, in both Europe and North America, and increasingly the Asian market."

This highlights another important point about the range of companies involved in green technologies and their representation in this book. That is, there simply is not a sufficient range of UK-traded stocks to build a viable portfolio (or indeed a fund or an ETF) from these alone. *Therefore, as a green investor you have to be thinking globally.*

Jolly green giants?

As climate change has moved up the political agenda, larger companies are increasingly moving into this space, although some have been quicker than others to seize the opportunity.

General Electric

Among the first large companies to move into the green sector was General Electric (NYSE: GE), one of the world's biggest companies. GE Energy is a leading global supplier of power generation equipment for coal, oil, natural gas and nuclear energy, as well as renewable technologies.

Since 2002, GE has installed over 12,000 units of its workhorse 1.5MW turbine globally – making this one of the world's most popular wind turbines. The company is now competing head-to-head with Siemens on next generation technologies such as direct-drive turbines and advanced carbon fibre blades.

In solar power, GE has stakes in PrimeStar Solar (thin-film), SolarEdge (power control systems for solar panels), Soliant Energy (CSP, or concentrating solar power, for commercial rooftops) and Fotowatio (a Spanish solar power developer). In smart grids, GE has invested heavily in metering and software start-ups and is developing complete smart grid networks. It has also developed a 'smart charging station' for electric vehicles (EVs). The company has significant interests in power storage and is a major investor in lithium-ion specialist A123 Systems. It has developed advanced batteries for a hybrid train and built a new $100m battery plant in the US.

These investments form part of their *ecomagination* programme, which aims to position GE as a champion of green technologies. However, the company is still investing heavily in oil, gas and power infrastructure. Cynics say that GE is planning to have its cake and eat it too – the ecomagination portfolio includes sales of jet engines as well as oil and gas exploration equipment.

Siemens

The European engineering giant Siemens (ETR:SIE) is going head-to-head with GE in many key areas of renewable energy. Roughly a quarter of its total revenues come from wind power and it is a global leader in offshore wind turbines.

In solar, its main focus is on the development of large-capacity solar plants in the Mediterranean region and it is also a major supplier of steam turbines for solar thermal plants. In power supply, the company's high-voltage systems will make the transmission of renewable power across large distances more economically feasible. It also has interests in advanced electric propulsion and hybrid engines for ships, and a stake in tidal energy company Marine Current Turbines.

Siemens had anticipated around €15bn in new orders for infrastructure projects as a result of the various government stimulus programmes announced in 2009, with around 40% of that focused on green technologies. The company's target is to increase annual sales of environmental technologies to €25bn by 2011.

United Technologies (UTC)

Another global corporation with growing interests in green technologies is the US industrial conglomerate United Technologies (NYSE: UTX). It has divisions that make helicopters, aircraft engines, elevators and security systems but it also has significant investments in geothermal power (through its subsidiary Pratt & Whitney) and fuel cells. The company diversified into wind power in 2009 when it took a 49.5% stake in ailing turbine manufacturer Clipper Windpower, hinting that it might increase this stake in time. The company has expressed an interest in further investments in renewable energies.

Panasonic and other Asian companies

Japanese giant Panasonic (TYO: 6752) has apparently undergone a green transformation, shifting its focus from consumer electronics to energy-saving products for homes and buildings. In 2009 Panasonic bought a controlling stake in rival Sanyo (TYO: 6764) for $4.6bn, thus acquiring the world's largest manufacturer of lithium-ion batteries as well as one of Asia's largest solar cell and thin-film manufacturers.

Panasonic already makes fuel cells and LED (light emitting diode) lighting, and has interests in smart grid technologies. The company's next step is selling complete, wired-up 'green homes' outfitted with energy-saving appliances. The company says that it will invest $1bn over the next three years in integrating energy-saving and renewable technologies into homes and buildings.

Samsung, South Korea's largest company, announced in May 2010 that it plans to 'go green', investing around $20bn in healthcare and green energy over the next decade. It plans to expand principally in solar cells, rechargeable batteries for hybrid vehicles, LED systems and medical technologies.

Elsewhere in Asia, shipbuilding and other industrial conglomerates are moving into the wind turbine business in a big way (see p.63 for more details). Throughout this book, in areas as diverse as building technologies and green transport, there are many more examples of this kind.

Google

One of the more high profile conversions has been search giant Google (NASDAQ: GOOG), which some commentators believe is moving from being an internet company to a renewable energy company. In 2008 Google presented its Clean Energy 2030 plan, which outlines a pathway to wean the US off fossils fuels and into carbon-free energy by 2030. The company has since made investments of more than $45m in three main areas (concentrated solar thermal, enhanced geothermal and high-altitude wind) with the stated aim of making renewable energy cheaper than coal. In addition, it also took an equity stake of $38m in two North Dakota wind farms in May 2010. Naturally enough, it is also investing in home energy management software (smart metering) and is working with GE on applications to integrate electric cars into smart grids. More surprisingly, the company has recently gained a licence to become an electricity wholesaler in the US market.

Deciding whether to invest in these large companies

Whether or not you choose to invest in these larger companies will depend partly on your attitude to green investing in general – are you looking for pure-play companies that are completely involved in green or ethical industries, or are you prepared to diversify your portfolio (and perhaps reduce your risk) with broader choices?

It is worth bearing in mind that, even though green technologies constitute only a proportion of these company's total revenues, because the companies are so big, when they start moving in the right direction the amount of revenues coming from that particular area are going to be much higher than they would be from a small or medium-sized company which is 100% green.

Basic green energy glossary

ARRA: American Recovery and Reinvestment Act (stimulus bill)

CO2:   carbon dioxide

DECC: Department of Energy and Climate Change (UK)

DOE: Department of Energy (USA)

FIT: feed-in-tariff (payments to consumers for generating their own renewable energy, either for their own consumption or for feeding in to the grid)

GHG: greenhouse gas

GHGE: greenhouse gas emissions

GW: gigawatt

kW: kilowatt

kWh: kilowatt hour

MW: megawatt

MWh: megawatt hour

TW: terawatt

W: watt

WHERE TO INVEST

II

Now we come to look at the ten main areas of environmental services and technology, which are:

- Solar power

- Wind power

- Marine energy

- Geothermal

- Power storage

- Smart grids

- Hydrogen and fuel cells

- Green transport

- Green buildings

- Waste and energy resources

Each chapter within Part II outlines current trends within one of these ten industries, including an investment overview that provides thoughts on where these sectors are heading. This is followed by a detailed round-up of some of the individual companies in the sector. Pure-play companies that are quoted on accessible stock exchanges are highlighted in **bold** and these companies will also have a listing in the Directory (Part III). Companies that are at the development stage or that are privately held are highlighted in *italics*, and these companies are listed under 'Companies to watch' at the end of each chapter. Those companies that are listed on stock exchanges but which are not pure-play investments will have their ticker symbol next to their name at their first mention.

SOLAR POWER 1

"Like the first silicon revolution, the next one will see industries transformed and massive wealth created. Solar millionaires and billionaires will emerge, and markets may even experience a bubble or two of speculative excitement. However, in the end … we will arrive at a world that is safer, cleaner and wealthier for industrialised countries and developing ones and in which solar energy will play a dominant role in meeting our collective energy needs."

Solar Revolution: The Economic Transformation of the Global Energy Industry[16]

Introduction

Solar energy is by far the most abundant source of power we have available and has the capacity to provide for the energy needs of the earth's population many thousands of times over – if an economical way of harvesting it can be found. The most commonly quoted figure is that 120,000 terawatts (TW) of solar energy hits the land parts of earth every year and the world currently uses only a fraction of this amount – between 13 to 16TW – annually, a figure that is expected to rise to 20TW by 2020.[17]

Although the energy from the sun itself is free, capturing and converting it into energy is anything but. The challenge has been to achieve this at a reasonable cost in order to arrive at grid parity – the point whereby solar power costs the same or less than conventionally generated fuels. This moment is predicted to arrive soon in several places that have high electricity costs and lots of sunshine.

Globally, the solar industry has taken huge strides in recent years to improve efficiency, bring down costs and develop new ways of capturing the sun's energy. At the same time, the industry has had a rough ride. A shortage of polysilicon (the material from which solar cells are made) was rapidly followed by a glut; cut-throat competition has led to disruption throughout the supply chain; and uncertainties over government incentives, as well as the global recession, have had a destabilising impact.

During these challenging times, many investors and fund managers have kept solar out of their portfolios, or reduced their exposure to a minimum. But there are signs that the worst is behind us and green fund managers are re-appraising solar companies.

Solar technology is advancing at an extremely rapid pace, as this relatively young industry expands globally. The diversity of technologies is also increasing, so before plunging into it investors should take some time to distinguish their CIGs from their CPVs and power towers from parabolic troughs.

Solar efficiencies

Energy efficiency is a key metric in determining power output (and profitability) for solar companies. The first solar cells in the 1950s had an energy conversion rate of around 6%. Commercial multicrystalline cells today can reach 16-18%, with laboratory modules as high as 40%. The best performing thin-film technology is copper indium gallium selenide (CIGS), which currently delivers 10-12% in production (and 20% in the laboratory). Cadmium telluride (CdTe) and amorphous silicon (a-Si) perform less well, although improvements are constantly being made.

Investing in solar power

"Although the solar industry has a huge amount of upside, there will periodically be bumps on the road when stock prices become overvalued and when profit margins decline to possibly push the weaker players out of the market. It is therefore important to focus investment dollars on the high-technology players that have strategically-defensible positions in the industry and that will be the leaders in driving the production cost reductions."

Profiting from Clean Energy[18]

Overview

Bull points

- There is huge growth potential in what is a very young industry.

- Costs are rapidly approaching grid parity.

- Solar cells are getting more efficient.

- Legislation is driving growth.

- Innovation pipeline is strong.

- Solar power is less conspicuous and attracts less objections than onshore wind farms.

- Solar technology can be placed in locations where it doesn't compete with food production, such as on rooftops or in deserts.

- Solar panels are relatively maintenance free.

Bear points

- The silicon supply is subject to boom/bust cycles.

- Solar is still dependent on government subsidies.

- Industry shake-out is still causing problems.

Solar stocks might have appeared to be a bit of a hot potato for investors in the last few years. The recent solar story, and the reason for this instability, goes something like this: due to the introduction of government subsidies and feed-in tariffs in Spain and Germany, demand for solar panels escalated rapidly in 2007 and 2008. This new demand resulted in a massive expansion in production capacity from 2008-2009, particularly in Asia. This eventually transformed into a huge excess of solar panels and then the recession occurred, leading to a reduction in the number of panels being ordered and more surpluses. Spain then shut down its subsidy programme, making the situation even worse. Germany has since announced, in early 2010, more reductions in subsidies. These events created considerable instability in the solar photovoltaic industry, which is now having to deal with lower module prices, lower demand and lower profits.

Analysts anticipate that this recent period of instability will soon give way to an era of expansion, fuelled by government incentives, outlined overleaf.

Expansion of the solar sector

Incentives from Asian governments

Even though some European countries are scaling back subsidies, other countries are stepping in with incentives for solar – particularly in Asia.

China has a *Golden Sun* programme, which will help build out an extra 624MW of solar throughout the country; the programme will cover hundreds of projects at major industrial sites, some 35 large-scale solar farms and 27 projects to bring solar power to off-grid regions. Major manufacturers including Suntech Power, Renesola and Yingli Green Energy have all announced expansion plans on the back of this programme. China currently has an installed base of around 140MW and their target is 20GW by 2020 – so there is enormous scope for producers in helping to meet this goal. China is also expected to announce a new FIT in 2010, which will boost growth.

Not to be outdone, India has unveiled plans for its own national solar programme, with plans to install 20GW by 2022. The first tranche of projects, costing $900m, will see 1GW of capacity installed by 2012, primarily across the desert regions of northwest of the country. Both PV and CSP are competing in this market.

In December 2009 the US administration signed a green partnership with India, whereby the countries will cooperate on clean technologies including solar. More than 12 Indian and US cities will partner to jointly promote solar power, with the US National Renewable Energy Laboratory (NREL) helping India's Solar Energy Centre to map out the country's solar potential.

In Taiwan, the government has allocated $1.3bn for green technologies, with a strong emphasis on solar. In South Korea, the government's Green Energy Roadmap will see $339m invested in solar PV by 2012, with the goal of 2GW of manufacturing capacity in 2010 and 3GW thereafter.

It is predicted that there will be a big shift from traditional solar markets to the Asia Pacific region as these programmes kick in.

US growth forecasts

The US is also on course for a huge upsurge in solar, according to a report from GTM (Greentech Media) Research. Demand for PV projects in the United States is rapidly expanding as a result of falling system prices, federal funding under the stimulus bill and new state incentives. As the recession retreats, the US is poised to become the largest global centre for solar power, with demand for PV installations growing by roughly 50% annually to between 1.5GW and 2GW in 2012.[19] The Solar Energy Industries Association (SEIA) reported in April 2010 that overall US solar electricity capacity grew 37% in 2009, driven primarily by strong demand in the residential and utility-scale markets, state and federal policy advances and declining technology prices. As a result, total solar industry revenue reached $4bn, a 36% increase on 2008's figure.

The MENA boom

The Middle East and North Africa (MENA) region is a prime market for solar power because it gets a lot of hours of sunshine. Although the market for solar power is less developed at this stage than other world markets, governments are slowly waking up to the potential. This is partly thanks to the Desertec initiative, which has put solar in the Sahara firmly on the map. Some experts believe this could lead to a bonanza for CSP across the region.

Algeria is amongst the first to set future targets, announcing an aim of 5% of energy to be drawn from renewables by 2015. The state-owned energy company Sonelgaz has also announced that it is investing $100m in a solar module factory. The 50MW plant is scheduled for completion in 2012 and represents the first step in turning Algeria into a strong and competitive player in the emerging fields of solar thermal and PV energy.[20]

Other projects are being initiated in Morocco, Egypt and Abu Dhabi.

Desertec: CSP from the Sahara

A group of mostly European companies have formed a joint venture to supply power to Europe from large-scale CSP plants in the North African desert. The concept, known as Desertec, has been around for some time but took a step closer to reality when 12 companies (including banks, utilities, engineering and solar technology firms) signed an agreement in October 2009 for an accelerated implementation of the proposal. The plan calls for a massive expansion of CSP in the deserts of Algeria, Libya and Morocco, with the objective of meeting 15% of Europe's energy needs by 2050. Expected to cost around €400bn, the project will also require a network of new transmission lines as part of the European super grid (see feature on p.136). The consortium has pledged to provide electricity for local needs as a priority, but New Energy Finance cautions that "the project will not be realised without solving the daunting political and security issues". Even if the shape and size of the project is likely to differ from the original plan, they conclude that "some form of electricity transmission form MENA countries to Europe will almost inevitably happen in coming decades." 21 Members of the consortium (who may well benefit in the long run) include ABB, Abengoa, First Solar, Schott Solar, Siemens, Solar Millennium and utilities firms.

Grid parity

"It is absolutely critical to solar stock investing not to lose sight of the big picture and to remember that at all times the industry remains dependent on public policy until grid parity is reached in markets sufficiently endowed with enough demand to sustain the industry."

Investing in Solar Stocks[22]

In order for there to be widespread take-up of solar power, the consensus is that the cost needs to fall to around $1 per watt. This is known as grid parity, whereby solar costs the same as energy supplied by fossil fuels. Grip parity is the holy grail of renewables and remarkable progress has been made towards achieving this goal, considering that the average cost of solar power stood at around $100 per watt in 1975. "When we reach grid parity, demand could well be infinite," according to the head of one major solar company.[23]

Increases in efficiency and the brutal price war of the last couple of years have led to some manufacturers already offering panels at around the $1 mark (you need to add another $1 per watt for the 'balance of system' to get the final installed cost per watt). China's LDK Solar, for instance, was offering wholesale prices of this order in 2009.

Thin-film manufacturers are even more optimistic (although bear in mind the lower efficiency rate of thin-film PV). The pioneer in this field, First Solar, already claims a production cost of 90c per watt – breaking the important $1 per watt barrier for the first time – and 50c per watt is forecast by 2013.

Grid parity will be achieved first in countries or regions with high electricity prices or sunny climates, or a combination of both. The European

Photovoltaic Industry Association expects Spain and Italy will reach grid parity in 2010 and 2012 respectively. The target should be reached in Germany by 2015 and most other European countries by 2020.[24]

"Achieving grid parity in the first key markets such as Italy, California and Japan will provide an enormous boost to the PV industry," writes Mattias Fawer, vice president of Bank Sarasin, adding that "the non-European markets will tend to grow even quicker up to 2020. Here there are some very sunny regions that have enormous pent-up demand for PV energy."[25]

What the experts say about the solar sector

Fund managers are starting to cautiously re-appraise solar after the bloodbath of 2008-2009. Clare Brook of the WHEB-AM Sustainability Fund, for example, says that valuations are starting to look better than they were. "We think that we're getting to the stage where it could be interesting to have a lot more solar exposure in the fund," she says.

Simon Webber of Schroders Global Climate Change Fund is also starting to build into solar. He says: "The industry still has massive over-capacity and therefore pricing is under pressure, and that's not very good for profits short term. It is great for the long term and great for the industry, because solar is expensive so the costs need to come down for it to grow."

Bozena Jankowska, fund manager of the Allianz RCM Global EcoTrends Fund, recommends waiting. "We're very cautious on solar at the moment," she says. "It is a sector which is basically going through a very, very tough time, and we continue to remain quite cautious on the solar space. Longer term we do like it but at the moment we think there are still more headwinds for the industry."

Michael McNamara, analyst with the cleantech division of research house Jefferies International, believes that there are two main trends affecting the majority of solar players: an increase in demand, combined with a collapse in module prices. "We're seeing a significant rise in global demand driven by a combination of stable incentive programmes, and a significant decline in module prices. So the returns to project investors are going through the roof," he says. "More encouragingly, there are signs that there is a significant amount of demand that's going to hit the market in 2010," says McNamara. "However, all this is happening at very low price points. The way we see it is that we're bullish on demand but bearish on margins," he adds.

As well as the sustained downturn in margins, there has also been a drop to lower absolute levels of revenues. For this reason, McNamara believes bankruptcies are inevitable:

> "Now what we're seeing is that a lot of the companies, particularly in Europe, have overhead costs and also debt levels that simply do not function well with a 40% to 50% decline in gross income. There are a few companies out there which won't be around in a couple of years time. At the same time, even the ones that survive are going to survive at a lower valuation because they have got less profits and more debt.
>
> "We do see some very, very attractive companies out there and it is no secret who they are but unfortunately their valuations are through the roof now in our opinion,"

he says, citing the German company SMA as an example.

Another concern is the continuation or otherwise of various European FIT schemes. The fears were confirmed when Germany announced a 15% cut in 2010 (to follow on from the 10% it had already announced in 2009), and France followed with a 24% reduction. At the same time, Britain introduced new FIT rates in April 2010, which should give the European industry a boost. A generous FIT in Italy is also currently fuelling a major solar boom.

On the positive side, not only are the US and Japanese markets growing steadily but China and India also have strong policies now. "We're expecting to see some pretty aggressive installation targets coming out of China, and possibly out of India," says McNamara. He cautions, however, against over-optimism on the Chinese markets because the support levels may be too low to make much difference.

In the medium term, McNamara suggested that it might be time to re-appraise solar sometime in mid-2010.

Solar technology and companies

We will now take a look in turn at the various technologies involved in the solar sector, which include:

- silicon photovoltaic solar panels

- companies that manufacture equipment used in the making of solar products

- those that produce components used within panels

- thin-film photovoltaic panels

- solar thermal energy

- concentrated solar power systems

- concentrated photovoltaic (CPV) systems

- concentrated photovoltaic thermal (CPVT) and hybrid photovoltaic thermal (hybrid PVT)

- organic photovoltaic panels.

Silicon photovoltaic solar panels

Silicon solar panels use arrays of photovoltaic cells to convert light into an electric current. It is not technically complicated, but producing highly efficient panels at a low cost is difficult.

The PV cells are built into panels which can be linked together on any scale required, right up to a utility-sized plant. Silicon panels are extremely reliable, but they have drawbacks. Polysilicon is relatively complicated and expensive to manufacture, and the panels are bulky and costly to install. The upside is that maintenance costs are low.

Silicon producers

The world's largest polysilicon producers are Hemlock Semiconductor (jointly owned by Dow Corning, Shin-Etsu Handotai and Mitsubishi Material Corporation), Wacker Polysilicon (part of Wacker Chemie, which also makes numerous other products including paints, sealants, polymer powders and pharmaceutical, cosmetics and food additives), **Renewable Energy Corporation (REC)**, Tokuyama, **MEMC**, **PV Crystalox Solar**, Mitsubishi and Sumimoto.

The UK company **PV Crystalox Solar** has been producing silicone ingots since 1996 and is one of only a handful of UK-listed solar companies.

PV manufacturers and installers

There are a vast number of companies making solar PV cells, solar modules or PV arrays. These include large Japanese conglomerates such as Sharp, Sanyo, Canon, Mitsubishi and Kyocera.

However, China has recently overtaken Japan as the world's biggest PV producer, largely thanks to low manufacturing costs. Chinese solar companies with London listings include **Jetion Solar Holdings** and **Renesola**. Chinese companies with US listings including **China Sunergy, J A Solar Holdings, LDK Solar, Solarfun Power Holdings, Suntech Power Holdings, Trina Solar** and **Yingli Green Energy**. Also US-listed is **Canadian Solar**, which has a manufacturing plant in China but headquarters in Toronto, Canada.

The largest US-based solar company is **SunPower** and another is **Evergreen Solar**, although Evergreen are in the process of transferring production to China.

Canadian company **Day4 Energy**, with a Toronto listing, is that country's largest PV manufacturer.

Germany, which until recently was the world's biggest market for PV products, is also home to one of the largest pure-play independent solar companies, Frankfurt-listed **Q-Cells SE**. **SolarWorld AG** (based in Bonn) and **Phoenix Solar** (of Frankfurt) are other important German companies.

In the UK, AIM-listed **Romag Holdings** is a leading player in the building-integrated photovoltaics (BIPV) market.

Solar manufacturing equipment

Another route into solar investment is via the companies that manufacture the equipment to make solar products. These include New Hampshire-based **GT Solar**, a global market leader in polysilicon reactors and converters, and **Spire Corporation**, also based on the US east coast. A major supplier to both the crystalline silicon and thin-film markets is Santa Clara-based **Applied Materials**.

Other key players are the German manufacturers **Roth & Rau AG** and **Singulus Technologies**.

Solar components

All solar panels need an *inverter* to convert the direct current generated in PV cells into alternating current suitable for the grid. In addition, the inverter acts as a system manager, responsible for yield monitoring and grid management. Currently, there is talk of a global shortage of inverters. The market for these and similar devices is projected to reach close to $700m over the next five years.

At present the market is dominated by the German company **SMA Solar Technology AG**, with a 42% market share. Other major suppliers include electronics companies such as Fronius International, Kaco New Energy, and Vancouver-based Xantrex Technology, which was recently acquired by the French electronics and automation specialist Schneider Electric (EPA:SU).

Most solar panel systems today rely on central inverters, such as those produced by SMA and Xantrex, but there is a problem if the central device fails, because it can bring down the whole system. Several companies are bringing a new type of inverter onto the market which they hope will solve these problems and increase the overall efficiency of solar arrays. Known as micro-inverters, these are basically miniature inverters which are fixed to each panel.

Start-ups operating in this area include Enphase Energy, who say that their micro-inverters can save up to 25% of energy output. Enphase raised $15m and shipped their 100,000th unit in 2009. National Semiconductor (NYSE: NSM) has also waded into this market with its award-winning SolarMagic power optimiser. Another contender in this field is Israeli start-up SolarEdge (GE Energy Financial Services joined a US$23m funding round in October 2009). Not to be outdone, SMA bought the Dutch company OKE-Services, a specialist producer of micro-inverters, in 2009.

Thin-film photovoltaics

Thin-film photovoltaic technologies do the same job as traditional PV cell panels but use much smaller quantities of semi-conducting materials (usually around 1% of material for the same output) and can be printed out onto different surfaces (glass, metal or flexible plastic sheets). This means that they are cheaper, lighter in weight and more flexible than traditional silicon panels. However, although thin film is cheaper, it is not as efficient – so you need a lot more of it (and therefore more space) to produce the same power.

The fact that thin-film PV is lighter and more flexible than traditional panels has opened up whole new markets in building integrated photovoltaics (BIPV), which incorporate PV modules directly onto roofs and other building surfaces. This has aesthetic as well as cost advantages. Thin film has also created a small but growing market for electronic integrated PV (EIPV), in which solar modules are incorporated directly into consumer goods such as electronic devices and luggage (backpacks that charge mobile phones are already on the market).

Investing in the thin-film sector

Thin-film PV has gone through something of a roller-coaster ride in the last couple of years. The fall in the price of crystalline silicon panels has undoubtedly been a blow to thin-film manufacturers, but given the advantages of thin-film PV – automated manufacturing and much lower material costs – many analysts believe it will capture increasingly significant market share in the future. It currently accounts for around 14% of solar production, but analysts iSuppli expect this to increase to 31% by 2013.[26] Despite the problems this sector is currently experiencing, NanoMarkets predicts that thin film will be worth $5bn in revenues by 2015.[27]

Despite these bullish estimates, for investors most of these stocks are high risk. The exception is **First Solar**, which almost single-handedly sparked the global frenzy in thin-film technologies, but it trades on a hefty premium. No other company working with cadmium telluride (CdTe) technologies is anywhere near First Solar in terms of production or sales. New entrants include Colorado-based Abound Solar (formerly AVA Solar), who opened their first production facility in 2009 after completing a $104m financing round.

For the moment the best approach may be to wait for public floatations of companies involved in copper indium gallium selenide (CIGS) and CdTe technologies. California-based Solyadra, which makes cylindrical thin-film modules designed for commercial rooftops, is expected to go for an IPO in 2010.

Large corporations

Several large corporations have placed big bets on thin film:

- General Electric has re-structured its solar business, closing down its crystalline cell production facilities and increasing its stake in the Colorado developer PrimeStar Solar with the goal of bringing thin-film panels to market by 2011 (GE also has other solar bets, namely on inverters, power control systems and CSP).

- Sharp (TYO: 6753) is one of the world's major crystalline cell producers and has been working on thin film since 2005. They have recently opened a new thin-film plant in Sakai City, Osaka, that will expand their capacity for thin-film production to 1GW. The company has a hugely ambitious target of gaining more than 50% of the thin-film market by 2012 and increasing their total thin-film production to 6GW by 2014.[28]

- Sanyo has formed a joint venture with Nippon Oil (Eneos) to produce amorphous silicon (a-Si) thin film. The new company, Sanyo Eneos Solar, plans to start mass production in 2010 with an initial 80MW capacity, scaling up to 1GW by 2015.

Copper indium selenide thin-film manufacturers

Manufacturers of copper indium gallium selenide (CIGS) – which is used in thin-film solar cells – have also been attracting attention from outside investors. Norsk Hydro, one of the world's largest aluminium suppliers, has invested nearly $25m in Colorado-based **Ascent Solar Technologies**.

There are numerous development-stage companies working on CIGS thin-film, some of them closer to market than others. Most are based in North America (these include Nanosolar, Solyndra, MiaSolé, SoloPower and HelioVolt).

Dow Chemical Company (NYSE: DOW) is launching roofing shingles with embedded CIGS cells in partnership with building companies in North America. The company has developed its flexible 'solar shingles' in conjunction with Global Solar Energy of Arizona.

The California-based company **XsunX** is charting a new course in the production of CIGS by using manufacturing techniques developed for hard disk drives. The company claims that this technique will increase solar cell efficiency, improve production yields and lower the overall cost of thin-film PV.

Amorphous silicon (a-Si) thin-film manufacturers

Amorphous silicon can be deposited in thin films and then used as a photovoltaic solar cell material. Some analysts doubt that a-Si will be viable in a market where prices for competing thin-film products (which work more efficiently) are falling.

One of the first companies to create BIPV products from a-Si was United Solar Ovonics, a subsidiary of **Energy Conversion Devices.**

Another company using a-Si for BIPV products is Iowa-based **PowerFilm**, who also make flexible thin-film solar rechargers for applications such as consumer electronics and outdoor equipment including field shelters.

Solar thermal

Solar thermal uses panels or evacuated tubes to collect the sun's energy and to supply hot water or space heating in homes or commercial buildings. However, most of these are made in China by companies not listed on easily-accessible stock exchanges.

Concentrating solar power (CSP)

CSP uses mirrors or reflective surfaces in various configurations to focus the sun's energy on receivers containing fluids. The fluids are heated to create steam that drives a turbine and generates electricity.

CSP technologies have been around for quite some time – there are plants which have been running for 20 years or more – and their usage is expanding rapidly. Since they use standard materials, building out on a large scale is easily achievable and CSP plants are usually around 50-250MW in size. There are several estimates which claim that CSP built across an area of desert just 92 square miles could generate enough solar power to meet all the energy needs of the US.

Parabolic trough

At present CSP installations are dominated by parabolic trough technology, which has a proven track record. Long, trough-like parabolic mirrors reflect sunlight onto a tube containing oil, which is heated to create steam and run a turbine. The reflectors track the sun along a single axis during the day.

The first parabolic trough plants were built in California's Mojave Desert by a pioneering company called Luz Industries in the late 1980s. Called the

Solar Energy Generating System (SEGS), this series of nine plants is still generating energy and is estimated to have supplied more than $2bn worth of power to the grid in their lifetime, with a 99% availability rate.[29] SEGS has fulfilled a valuable role in demonstrating the long-term durability, as well as low operating and maintenance costs, of CSP.

The next generation of parabolic trough plants is now taking shape in Spain – parabolic troughs represent more than 96% of all CSP projects currently under construction in the country. On the Guadix plateau near Granada, two 50MW plants are already producing power with a third due to come on-stream in 2011. The Anadasol installations are the first parabolic trough power plants in Europe and, in terms of collector area, they are also the world's largest – covering around 6km² of land. Using molten salt for heat storage, the Andasol plants can generate electricity for over seven hours after the sun has gone down.

One of the main advantages of parabolic troughs is that systems are modular and can be expanded easily, so building large scale plants is feasible. The high cost of the mirrors is a disadvantage, but large scale manufacturing should bring this cost down. Some companies are also offering innovative alternatives to mirrors.

A variation on parabolic troughs are Linear Fresnel Reflectors: these also use long lines of reflectors, however they are flat mirrors – cheaper than parabolic mirrors – and more of them can be used for the same amount of space.

Power towers

Power tower systems use fields of thousands of flat mirrors mounted on tracking motors, which focus sunlight onto a boiler mounted on top of a tower. The boiler produces superheated steam which is sent down to a turbine on the ground.

The current generation of power towers started with Abengoa's PS10, which began operations at Sanlúcar la Mayor in Spain in 2007. It was later joined by PS20, which is twice as powerful, in April 2009.

Although power towers only account for around 5% of the CSP market at present, they are widely considered to be the next step for solar thermal. Their higher thermodynamic efficiency has led Brian Fan of the Cleantech Group to suggest that power towers "will be the next generation of CST plants past 2012."[30] Additionally, power towers are more flexible when it comes to siting: troughs require level ground, but power towers can be placed on uneven terrain if necessary.

Growth of the CSP sector

To date, the global installed base of CSP is relatively low (around 679MW). However, this is growing rapidly, with around 2GW under construction globally.[31] According to analysis from Emerging Energy Research, CSP is entering a new growth phase.[32] Sebastian Waldburg of the private investment fund SI Capital believes that CSP has huge potential based upon its two key advantages – storage and scalability. " Here in Spain on some days there is so much wind-generated electricity in the networks that they have to switch off some of the turbines," he says. "So clearly storage [a possibility offered by CSP] is a huge advantage over other renewable technologies."

Supporting the idea that CSP will be important in future electricity generation in the United States, the US Department of Energy expects CSP to be cost competitive by 2015 and to provide a sizeable amount of electricity to the US grid by 2020. To this end, America's National Renewable Energy Laboratory has launched a research project to look at new thermal storage materials and technologies to enable CSP plants to operate at higher temperatures, with lower costs.

Hybrid CSP plants are now starting to be developed. These use another fuel to generate power when the sun is not shining, thereby enhancing output and efficiency. Several next-generation CSP installations (such as those being built in Algeria and Egypt) are hybrid solar and natural gas. CSP can also be integrated with biomass firing, using agricultural or forestry waste to produce round-the-clock power.

The country with the largest share of CSP is Spain; it has 22 projects with a capacity of over 1GW under construction, all of which are projected to come online by the end of 2010.

The US trails a long way behind Spain (with just 75MW of capacity currently under construction) but has huge potential, with 8.5GW scheduled for installation by 2014. "Ultimately, the US market is considered to have the greatest upside for CSP potential given its solar resources, space availability, proximity to load and growing pressure to mitigate carbon emissions," says Reese Tisdale, research director at EER. According to Tisdale: "The US market has a greater technology mix, as the highly cost-competitive marketplace encourages innovative technology development, such as central receiver, dish engine and linear Fresnel."

India could also become a major player in CSP, with a number of established players (including Solar Millennium and Abengoa Solar) as well as early-stage companies (such as BrightSource, Ausra, and Australia's Wizard Power) announcing project plans for the sub-continent. Chile and the Sudan are another two countries that have recently unveiled plans for CSP.

The World Bank is investing $750m to accelerate deployment of CSP, with funding going towards 11 commercial-scale plants and transmission links in five Middle East and North African countries. The bank hopes this will trigger an additional $4.85bn of investment into this technology from other sources. Morocco is planning five new CSP plants as part of its push to become a major player in solar power. The first of the new plants, which will eventually link into the massive Desertec plan (see p.35), is a 500MW installation near the southern town of Ouarzazate.

One industry estimate is that the market for solar thermal power plants will show annual double-digit growth rates and attain a volume of over €20bn by 2020.[33] According to the European Solar Thermal Association, CSP could supply up to 7% of the world's energy by 2030 and up to 25% by 2050.[34]

Indeed, the future looks promising for CSP, according to entrepreneur Vinod Khosla, founder of Khosla Ventures. "Solar thermal power technology offers the greatest potential to produce base-load, large-scale power that could replace fossil fuel plants (presently principally coal based) at low technical risk and with characteristics similar to coal, thus reducing adoption risk," he says. "The key advantage of this technology is its capacity to store heat energy at low cost, making 'utility grade' solar power reliable and available around the clock."[35]

CSP companies

One company at the forefront of the development of parabolic trough plants is Frankfurt-listed **Solar Millennium AG**.

In Spain, major construction and energy companies such as ACS/Cobra and Acciona, as well as renewables developers such as **Iberdrola Renewables**, are involved in CSP. Another Spanish company, Madrid-listed **Abengoa**, has been involved in nearly all varieties of CSP technologies, including power towers, parabolic troughs and Stirling dishes.

European engineering giant Siemens is a world leader for supplying steam turbines for solar thermal power plants, with an 80% market share. Siemens has recently strengthened its position in the CSP sector, buying the Israeli company Solel Solar Systems (one of the world's two leading suppliers of solar receivers, a key component in parabolic trough plants, as well as being a leading developer of solar farms) and taking a stake in the Italian company Archimede Solar Energy, which makes parabolic trough plants with molten salt storage facilities. Archimede is developing plants in Sicily and Umbria.

Another major supplier to the CSP industry is Schott Solar, a subsidiary of Schott AG. The company has been making solar receivers for over 30 years and has factories in the US, Spain, Germany and the Czech Republic. Its third plant in Albuquerque, New Mexico, which opened in 2009, is said to be the world's first dedicated production site for utility-scale CSP receivers with an annual production rate expected to reach 85MW.

It is a sign of the growing maturity of this technology that a small Californian start-up, Ausra, was bought by the French nuclear giant Areva SA in February 2010 for a rumoured $200m despite having developed just two small demonstration projects using its Compact Linear Fresnel Reflector technology (a 5MW plant in California and a 3MW plant in Australia). Areva SA, the world's largest maker of nuclear reactors, subsequently predicted that the global use of solar-thermal power will grow by about 30-fold this decade. "It is a very attractive market," Anil Srivastava, Areva renewable energies executive vice president, told Bloomberg, adding that the Paris-based company aims to become a world leader in solar thermal.[36] The company already has interests in wind (having acquired 51% of Multibrid, a German manufacturer of offshore wind turbines, in 2007), and biomass-based power. Ausra's most recent contract is for a 100MW plant in Ma'an, Jordan.

The Barcelona-based firm SI Capital has invested in Enerstar, who have several CSP projects in development in Spain and elsewhere. Enerstar is exploring the potential of co-firing with biogas or biomass, which increases the efficiency of the plant. For instance, it takes 90 minutes or so for CSP systems to warm up enough in the mornings to start working. But if the system is already pre-warmed with biomass, it can start generating power much more quickly.

CSP start-ups

With CSP in the ascendant, numerous new companies are springing up to take advantage of growing interest globally. These include:

- *BrightSource Energy*
- *Solar Reserve*
- *eSolar*
- *SkyFuel*

None of these are currently listed on stock exchanges. You can find details about them in the 'Companies to watch' section at the end of this chapter.

Concentrated photovoltaic (CPV)

Concentrated photovoltaic (CPV) technology uses lenses, mirrors or other optical concentrators to focus sunlight on to a small area of solar cells. The aim is to replace the most expensive part of a solar panel (the silicon cell) with cheap optics such as plastics or glass. The cells used are also much more efficient and therefore give an increased energy yield.

Other advantages of CPV are that it doesn't use any water and units take up very little space (the land underneath can be used for grazing, for instance). According to the CPV Consortium, CPV also offers a much shorter payback time than other solar technologies and in areas with high irradiance and strong levels of direct sunlight, it can provide the highest levels of energy production at the lowest cost.[37] CPV needs direct sunlight though, so tracking devices are required.

It is only recently that technical improvements in the core components of the system have paved the way for significant advances in CPV usage. Developers are now hoping that this will become the technology of choice in very hot regions, where crystalline PV cells can degrade in the heat. Already, a pilot plant in Spain is said to be operating at 23% efficiency and yielding twice the power of conventional PV on clear, sunny days.[38]

CPV has had some teething problems, but if reliability can be improved and costs reduced the scope is huge. This potential is just beginning to be recognised. For instance, IBM is working on CPV technology in conjunction with the Saudi Arabian national research and development organisation and aiming for a CPV system that can operate at the equivalent of the concentration of 2000 suns. Boeing are also seeking to commercialise their XR700 CPV system and are currently installing a 100kW facility at California State University.

Growth of CPV

This technology is still in its infancy and lags a long way behind other solar technologies in terms of installed or projected capacities – one estimate is of 30-50MW installed globally during 2009. This is tiny, but nonetheless it is a big jump up from the 8-10MW installed in the previous year.[39] To put this in perspective, CPV has gone from providing the power of two normal wind turbines in 2008 to providing the power of around a dozen or so in 2009.

Whilst this might be a negligible amount in terms of power supplied, this is a very young and fast-growing segment of the solar industry which has expanded from just a handful of contenders to at least 40 development-stage companies in 2010.[40]

CPV companies

One of the few listed companies in this field is Emcore (NASDAQ: EMKR) but it is also a provider of semiconductor components and products for the broadband, fibre optic, and satellite industries and therefore can't be considered a pure-play in this field. The Spanish company Isofotón is a market leader in this area but it is not publicly listed.

CPV start-ups

There are a number of start-ups working in CPV. In Germany, Concentrix Solar is a spin-out from the Fraunhofer Institute for Solar Energy Systems and has three installations up and running in Spain. It was recently bought by the French microelectronics company Soitec (EPA:SOI). It is also worth monitoring *QuantaSol, Whitfield Solar* (both of the UK), *SolFocus* of California and *Morgan Solar* of Canada.

Investing in CPV

CPV is a wide-open game, and the next few years will be critical in seeing if it can succeed in scaling up to a decent level. This is a highly promising field, and it wouldn't be at all surprising if some of the big energy corporations started to move in and set off a feeding frenzy on these companies.

Concentrated photovoltaic thermal (CPVT) and hybrid photovoltaic
thermal (hybrid PVT)

Hybrid photovoltaic thermal (hybrid PVT) systems produce both electricity
and heat from one panel or collecting surface. In most cases the system
consists of a PV panel combined with a thermal collector behind it. Thermal
energy is drawn from the back of the panel and used for space heating inside
a building. This has the added bonus of improving the performance of the
PV cells, because they operate more efficiently at lower temperatures.

Although more expensive than a conventional panel, these hybrid systems
are said to increase electrical efficiencies by up to 10% and can generate four
times the energy from the same surface area (if the heat gain is included).

The first ever full-scale demonstration was an installation at the Beijing
Olympics village in 2008. Researchers in several countries are currently
exploring similar hybrid systems under the title of combined heat and power
solar (CHAPS) systems.[41] A variation on this is concentrating photovoltaic
thermal (CPVT), which uses CPV and thermal combined.

CPVT and hybrid PVT companies

This is such a new direction for solar power that there are as yet very few
opportunities for investors. The one publicly listed company operating in
this field is **Entech Solar** – see the entry in the company directory on p.230
for more information.

The market leader in hybrid PVT is Toronto-based Conserval Engineering,
a privately held company which installed the panels at the 2008 Beijing
Olympics village. The company has also undertaken other installations of
its SolarWall technology, which follows the same principles except (as the
name implies) it is part of the building wall rather than on the roof.

A glimmer of the potential for these technologies is appearing on the horizon
as other developers start getting products to market. Colorado-based
BrightPhase Energy, for instance, has launched its Photensity modules which
combine solar PV, solar thermal and daylight management – the first
commercial installation was completed in October 2009.

Another variation on this is provided by the Swedish company ClimateWell,
who have developed a solar air-conditioning device which stores energy
from a PV panel in a battery using salt, which can then be used to generate
heating or cooling.

Serial solar entrepreneur Peter Le Lievre, a co-founder and former CEO of solar thermal specialist Ausra, has set up a new company, *Chromasun*.

Organic photovoltaic

This is the next wave of technologies to harness solar power; it is being called third-generation solar. Cheap, flexible and easy to make, this technique uses organic molecules to capture sunlight and convert it to electricity. Although efficiency levels are currently low (around 6.5% at best), this should improve.

The organic PV layer can be printed, coated or sprayed inexpensively on to different surfaces using roll-to-roll manufacturing. This means that it can be turned into a wide range of end products, such as café umbrellas with plugs in so that you can charge your laptop or mobile on the go.

The leader in this field is *Konarka Technologies*, who received the corporate seal of approval in March 2010 with a $20m investment from the Japanese technology company Konica Minolta. Another company working in the area is Dresden-based *Heliatek*.

Another form of organic PV is known as a dye solar cell (DSC). With this technology, dye-coated semiconductor nanocrystals are sandwiched between glass panels or embedded in plastic along with an electrolyte. The ink or dye absorbs light and creates electrons, transferring them to an electric circuit. One of the market leaders in DSC is *Innovalight*, which claims to have reached 18% efficiencies with its silicon inks. The company is planning to bring products to market in 2010.

A further ambitious company in this area is Cardiff-based G24 Innovations, whose first commercial product is a backpack coated with cheap, lightweight and flexible solar cells for on-the-go recharging of portable gadgets. The company says that its cells are over 12% efficient at converting light into electricity. G24 uses dye technology under license from the award-winning Australian company **Dyesol**.

Solar ETFs

There are two main solar ETFs. The first is the Claymore/MAC Global Solar Energy Index (NYSE: TAN). Launched in March 2008 it tracks the MAC Global Solar Energy Index (SUNIDX).
www.claymore.com/etf/fund/tan

The second is the Van Eck Market Vectors Solar Energy (NYSE: KWT). Launched in April 2008, it tracks the Ardour Solar Energy Index (SOLRX). www.vaneck.com

Both these funds offer exposure to solar stocks and carry a 0.65% expense ratio, although there are some differences in the way that the indices are constructed.

Companies to watch

Amonix (US) is currently marketing its seventh generation CPV system, which it claims generates over 40% more energy than conventional panels. Some of their panels, in use by utilities, have been continuously operational for more than a decade. It has installed a total of 13MW of CPV capacity so far. The company has won $5.9m in federal funding to build a new plant in Nevada and a further $3.6m for a manufacturing plant in neighbouring Arizona. Both plants are expected to be commissioned in 2011. Amonix intends to increase its manufacturing capacity after a successful $129.4m fund-raising round in April 2010, led by Kleiner, Perkins, Caufield & Byers (KPCB). www.amonix.com

BrightPhase Energy (US) has developed a system that provides single story commercial buildings with electricity, heating and lighting. It consists of a network of rooftop modules tied to a central system controller that monitors conditions to generate the maximum value energy stream at any time. Firstly, the rooftop diffusers provide daylight from between their louvers; secondly, power is generated from PV cells on the back of the modules; and finally solar energy not converted to electricity is trapped by glycol fluid circulating in the louvers and passed to heat storage tanks. www.brightphaseenergy.com

BrightSource Energy (US) is a new company with old roots: its founder and chairman, Arnold Goldman, was the entrepreneur behind Luz Industries, which built the original SEGS parabolic troughs. It has been developing its Luz Power Tower 550 at a test centre in Israel's Negev Desert and claims that it has one of the highest operating efficiencies and lowest capital costs in the industry, with the potential to deliver renewable energy at a cost competitive with fossil fuels. BrightSource emphasises the fact that its power towers are cooled by air rather than water, an important consideration in desert environments. The company estimates that air-cooling reduces their water usage by 90%. The water they do use is re-circulated during energy production and then reused to clean the heliostats.

BrightSource is currently developing its first solar power complex in California's Mojave Desert, with the first phase scheduled to be completed by 2012. This plant will deploy a Siemens' turbine which will become the largest ever solar-powered steam turbine generator. BrightSource has raised more than US$300m in backing from investors including Vantage Point Venture Partners, Google.org, BP Alternative Energy, Alstom, Chevron Technology Ventures and Statoil Hydro. It also won $1.37bn in loan guarantees from the US Department of Energy in early 2010. www.brightsourceenergy.com

Chromasun (US) was set up by serial solar entrepreneur Peter Le Lievre (he is also the co-founder and former CEO of Ausra). Chromasun's solar collector uses a Fresnel lens to focus energy onto a high-performance receiver tube. A wide variety of fluids can be heated in the unit, which has been designed specifically for rooftop integration. The heated liquid is then used in an absorption chiller for air conditioning. The collector is low profile, lightweight and has no external moving parts, so it is simple to mount and easy to maintain, says the company. The idea of a solar-powered air conditioner makes sense because people turn on air-conditioners when it is hot, so solar cooling technology can benefit a building just when the need is greatest. Chromasun raised $3m from investors including VKR Holding and GoGreen Capital in April 2010. www.chromasun.com

eSolar (US) is backed by $180m in funding from Idealab, Google.org, and Oak Investment Partners, and has secured rights to support the production of over 1GW of power in the southwestern US. It also has licensing agreements in India and Southern Africa. They unveiled their first development, a 5MW tower in California's Antelope Valley, in August 2009. eSolar claims that it has solved many of the problems associated with CSP and that their pre-fabricated plant is based on mass manufactured components which have been designed for rapid construction, uniform modularity and unlimited scalability. In January 2010 eSolar won a contract to supply its technology to a Chinese company, who will build 2GW of solar thermal plants by 2021. www.esolar.com

Heliatek (Germany) is a spin-out from the University of Dresden, that has developed organic cells manufactured on foil substrates in a continuous vacuum-coating process. The company is aiming for efficiencies in the region of 8-10% and has raised US$27m from investors including Bosch, RWE Innogy Ventures and BASF Venture Capital to build a production facility in Dresden. www.heliatek.com

Innovalight (US) has developed a proprietary silicon ink which combines the best properties of silicon with the cost advantages of inkjet manufacturing. The company has worked closely with leading research institutions such as the US National Renewable Energy Laboratory (NREL) and has over 60 patents pending. The company claims that its first product will have a similar look and feel to today's crystalline-based solar cells and modules but with a significantly higher power output per area. Innovalight is one of seven companies that have been selected for Chevron's high profile Project Brightfield experiment in Bakersfield, California, which is testing advanced solar products. www.innovalight.com

Konarka Technologies (US) was founded in 2001 and has attracted investments of over $150m in private capital and $20m in government research grants to date. In 2009, the company opened a large-scale manufacturing plant for its PowerPlastic panels. PowerPlastic can be printed directly on to numerous different surfaces. www.konarka.com

Morgan Solar (Canada) has taken an entirely different approach to CPV. It has developed a thin optical structure, made from simple acrylic and glass components, which concentrates sunlight internally. Light is redirected onto tiny slivers of PV attached directly to the optic, which they say eliminates the bulkiness of traditional CPV systems. The company has attracted investment from the world's largest renewables developer, Iberdrola, and also won C$2.3m from Sustainable Development Technology Canada in early 2010. The company's SunSimba panels, designed for large-scale solar farms, are said to operate at 25-30% efficiencies. In January 2010 Morgan increased their first-round investment to US$8.2m from the US$4.7m announced in 2009. As well as Iberdrola, strategic investors include Nypro Inc and Turnstone Capital Management LLC. www.morgansolar.com

SkyFuel (US) has developed a highly reflective, silverised polymer film which takes the place of the heavy and expensive curved mirrors normally used in parabolic trough collectors. SkyFuel says that its SkyTrough collectors built with mirror film are 35% less expensive than normal troughs and twice the size of any troughs in commercial use. The company has also designed a lightweight aluminum space frame to hold the film in place. The company has raised $18m in private finance (led by the Leaf Clean Energy Company) and $900,000 in government grants. www.skyfuel.com

Solar Reserve (US) has licensed its technology from Rocketdyne, a subsidiary of United Technologies, which was involved in the solar power towers built in the Mojave Desert in the 1980s. The company has raised $140m from investors including the US Renewables Group, Citi Alternative Investments, Good Energies, Credit Suisse and Sustainable Development Investments. Its first project is being developed near Alcázar de San Juan, south of Madrid. It has also applied for permits to build a 150MW plant in the Sonoran Desert east of Palm Springs, California. www.solar-reserve.com

SolFocus (US) has developed CPV technology, which combines high-efficiency solar cells and advanced optics to provide cost-effective power. The company has European operations based in Madrid and manufacturing in Arizona, India and China. SolFocus, which has raised $78m, recently expanded its Arizona facility to provide the capacity to produce two million concentrating reflectors annually. Its most recent order was for a full-scale 8.5MW unit to be installed at the headquarters of the Portuguese utility Águas de Portugal. Project deployment began in early 2010 for the first 2MW, with the balance to be constructed in stages. www.solfocus.com

QuantasSol (UK) is a spin-out from Imperial College London. It claims to have developed the most efficient single junction solar cell ever manufactured. Aimed at CPV systems, the cell has been independently tested and achieved 28.3% efficiency at greater than 500 suns. They are also developing very high efficiency (34%) multi-junction cells for CPV applications. Their technique combines several nanostructures in order to obtain synthetic crystals that greatly enhance the PV conversion efficiency. The company is jointly owned by Low Carbon Accelerator and Imperial Innovations. www.quantasol.com

Whitfield Solar (UK) has carried out successful trials in Spain of its concentrator platform, which they claim has key advantages because it uses electric rather than hydraulic systems to track the sun's movement. This makes them much lighter than existing systems, and better suited to installations where load capacity is a key issue, such as rooftops. It is scheduled to launch its first factory-produced 2-axis concentrator units in 2010. The company closed a second funding round totalling £1.4m in 2009 from existing shareholders Carbon Trust Investments Limited (CTIL) and new investors Kilsby Ltd. www.whitfieldsolar.com

Glossary

a-Si: amorphous silicon

BIPV: building-integrated photovoltaics

CdTe: cadmium telluride

CHAPS: combined heat and solar power

CIGS: copper indium gallium selenide

CLFR: compact linear fresnel reflector

CPV: concentrating photovoltaic

CPVT: concentrating photovoltaic thermal

CSP: concentrating solar power

EIPV: electronic integrated photovoltaics

GaAs: gallium arsenide cells

Hybrid PVT: hybrid photovoltaic thermal

NREC: National Renewable Energy Laboratory

PV: photovoltaics

SEGS: Solar Energy Industry Association

SOLRX: Ardour Solar Energy Index

SUNIDX: MAC Global Solar Energy Index

UHCPV: ultra-high concentrator photovoltaic technology

UMG: upgraded metallurgical silicon

WIND POWER

2

Introduction

"We're very bullish on wind right now. All the growth elements are in place: reliable technology, industry experience and maturity, and heavy investment from global manufacturing giants, large influential electrical utilities, and many of the world's largest and most respected financiers."

The Cleantech Revolution[42]

Wind power is one of the most efficient and most affordable means of delivering large-scale reductions in carbon dioxide emissions. Wind power doesn't emit any pollutants and within six months of operation a modern turbine will have offset all the emissions attributable to its construction, therefore providing carbon-free electricity for the rest of the time it is operational. A modern, lightweight wind turbine will pay for itself more than 35 times over in energy produced during its lifetime.

Wind farms can be built remarkably quickly compared to other forms of energy supply. Planning issues and delays in grid connection are well-known bottlenecks in some locations but given a lack of obstacles of this kind an onshore wind farm can be constructed within one year. Even offshore wind farms, with their more complex infrastructure and grid connections, can be built in two years. This compares with a time frame of decades for nuclear reactors.

Wind farms and turbines also have other good green credentials. As farms near the end of their design life, they can be upgraded with newer, more efficient and more powerful turbines. This also creates green, sustainable jobs in manufacturing and servicing. The old turbines can also be recycled: Vestas, for instance, say that 80% of their turbines can be reused. Further, unlike conventional power plants, wind power doesn't require the use of scarce water resources, and most activities (such as farming or ranching) can carry on as usual below wind turbines.

New records are frequently being achieved for the amount of electricity generated by wind: Ireland's transmission operator, EirGrid, reported that wind met 39% of the country's power demand on 31 July 2009.[43] Spanish grid operator Red Electrica de Espana topped that with a report that 45% of Spain's energy requirements were met by wind on 8 November 2009.[44] These figures are an illustration of the continuing strength of wind power to generate meaningful levels of energy.

Wind power is a proven technology, refined and optimised over the last 30 years. It is clean, reliable and can be built quickly. On a good windy site wind power is already cost competitive with gas or new coal-fired electricity and, unlike with fossil fuels, there is no fuel price risk.

Given all these factors it is hardly surprising that wind power is the fastest-growing form of electricity generation in the world today, with the level of installed capacity expanding at an average rate of around 30% a year for the last five years. It is this phenomenal growth rate – which was been maintained even through the 2007-2009 recession – that makes wind power such an attractive proposition for investors.

Growth of the wind power sector

"We believe that for the next two decades or more, the growth of the industry will be strong and sustained, surpassing previous estimates. We estimate that, conservatively, we'll continue to see 25% annual growth rates for the foreseeable future, creating more than $4bn in new wind projects annually."

Investing in Renewable Energy: Making Money on Green Chip Stocks[45]

General overview of global expansion

The year 2009 was another record year for new installations, with global wind energy capacity growing by over 30%, adding 38GW to take the total global capacity up to 158GW, according to the Global Wind Energy Council (GWEC). The council said that the global market for turbine installations was worth €45bn ($63bn) in 2009 and that the sector now employs in the region of 500,000 people around the world. The GWEC anticipates that global installed wind capacity will reach 409GW by 2014, up from 158GW at the end of 2009. This assumes an annual growth rate of 20.9%, a relatively modest rate compared to the past ten years when growth rates have exceeded 28%.

The biggest growth in 2009 was in China, which more than doubled the number of wind farms built and reached 25GW of capacity. The US also shattered all records in 2009, adding nearly 10GW to reach a total capacity of 35GW. In Europe also, wind farms expanded by around 10GW to reach about 75GW of installed capacity.

What is a ROC?

The Renewables Obligation is the main support scheme for renewable energy in the UK. It places an obligation on utilities to source an increasing proportion of their electricity from renewable sources. The system is managed through Renewables Obligation Certificates (ROCs), which are issued to renewables developers. Originally, the scheme issued one ROC for each MWh of eligible output generated. However this was changed in 2009 to take account of the fact that certain technologies are more commercially viable than others and so technologies that need more support for effective market deployment can receive it. The new 'banded' system uses onshore wind power as a reference technology, so any technology which needs more support is granted additional ROCs and similarly more commercially viable technologies are granted less ROCs. However, this system is now under review by the government.

Asian advances in wind power

A number of countries in Asia are making advances in wind power:

- China is the world's fastest growing wind power market and is also expected to become the biggest manufacturer of wind energy equipment in the near future. Some of the largest wind farms ever built are currently under construction in the country. China's official target is to reach 30GW by 2020 but most observers predict that it will reach this target well ahead of time, with somewhere between 100-150GW installed by the end of the decade. China has the potential to go further than this according to a report in the journal *Science*, which claims that the country could get 100% of its electricity supplies from wind by 2030.

One of China's largest wind operators, China Longyuan Power Group, raised \$2.3bn from its Hong Kong IPO in late 2009 – the issue was oversubscribed by investors keen to take part in the fast-growing Chinese wind market.

- In Taiwan, the government has set a target of 15% (8.5GW) of the nation's electricity to be generated from renewable resources by 2025. Offshore wind is considered to be the fastest way to reach that goal, with around 3GW of capacity currently pencilled in.

- In Japan, the new government's ambition to reduce carbon dioxide emissions by 25% relative to 1990 levels before 2020 bodes well for wind power investments. The introduction of tariffs for renewable energy will contribute to propelling developments in the Japanese market.

- India is considered a highly promising country for wind: it already has a burgeoning wind industry, and wind farms can be deployed at a very large scale in a very short period of time. It is thought that wind could provide nearly a quarter of India's power demand by 2030 and create over 200,000 green-collar jobs.[46]

European advances in wind power

Wind power is the fastest growing power generation technology in Europe, with the European Wind Energy Association (EWEA) forecasting that 230GW of wind power will be installed by 2020.[47] Spain was the fastest growing market in 2009, with an additional 2.5GW of capacity, closely followed by Germany with 1.92GW. Britain, Italy, France and Ireland have also experienced notable growth in the area:

- Britain is Europe's third largest market, with cumulative capacity expected to be around 14.3GW by 2013. Around 4GW of this is expected to come from offshore wind farms.

- Italy is experiencing significant growth in new wind farms, partly driven by the introduction of 'green certificates' similar to the UK's Renewables Obligation Certificates (ROCs).

- In France, wind power is now the country's fastest growing energy source, with the biggest potential thought to be in the north and the north east of the country.

- Ireland currently has just under 1.1GW of installed capacity and has set itself a target of generating 40% of its energy from renewables by 2020.[48]

Advances in wind power in the United States

In 2009, 10GW of new wind farms were installed in the US and this has put wind power on the same level as natural gas as a source of new electricity generation. The boost is largely credited to President Obama's American Regeneration and Recovery Act, which the American Wind Energy Association (AWEA) called a "historic success" in spurring the growth of construction, operations and maintenance, and in creating clean energy jobs.[49]

The AWEA warned, however, that targets in the form of a national Renewable Electricity Standard (RES) were needed in order to provide long-term stability for manufacturers and to seize the historic opportunity of building a thriving renewable energy industry. The five-year average annual growth rate for the industry is now 39% (up from 32% between 2003 and 2008).

In addition to stimulus funding, the federal government has earmarked $45m for research and development (R&D) spending on large-scale wind turbine drivetrain systems. "Wind power holds tremendous potential to help create new jobs and reduce carbon pollution," said US Energy Secretary Steven Chu. "We are at the beginning of a new industrial revolution when it comes to clean energy and projects like these will help us get there faster."[50] The latest estimates from the NREL indicate that the US has a total of 10,500GW of developable potential, which is far higher than previous assessments.

Offshore – the new wind frontier

Offshore wind is expected to be one of the most promising areas for clean energy in the next ten years. Estimates are that offshore wind capacity globally will grow at a compound annual rate of 32% over the course of the next decade, soaring from the current installed base of just 2GW to 55GW by 2020.[51]

Growth of offshore wind will be assisted by the key advantages it has over onshore wind. Wind speeds are generally higher at sea, the wind tends to blow more consistently, and turbines can be larger (since it is easier to transport them by sea) and more powerful – generally providing 25% more energy than onshore machines.[52] Part of the reason for the higher growth rates of offshore wind power (relative to that onshore) is that some countries have reached saturation point on the best sites onshore and local community objections are also preventing further growth.

The one major issue with offshore wind is that costs are higher, due to the more complex foundations required and the need to protect turbines from the corrosive effects of salt spray. Underwater cable connections are also expensive. On the other hand, you do not need to build access roads and the neighbours rarely object (studies have also shown that offshore structures increase fish populations by providing artificial reefs for fish communities). Also, as more wind farms are built out, the cost of offshore installations is likely to fall dramatically. RenewableUK predicts a drop of 15 to 20% in the cost of offshore wind if economies of scale can be achieved and the market becomes more competitive.[53]

A survey of developments in offshore wind in different regions is presented on the next few pages.

Europe

Europe is the world leader in offshore wind with nearly 900 offshore turbines and a cumulative capacity of 2GW spread across 38 wind farms. Currently, 17 offshore wind farms are under construction in Europe (totalling more than 3.5GW) with a further 52 having been given full consent. According to the EWEA offshore wind power capacity in Europe grew by 54% in 2009.[54] They also reported that the turnover of offshore wind industry was approximately €1.5bn in 2009, a figure that is expected to increase to around €3bn in 2010. The sector has been further boosted by an injection of €255m under the EU's European Economic Recovery Plan. The UK is the current leader in installed capacity with a 44% share and around half the current offshore wind farms being built are in UK waters. In April 2010 the UK officially passed a landmark 1GW installed offshore as two new wind farms came online.

The UK's early lead in this field has been supported by the Crown Estate, the national agency which owns the coastal seabed. Offshore zones have been leased to wind power companies in several tranches, with the most recent Round 3 licences awarded in early 2010. The successful bidders for these nine zones were awarded development rights for a total combined capacity of 25GW, with construction scheduled to take place between 2013-2015. Combined with the 8GW from Rounds 1 and 2, the 33GW total will represent 38% of the UK's overall generation capacity (estimated to be 84GW), which is sufficient to provide all of the UK's needs for household electricity. The Carbon Trust has predicted that a successful Round 3 would propel Britain towards a £70bn wind and wave market that could provide up to 250,000 jobs.[55] Since the Round 3 announcements, major corporations including Siemens, GE and Mitsubishi have announced investments in offshore manufacturing facilities in the UK.

Britain's biggest project at present is the London Array, which will comprise 341 turbines generating around 1GW of power (enough to power a quarter of London's homes). The project is being developed by E.ON, Dong Energy and the Abu Dhabi cleantech investor Masdar. When finished it will be the world's largest offshore wind farm. Other equally huge projects are being planned; a consortium of utilities is already eyeing up the enormous 10GW Dogger Bank project.

Following behind the UK in terms of offshore capacity is Denmark, with a 30% share of installed capacity. Sweden, Norway and Germany also have some offshore farms but the potential is still huge. Germany, for instance, which has led Europe in the installation of solar power, only completed its first offshore wind farm in 2009. However, the German government has announced that 40 new arrays are to be built between 12km and 200km offshore, adding some 12GW to capacity.[56] Holland recently awarded its Round 2 contracts, and is hoping to have 6GW installed offshore by 2020. France announced plans for ten offshore zones in May 2010, with an initial 3GW of capacity along its Atlantic and Mediterranean coasts.

Asia

In Asia, China's potential offshore resource is phenomenal. According to Barbara Finamore, director of the US Natural Resource Defense Council's Beijing office, "China has the largest wind resources in the world, and three-quarters of them are offshore."[57] The country's first wind farm, a 102MW array near Shanghai, came on-line in April 2010. The government has invited bids for a further 1GW of developments and there are plans to install up to 30GW by 2020. Both Japan and Taiwan are also planning significant offshore wind developments.

United States

To date, the US has no offshore wind installed, although the potential is huge – particularly on the east coast. Winds in the Gulf of Maine, for instance, reach 35mph in the winter (when demand is highest). The Global Wind Energy Council estimates that the resources available in the shallow waters off the east coast, from Massachusetts to North Carolina, are roughly four times the energy demand in what is effectively one of the most urbanised, densely populated and highest-electricity consuming regions of the world.[58]

Despite the lack of progress so far, the federal government has forged a new agreement between federal, state and local agencies to help to speed up the development of offshore wind. Duke Energy is likely to be the first to install offshore wind, with plans for three turbines off the coast of North Carolina, and a group called the Virginia Offshore Wind Coalition is lobbying for major developments offshore from Virginia.

There are proposals in the pipeline for nearly 2.5GW on the Atlantic coast and there is considerable potential in the Great Lakes; the New York Power Authority is developing up to 500MW in the waters of Lake Ontario and Lake Erie, and Canadian developers are proposing 30MW projects in Lake St Clair and Lake Erie.

The US's most controversial project, the Cape Wind scheme in Nantucket Sound off Cape Cod, has been held up by a small but vocal minority of objectors for nearly a decade. It gained federal approval in April 2010 but opponents are still likely to mount legal challenges.

Important companies

Globally, the two companies with the lion's share of the offshore turbine market are Vestas (56%) and Siemens (39%). However, Siemens is expected to grow its market share significantly based on installed turbines and firm orders up to 2012, which analysts predict will see it overtake Vestas. The Spanish turbine manufacturer Gamesa moved into this area by taking a stake in the German offshore wind engineering firm Bard in early 2010. They are also considering a UK manufacturing facility to take advantage of the North Sea offshore boom.

Of the current 20GW under development in Europe, 90% is being built by large utilities such as RWE, E.ON, Dong, Vattenfall, Stakraft and Iberdrola.

These companies have the strong balance sheets and industry expertise to deal with the risks and high costs associated with offshore wind farms, and these companies will challenge the dominance of Siemens and Vestas in the next few years.

Masdar City: the renewables powerhouse

Abu Dhabi has seen the future and decided that it is green. Abu Dhabi is one of seven states of the United Arab Emirates and holds around 8-10% of the world's remaining oil reserves and 5% of its natural gas. But as part of its long-term strategy to retain its leadership in the energy business and to diversify away from fossil fuels, the emirate is investing $22bn in renewable technologies – making it the largest single government investment of its kind in the world.

At the heart of this plan is the world's first zero-carbon conurbation, Masdar City. This flagship project, to house 50,000 residents, is being designed along classic vernacular lines, surrounded by walls to keep out the desert dust, with low-rise buildings clustered around souks and shaded alleyways. The only form of transport will be all-electric autonomous pod cars (being built by Dutch company 2GetThere). The first phase is scheduled to be completed by 2013.

Masdar City will house the Masdar Institute of Science and Technology (being developed in conjunction with the Massachusetts Institute of Technology) and the headquarters of the newly formed International Renewable Energy Agency. It hosted the 2010 World Future Energy Summit and has entered into a partnership with Britain's Department of Energy and Climate Change (DECC) to support renewable energy policy research.

Some of the technologies being developed here include solar, hydrogen, geothermal, advanced waste handling systems (plasma and pyrolysis), smart grid management and water treatment.

Solar power

Masdar is aiming to develop a solar manufacturing cluster which will embrace crystalline, thin-film and concentrating solar power. It has invested $600m in two thin-film manufacturing facilities, one in Germany and the other in Abu Dhabi. The combined output will be over 200MW annually, using Applied Materials' SunFab production lines. Masdar is also developing projects which are breaking new ground in Concentrating Solar Power. Most 'power tower' CSP plants use mirrors to concentrate the sun on to a boiler at the top of the tower. Masdar is reversing this process and experimenting with 'beam down' technology whereby the receiver is placed at the base of the tower. They believe this will reduce energy losses, raise efficiencies and reduce electricity production costs. The project is a collaboration with the Tokyo Institute of Technology and Japan's Cosmo Oil (TYO: 5007).

Masdar is involved in a power tower project to use molten salt instead of synthetic oil as a heat transfer fluid, with cold salts being pumped up to the tower receiver and heated up to 565°C before being stored in a hot salts tank. The Gemasolar plant near Seville, part-funded by €80m from the European Investment Bank, should be able to produce power for 15 hours after the sun has gone down. The 17MW project is 60% owned by the Spanish engineering group Sener and 40% by Masdar.

Hydrogen

Masdar has joined with BP to develop the world's first industrial scale plant to convert natural gas to hydrogen and carbon dioxide. The $2bn project will take gas from the Abu Dhabi National Oil company, and reform it into hydrogen and carbon dioxide, using the hydrogen to generate electricity with fuel cells (producing around 5% of Masdar City's power needs) and selling the carbon dioxide back to the oil company to enhance oil recovery. Construction is expected to start in 2011.

Geothermal

Pioneering the first ever geothermal project in the Gulf region, Masdar plans to generate up to 5MW from boreholes drilled 4km beneath the city. An Icelandic start-up, Reykjavik Geothermal, has been awarded a $1.6m contract for the exploratory work. One drawback could be providing enough water for the wells, which could use vast quantities.

Biofuels

A joint research project has been set up in conjunction with Boeing, UOP Honeywell and Etihad Airways to investigate next-generation biofuels made from saltwater-tolerant crops grown in the desert. The plan is to combine inland fish farms with tracts of mangrove trees and salicornia, an oil-rich plant which can be converted into fuel.

Wind

Masdar has a 20% stake in the London Array, the flagship 1GW project that will be the world's largest offshore wind farm when completed. Masdar is also an investor in the Finnish wind company WinWind. www.masdar.ae

Investing in wind power

Overview

Bull points

- The most secure and fastest-growing of all renewables.

- Well-understood technologies and installation processes.

- Support through government subsidies and tax breaks.

- No fuel price risk – the cost of the wind is zero.

- Wind farms can be erected rapidly, once permits are agreed.

- Efficient means of delivering large-scale reductions in carbon dioxide emissions.

- Profitable return on capital investment.

- Technological developments are making turbines smaller, lighter and more powerful.

Bear points

- The big players in wind are multinational utilities, manufacturers and traditional energy companies – there are very few breakthrough opportunities for niche companies.

- Community resistance to onshore wind.

- Uncertainties over government subsidies and tax breaks.

- Commodity price risk, i.e. rising cost of steel.

- Competition from low-cost Asian production.

What the experts say about the wind sector

Wind power is enjoying a favourable climate amongst investment managers at present, who see it as an interesting long-term proposition that is currently one of the cheapest and most easily scalable of renewable technologies.

Simon Webber, co-manager of the Schroders Global Climate Change Fund, is bullish on all areas of wind power:

> "We like a range of companies in the value chains – gear boxes, component makers, turbine makers and the developers who actually build the wind farms. You are getting good economics now on building a wind farm. The markets are taking off in places like China, the US will grow stronger next year as well – it is growing globally."

Other analysts have a preference for the developers and owners of wind farms because turbine manufacturers are being squeezed on margins and competition from China. Michael MacNamara of Jeffries International in London sees a distinction between utilities (whom he considers low risk) and capital goods suppliers (who are a more risky proposition). He says:

> "At the moment our top picks are low-risk players such as Iberdrola and EDPR. These are well-capitalised companies with considerable experience of building wind farms who can deliver what's required. There are customers out there willing to pay a high price for wind, driven by renewable energy standards – and in tough times, the pool of players that can supply that wind energy is lower, so they are in a very strong position."

These companies are benefiting because they can maintain their pricing, their margins are improving because they are getting more and more scale in their wind operations, and the cost of building a wind farm is down anywhere form 15 to 30% from its peak because of lower turbine costs, lower steel costs, lower transportation costs and lower civil engineering costs.

MacNamara believes the policy drivers worldwide are better than they have ever been and new markets are coming on-stream – not just China and India, but huge tenders are now going out for projects in Brazil and elsewhere in South America. The recession and subsequent lack of availability of long-term funding has been the main factor holding back growth in wind but once this situation eases then demand will take off. The only thing holding back the growth in wind is the law of big numbers – it is hard to maintain growth at these current high rates indefinitely.

Wind ETFs

There are two New York-listed wind ETFs, which offer a convenient way to play the wind market:

1.   PowerShares Global Wind Energy Portfolio (NASDAQ: PWND)

2.   First Trust Global Wind Energy fund (NYSE: FAN).

See p.321 for more details.

Wind power technology and companies

Wind turbine manufacturers

Here is a survey of the companies working in the area of wind turbine manufacture:

- Danish company **Vestas** has installed around 40,000 wind turbines in 63 countries since 1979.

- Second to Vestas in terms of global market share is General Electric. The company has installed over 12,000 turbines globally and is currently working on next-generation offshore turbines and advanced turbine blades. GE is also building what will become the world's largest onshore wind farm at Shepherd's Flat in Oregon; it will comprise 338 turbines and have a generating capacity of 845MW (sufficient to power well over 500,000 homes) when completed in 2012. GE has signalled its commitment to the growing European offshore sector with plans to invest €340m to develop or expand its wind turbine manufacturing, engineering and service facilities in the UK, Norway, Sweden and Germany.

- The world's third largest manufacturer in terms of global sales is the Spanish firm **Gamesa**, which has installed over 16GW of turbines in over 20 countries.

- The German turbine manufacturer **Nordex** recently completed its Highland wind farm in Pennsylvania – this is one of the first in the US to use large, 2.5MW turbines.

- The privately held German company EnerCon developed turbines without gearboxes in 1992; their innovative drive system with few rotating components enables almost friction-free energy flow and reduces mechanical stress, operating costs and maintenance costs.

- Another major German turbine manufacturer is **REpower**, whose MD 70/77 range has become one of the most successful turbines in its class. To date, they have installed over 1400 turbines globally.

- Siemens Wind Power is part of the company's power generation division (which also includes gas and steam turbines, generators and power plants, gasifiers and fuel cells). It has over 25 years' experience in the wind business and has installed nearly 8000 wind turbines worldwide. The company is active throughout the whole wind power value chain (from turbines to grid connections) and operates globally. Siemens is continuing to make important advances in wind technologies, including the use of direct drive systems and jointless blade manufacturing.

- California-based **Clipper Windpower** floated on London's AIM in 2005 and grew very rapidly to achieve revenues of $800m in 2008. However, it was taken over by United Technologies Corporation in 2009.

- Some of Asia's largest industrial conglomerates have started to enter the global turbine market in a big way. Samsung Heavy Industries of Korea, the world's second largest shipbuilder, is planning to build turbines in order to counter a slump in shipping orders. They have ambitious plans to sell turbines in China and India, and are equipping their first wind farm in Texas. The company says that this will act as a testing ground in preparation for entering the US market more fully in 2011. Along with another Korean company it has entered into a $6.6bn deal to build and maintain solar and wind projects in Ontario, Canada.

- Samsung is not the only Korean manufacturer moving into this area. Hyundai Heavy Industries, Hyosung Corporation and Doosan Heavy Industries have all begun investing in wind. The Korean industrial group Daewoo Shipbuilding & Marine Engineering bought the American turbine manufacturer DeWind in 2009 and plans to leverage its vast engineering and manufacturing capabilities to become what its chief executive describes as "one of the world leaders in the wind energy sector".

- Mitsubishi Power Systems, a subsidiary of Mitsubishi Heavy Industries, has been manufacturing turbines in the US since the 1980s. It has also announced £100m of investment in a manufacturing and R&D centre for onshore and offshore wind to be located in the UK.

Super turbines

A modern wind turbine is 180 times more efficient at generating power than its 1980s equivalent, at less than half the cost per unit. The average onshore turbine today generates around 2.5 to 3MW, enough to power 1500-1800 households. But turbines are getting more powerful, with several companies working on 10MW designs.

The move towards even bigger turbines is being driven by the requirements of offshore wind and is being made possible because of advances in superconducting materials (see feature on the superconductor revolution on p.147). American Superconductor is actively developing a 10MW design using high temperature superconductors (HTS) and Zenergy Power is driving towards the same goal in collaboration with French power conversion specialists Converteam SAS.

The prize is huge. Using HTS wire instead of copper for the generator's rotor is expected to lead to turbines which are much smaller, lighter, more efficient and more reliable than conventional generators and gearboxes. In addition, direct drive generators eliminate the need for massive gearboxes, which is the component with the highest maintenance cost in normal turbines. It is expected that this could radically reduce the cost of wind power – Zenergy claim that the weight savings achieved through the use of superconductors could lead to a 25% reduction in the overall cost of offshore wind energy.

The outlook for wind turbine manufacturers

Competition between large conglomerates, alongside manufacturing starting up in low-cost countries such as China and India, may lead to a dramatic fall in the price of turbines – some industry experts suggest that the cost of wind turbines could fall by as much as 20% within three years.

Executives from some turbine manufacturers believe that soon they won't be able to compete with imports from Asia, and that they will become suppliers of technical services and R&D work rather than turbine builders. Others are less concerned, taking the view that their superior, more reliable technology is more cost effective over the lifetime of the wind farm than cheap Asian imports. But analysts warn that after a couple of years of ironing out any quality issues, Asian producers are going to be providing turbines of acceptable quality at significantly lower prices.

The vast new markets opening up in China, India and elsewhere in Asia will create opportunities for Asian turbine manufacturers. Already, Chinese wind turbine manufacturers have been winning huge contracts. Amongst those already established who will continue to benefit from this green gold rush are Goldwind (Shenzhen-listed), Sinovel (privately held) and Dongfang Electrical (HKG:1072). The latter is one of China's biggest enterprises and is also involved in nuclear power, so it is not a pure play in renewables.

One of the few pure-play companies accessible to outside investors in this sector is **China High Speed Transmission** (HKG:0658), which currently has a 90% share of the Chinese market for turbine gearboxes. The Nanjing-based company also makes marine gearboxes.

In recent contracts for wind farms, Chinese turbine manufacturers have won most of the bids. But there may still be some upside for foreign-owned companies. "Local equipment manufacturers are certainly going to get the lion's share," says Simon Webber of Schroder's Global Climate Change Fund, "but some of the foreign manufacturers will benefit. Vestas and Gamesa both have wind turbine businesses in China that will see some growth." Certainly, Vestas and Gamesa can be expected to work hard to remain as leaders in this industry – including work to develop lighter and more powerful models.

Other companies with a Chinese presence include GE, Siemens and **Suzlon**.

Wind power developers

Some of the most prominent listed companies in wind power development are spin-outs from major electricity utilities in European countries. These companies are listed below, as well as some companies in the US and smaller firms from around the world.

- **EDF Energies Nouvelles** is a subsidiary of the French utilities group Électricité de France (EDF). Wind power is EDF EN's main growth driver, accounting for 2.4GW (about 90%) of the company's renewables capacity.

- Another major European wind developer is EDP Renewables (EDP Renováveis), which is majority-owned by Grupo EDP-Energias de Portugal. EDPR has ambitious expansion plans to increase its wind power capacity to 10.5GW by 2012.

- A similarly ambitious expansion programme is being promoted by Spanish renewables group **Iberdrola Renovables** (a subsidiary of the power engineering and nuclear company Iberdrola), which is aiming to increase net capacity to 12.5GW by the end of 2010.

- The German utility giant RWE operates a renewable development arm, RWE Innogy, but has not yet spun this off. The group operates in the UK and Germany, with both onshore and offshore wind, and is aiming to invest at least €1bn annually on renewables.

North American companies

In the US, FPL Energy (part of the FPL Group) is the largest owner-operator of wind farms, with over 5GW spread across 50 facilities (comprising over

7500 turbines) in 16 states; its goal is to add a further 8 to 10GW of capacity before 2012, with investments of $20bn.

One of the small, independent developers active in the US is Renewable Energy Systems, part of the privately held Sir Robert McAlpine group. The company has installed over 3.6GW to date, and has several thousand megawatts under development in the US and the Caribbean. RES is also active in European offshore wind farms.

The Canadian wind farm developer **Western Wind Energy** is currently expanding its existing 34.5MW of capacity in California, with the addition of a further 30MW being provided by Gamesa turbines.

Small-scale European companies

In Europe, there are several small-scale publicly listed wind farm developers. These include:

- French company **Theolia,** which operates 421MW on its own account and manages a further 329MW for third parties.

- In the UK, **Renewable Energy Generation (REG)** is an AIM-listed developer with a portfolio of just over 21MW spread between seven small wind farms.

- Another small, AIM-listed wind power developer is Isle of Man-based **Renewable Energy Holdings**, which currently has a 40.5MW portfolio of German wind farms with a further 30MW in development in Poland.

- One of the latest wind-powered arrivals on AIM is **Indian Energy,** which launched on AIM in September 2009. The company is hoping to capitalise on the rapid growth of wind power in India.

- The UK's first publicly listed firm to focus exclusively on developing offshore wind farms is **SeaEnergy**, launched in 2009 from the former Scottish oil and gas services company Ramco. The company has a five-year global goal of building 1GW net of offshore generation capacity.

Component manufacturers and service companies

As mentioned above, Simon Webber of the Schroders Global Climate Change Fund suggested that there might be good companies among the developers who actually build components for turbines and wind farms. It is worth us taking a look at some of these companies here.

- One of the world's biggest manufacturers of gearboxes for wind turbines is the Belgian-based **Hansen Transmissions**. Part-owned by India's Suzlon Energy, Hansen supplies gearboxes to four of the five largest manufacturers of gear-driven wind turbines globally.

- NASDAQ-listed **American Superconductor** (AMSC) is a major component and turbine supplier to the wind industry globally. The company provides a range of technologies and solutions spanning the electric power infrastructure – from generation to delivery to end use.

- The world's leading supplier of wind turbine blades is the privately held Danish company LM Glasfibre, which has 12 production facilities globally and produces blades for eight of the world's top ten turbine manufacturers; the company has built over 120,000 blades in the course of the last 30 years.

- **Zoltek**, which supplies carbon fibre for blades, recently entered an agreement with the Dutch company Global Blade Technology to accelerate the design and manufacture of turbine blades utilising carbon fibre.

- In the US, one of the leading service supply companies to the onshore wind industry is **Broadwind Energy**. It moved up to a NASDAQ listing in April 2009.

Wind innovations

As the big corporations around the world continue to compete for massive contracts for large-scale wind farms, new entrants are nibbling away at the corners, looking for small, niche markets – whether it is small turbines designed to sit on top of factories or radical technologies that will improve the efficiency of existing turbines.

A new company called **Catch The Wind** is aiming to improve the efficiency of any wind turbine by at least 10%. A similar system has been developed in Denmark by the RISO Technical University of Denmark, LM Glasfiber and NKT Photonics. However, it is still several years away from market.

Other ideas under development include the ground-breaking work being carried out by *Artemis Intelligent Power* in Edinburgh, who are perfecting an innovative direct drive which will make wind turbines cheaper to build and maintain.

Whilst most manufacturers decided years ago that three blades was the most efficient wind turbine design, there are others who believe that earlier models, including two-blade designs, have something to offer. California-based *Nordic Windpower* is one of these.

Other companies experimenting with the design of wind turbines include *Broadstar Wind, FloDesign Wind, Leviathan Energy* and *WhalePower*.

Offshore innovations

As the offshore wind industry develops it seems that many new techniques and services will be investigated in an attempt to cope with the challenges involved. Whether these will present investment opportunities remains to be seen.

In Britain, a new £15m facility for testing offshore turbine blades of up to 100 metres in length is being developed at Blyth, Northumberland. Also, plans to develop the northeast as a hub for servicing North Sea wind farms have been boosted by a further £3m in grants under the Northern Wind Innovation Programme, announced in early 2010. Clipper Windpower is just one of several companies building facilities.

One of the consortia set to benefit from the new funding is *Xanthus Energy*, which is working to build a completely new type of foundation for offshore turbines.

Existing offshore turbines are only designed for depths of up to 30 metres, so new concepts are being developed for deepwater offshore turbines which can float. The world's first fully operational floating offshore wind platform was launched by the giant Norwegian energy company StatoilHydro (OSLO: STL) and connected to the grid in September 2009. The Hywind machine employs a Siemens turbine, while France's Technip (EPA:TEC) built the floater and Nexans (EPA:NEX) produced and laid the power cable to land. It is reported that Iberdrola may be the first to deploy floating turbines on a commercial scale at its recently acquired Baltic offshore wind farm.

In the US, the state of Maine is planning a vast offshore wind farm with over 1000 turbines floating in depths of 60-900 metres, some 35km from the coast. The University of Maine is working with around 30 companies on this scheme, which is estimated to cost around $20bn.[59]

A number of start-up companies are working on floating technologies, including *Principle Power, Blue H Technologies, OTM Consulting, Project Helm Wind* and *Sway*.

Opportunities in small-scale wind

There are currently limited opportunities for investing in small-scale wind (SSW) but recent reports from both the main wind industry trade associations in Britain and America have flagged up significant growth in demand in this area.

Unfortunately small wind systems have gained a poor reputation for actually delivering power. This is largely because so many turbines (particularly those mounted on the sides of houses) are badly placed in locations with not enough wind. Although building-mounted turbines can work, successful performance is highly dependent upon an adequate, unobstructed wind resource and appropriate siting. Free standing turbines frequently exceed their promised load factors if correctly sited.

Although domestic installations are currently the mainstay of SSW, this is forecast to change as larger systems (21-100kW) are deployed on industrial, commercial, agricultural and public housing developments. The Energy Saving Trust claims that "there are a vast number of commercial and domestic users ready to embrace this technology."[60]

An Italian company, Ropatec, has installed 27 of its 6kW turbines at Tesco stores throughout Britain. The company is also pioneering a financing deal which involves selling advertising on the rotor blades. McDonald's is an early customer in Germany.

With the UK enjoying the best wind resources in the whole of Europe, future technology cost reductions and fossil fuel price hikes could mean that many more potential sites will become commercially attractive. RenewableUK estimates the current installed base at around 10,000 systems, equivalent to just 20MW of power. However, they believe that over 600,000 small-scale wind turbines could be installed by 2020.[61] The newly adopted FIT in the UK should provide a boost to domestic installations. Renewable UK's *Small Wind Systems UK Market Report 2010* showed that the market expanded by 25% on previous records, with 8.6MW of installations in 2009, and projected growth of 181% in 2010.

In Britain the market leader in SSW is Proven Energy, based in Scotland. Their vertical axis turbines have a flexible blade, which enables them to generate power in light or strong winds – unlike many turbines which need to stop generating power to protect themselves at high wind speeds. Proven's latest product is a 3.2kW machine which the company claims can power a three-bedroom house. The technology fund Low Carbon Accelerator took a further £1.5m stake in the company in 2009 and converted its existing holdings to stock, giving LCA a controlling stake of 81% of Proven's share capital.

The US continues to command roughly half the global market share and is home to one-third of SSW manufacturers globally. The American Wind Energy Association projects 30-fold growth within as little as five years, for a cumulative US installed capacity of 1.7GW by the end of 2013.[62] The AWEA concludes that economies of scale are beginning to take shape and growth projections are the strongest in the industry's history. Growth is also being stimulated by the federal production tax credit, which contributes 30% towards the cost of small turbines.

One of the longest-standing SSW operators is Arizona-based Southwest Windpower. Founded in 1987, the company has sold over 140,000 machines but has only been marketing grid-connected turbines since 2006. Southwest received a major boost when General Electric led a group of investors (including Chevron Technology Ventures, the oil giant's VC arm) and put $10m into the company in 2009. Widely regarded as a corporate stamp of approval for small wind, the agreement will allow Southwest to expand in global markets as well as enhance its flagship 2.4kW Skystream machine. The company makes turbines in Arizona and China.

The only publicly listed small-scale wind company is **Helix Wind**, based in California. The company makes a series of vertical axis turbines ranging from 300W to 50kW capacity.

Small scale wind may be just that – small scale – at present, but with the increasing need for distributed generation this is an area to keep an eye on.

Companies to watch

Artemis Intelligent Power (UK) is developing digital displacement (DD) technology, which is an advanced hydraulic transmission system that replaces the gearbox and much of the power electronics on large turbines. It will be suitable for retro-fit to existing machines and also for use in the next generations of very large turbines. The company is also working with Pelamis on DD drives for their Sea Snake generators and on vehicle applications: Artemis has successfully tested a BMW 530i equipped with a DD hybrid transmission and demonstrated a 30% savings on fuel efficiency.

The company was named overall winner in the 2009 Carbon Trust Innovation Awards. www.artemisip.com

Broadstar Wind (US) has developed a ten-blade Darrieus turbine with a horizontal axis which they claim is ideally suited to rooftop applications and for placing in between conventional turbines in a ground-based wind farm. The company has signed up several high-profile customers for testing. www.broadstarwindsystems.com

FloDesign Wind (US) claims that a prototype of its jet engine-inspired turbine is three times more efficient than a conventional turbine. The 150kW turbine is built around a fan and a shroud, with a fin which directs it towards the wind. FloDesign closed a $34.5m Series B financing round in December 2009. www.flodesignwindturbine.org

Leviathan Energy (Israel) was founded in 2006 and the company designs aerodynamic cone-shaped structures that sit at the base of turbines in order to direct wind-flow to the critical area of the blades. The company claims that it can deliver a 15-30% increase in output as well as reduce maintenance costs. www.leviathanenergyinc.com

The first commercial product released by *Nordic Windpower* (US) is the two-bladed N1000 turbine, which uses a flexible hub link between the rotor and the generator driveshaft, enabling the blades to move in and out of the plane of rotation in response to gusts of wind. Nordic claims its design reduces costs by 20-25%. The company has been awarded a $16m loan guarantee from the US Department of Energy and raised $38m in fresh funding (led by new investors including Khosla Ventures and New Enterprise Associates) in early 2010. The N100 design has just started to win its first orders. www.nordicwindpower.com

WhalePower (Canada) is designing turbine blades with a series of ridges on the edges of the blade which they claim could increase efficiencies by up to 20%. The idea comes from humpback whales that tilt their fins at steep angles for more lift in the water. In low wind, blades with steeper angles could theoretically generate more power. www.whalepower.com

Offshore wind: companies to watch

Blue H Technologies (Netherlands) tested a floating two-bladed prototype off the coast of Italy in 2008 and now they are building the first operational

2.4MW unit. The company (which is planning to deploy its turbine offshore from Massachusetts) is part of a consortium which has been granted funding by Britain's Energy Technologies Institute. www.bluehgroup.com

OTM Consulting (UK) is developing a radical offshore turbine which looks like nothing ever seen before. The Novel Offshore Vertical Axis (NOVA) turbine is based on a pair of V-shaped giant wings which sit on a circular central generator. The project includes representatives from three UK universities and has been granted funding by the Energy Technologies Institute. www.otmnet.com

Principle Power (US) is developing WindFloat, a triangular-shaped, semi-submerged platform with a wind turbine placed on one corner of the triangle. The company has a memorandum of understanding (MoU) with Energias de Portugal to develop projects and has won $750,000 in DOE funding to explore the possibility of adding wave machines to the WindFloat platform, thus harnessing two sources of power at once. www.principlepowerinc.com

Project Helm Wind (UK) is a consortium led by E.ON Engineering and includes representatives from Rolls-Royce, BP Alternative Energy and the University of Strathclyde. No details are available for this highly secretive project, except that it involves "a new type of offshore-specific wind farm which will overcome issues such as turbine reliability and accessing equipment for maintenance". This project has received a grant from the Energy Technologies Institute.

Sway (Norway) has teamed up with Statoil Hydro and the turbine manufacturer Areva Multibrid (part of the French energy group Areva) to develop a prototype 'tilting' tower. In this concept, the wind turbine is mounted downwind, thereby allowing the floating tower to tilt (between 6-8 degrees) with the wind, thus reducing misalignment between the rotor and the wind in strong winds. The tower will also be able to revolve with the wind. The company has been granted a licence to deploy a 5MW prototype 7km offshore from Karmoy in Norway. www.sway.no

The SeaBreeze offshore wind turbine foundation systems designed by *Xanthus Energy* (UK) are low-cost alternatives for foundations in water depths up to 50 metres. They are built using prefabrication techniques for mass production and come fully assembled with the wind turbine, so it can be tested onshore. www.xanthusenergy.com

MARINE ENERGY | 3

"Of all the intermittent renewable sources, ocean power could be closest to providing a predictable generating profile and water's density means that lots of energy can be extracted from a small area. Significant developments in ocean power are expected over the coming decade, with over 1000 patents existing for ocean power generators. Tidal and wave power is at a similar stage of development to wind power 25 years ago."

Investment Opportunities for a Low Carbon World[63]

Introduction

During the first flowering of what was known as alternative energy in the 1970s, talk of marine renewables was dominated by just one device, the legendary Salter's Duck, which was said to have achieved efficiencies close to 90% in converting wave power to energy. Invented by Professor Stephen Salter at the University of Edinburgh, the eponymous duck had a curved, cam-like body but was never built. Britain's wave energy programme was shut down in 1982 – mostly due to pressure from the nuclear and coal industries.

Some 30 years after Salter's first experiments with wave machines, three Pelamis sea snakes were launched into the water off the coast of Portugal in September 2008 and the world's first commercial-scale wave farm was born. Then in January 2009 the world's first commercial tidal stream technology – Marine Current Turbines's SeaGen device – started sending power to the grid from Strangford Lough in Northern Ireland.

Although the last five years have been characterised by dozens of prototypes being produced, just a few full-scale deployments have been seen. From 2010 onwards the prognosis is for a significant increase in commercial-scale activities, with around 75 commercial size units forecast for deployment.[64] This industry is in its infancy compared to solar and wind, but the drive for clean energy is rapidly accelerating progress.

A report from Greentech Media claims that the emerging marine power industry will break through the 1GW barrier by 2012. The report identifies $500m which has been invested over the last decade in the 35 most active marine power companies. It forecasts expenditure of over US$2bn on R&D and a further US$2bn on building wave and tidal farms over the next five years.[65]

To date, the countries with the most significant developments in marine power are the UK, Portugal, the US and Canada.

The marine sector is divided into two different areas: *wave power* and *tidal power*. At present, this is represented by the focus being split between two main types of device:

1. Wave energy converters (WECs): these harness the power of waves to move pontoons, buoys or other devices up and down to generate electricity.

2. Tidal stream devices: these capture the energy from the flow of currents or tidal streams, often using two or three blades (the underwater equivalent of a wind turbine).

Other marine devices currently in use include tidal barrages (see box on p.92). There is also some interest in ocean thermal energy conversion, which exploits the temperature difference between warm water at the ocean's surface and colder, deeper water.

Advantages of marine power

Harvesting energy from the ocean has considerable advantages compared to other sources of renewable energy:

• It is much more predictable: tides and marine currents can be forecast years in advance.

• Water is over 800 times more dense than air so the energy potential is greater.

• Most of the hydrodynamic theory, engineering principles and marine construction techniques are well studied.

Disadvantages of marine power

The drawbacks of marine energy include the harsh marine environment and the challenges of delivering energy at a competitive price, given the high cost of installing and maintaining equipment. Other hurdles include getting electricity to population centres.

Just as wind and solar resources are not evenly distributed, neither is marine power. Waves are driven by wind: the best sites for wave power are coastal shelves in temperate zones with prevailing westerlies. Some of the most promising areas are the western coasts of Europe and the southern parts of South America and the Antipodes.

Tidal energy is also unevenly distributed. Although there are undoubtedly terawatts of power available in the world's oceans, many of these tidal streams are in locations far from land and at depths which would make them impractical to exploit. There are thought to be roughly 25 locations around the world where tidal streams are accessible and strong enough to generate power.

Survivability and reliability are key challenges. Any device (plus the associated infrastructure) will have to endure challenging (and changing) conditions offshore, nearshore and onshore. Machines have to survive the corrosive effects of seawater, punishing sea conditions and storm damage.

Britannia rules the waves

Britain is currently a world leader in marine power, with up to 25% of the world's wave technologies already being developed in the country. The Carbon Trust says that Britain could be the "natural owner" of the global wave power market, generating revenues worth £2bn per year by 2050 and supplying 20% of the country's electricity needs.[66]

This is largely thanks to abundant marine resources with long stretches of coastline (particularly in Scotland, Ireland and Cornwall) exposed to westerly winds. The UK also has considerable offshore experience from the oil and gas industries. The industry is supported by two major project-testing centres: the European Marine Energy Centre in the Orkneys and the Wave Hub in Cornwall.

Major European utilities – including EDF Energy, Eon, RWE npower renewables, Scottish & Southern Energy and ScottishPower Renewables –

have made significant investments in tidal or wave energy developers in the UK. The Carbon Trust has also handed out more than £12m in grants to over 60 marine technologies since 2003 through its Marine Energy Accelerator initiative. A further £22m has been handed out through its Marine Renewables Proving Fund, which supports companies making the leap from prototype to commercial generation. The government has also launched a Marine Action Plan which they hope will promote the mass deployment of marine energy and sets out a strategy for this sector up to 2030.

The European Marine Energy Centre (EMEC)

Located on the edge of the Pentland Firth, EMEC provides the only grid-connected facilities in the world for testing tidal and wave energy machines. Orkney was chosen because it receives uninterrupted Atlantic waves up to 15 metres high and has some of the strongest tidal currents in Europe (reaching speeds of four metres per second at spring tides).

The first device to be connected up here was Pelamis' wave energy converter, which successfully generated power to the national grid in May 2004. The first tidal device to achieve this goal was Open Hydro's turbine, which was connected in May 2008. Another first was achieved in November 2009, with the successful production of electricity from Aquamarine's Oyster (technically this is known as a near-shore wave energy converter).

Developers such as Ocean Power Technologies, Tidal Generation Ltd, Hammerfest Strom and others are planning to launch many more wave and tidal machines in the immediate future. EMEC has proved itself to be at the cutting edge of wave and tidal technology today. www.emec.org.uk

---

Wave power in Scotland

Scotland leads the way in marine renewables, a position which was reinforced by a recent leasing round with an unprecedented 1.2GW of wave and tidal projects given the go-ahead in March 2010 by the Crown Estate. Six sites have been allocated for wave energy devices and four for tidal projects around Orkney and the Pentland Firth off the north coast of

Scotland. The winning developers are Aquamarine Power, E.ON, Marine Current Turbines, OpenHydro, Pelamis Wave Power, ScottishPower Renewables, and SSE Renewables Developments. Scotland has also increased the subsidies available for marine energy to three ROCs for tidal and five ROCs for wave energy (compared to just two for all offshore renewables in England).

The Scottish executive, which estimates that Scotland has the capacity for 7.5GW of tidal and 14GW of wave power, is aiming to turn Scotland into the European leader in marine energy. To help further this aim, they are sponsoring the £10m Saltire Prize, which will be awarded to any wave or tidal energy company that achieves a minimum electrical output of 100GWh over a continuous two-year period in Scottish waters. The prize has attracted over 140 registrations of interest from 27 countries, with testing due to begin in June 2012.

"The UK, and particularly Scotland, is in a strong position to lead in the commercialisation of marine renewables, with all the benefits that would bring," according to *Renewable Energy World*. "Competition will be fierce, however, with many other countries also investing heavily and offering simplified feed-in systems. It remains to be seen if the UK government's new initiatives will be enough to secure the lead in the marine renewables race."[67] Alex Salmond, Scotland's first minister, believes Scotland is "the Saudi Arabia of marine energy."

The Wave Hub

The world's first large scale wave energy test centre is being developed 16km off the north coast of Cornwall. Called the Wave Hub, the £42m project is basically an electrical socket on the seabed which will allow developers to plug in their devices and connect to a sub-station on the shoreline. Whilst EMEC is designed for testing individual machines, the Wave Hub is designed for testing massed arrays of wave units. It has four berths, each covering 2km^2 of sea. The first developer to sign up is Ocean Power Technologies. The Wave Hub has become something of a barometer for the offshore wave sector, with the promise of megawatt arrays still looking elusive. Wave energy technologies, particularly those deployed further out to sea, are taking much longer to reach a commercial stage than many investors were anticipating.

Atlantic resources

Other European countries with strong marine energy programmes include Ireland, Spain and Portugal, all with Atlantic-facing coastlines.

In Ireland the government has set a target of 75MW of ocean energy by 2012 and 500MW by 2020, and operates a generous FIT. As part of its National Strategy for Ocean Energy, Ireland has allocated €26m towards a range of initiatives including a state-of-the-art National Ocean Energy facility in Cork, the creation of a wave test facility in County Mayo and the establishment of an Ocean Energy Prototype Fund.

Tidal barrages

Compared to tidal stream or wave devices, tidal barrages are a well-proven technology. The two largest in the world are at La Rance, France, and in Nova Scotia, Canada. Smaller barrages are operational in China and Russia. Britain's Severn Estuary has a tidal range of up to 14 metres and a barrage across the mouth of the river could potentially generate 8GW of electricity (about 5% of the country's energy needs). However, proposals for the scheme have been held up because of environmental concerns, finance issues and technological challenges.

If the scheme is approved, the biggest beneficiaries are likely to be large construction and engineering firms. Further barrages have also been mooted: four barrages in the Irish Sea (across the Solway Firth, Morecambe Bay, and the Mersey and Dee estuaries) could meet a further 5% of Britain's energy needs, claims the Northwest Development Agency.

Investing in marine energy

"Although substantial progress is being made in the area of wave power, the field has not yet approached the stage of development where investors can safely invest in the space. Investors interested in the technology are advised to wait until the technology proves that it is truly scalable."

Green Investing[68]

Overview

Bull points

- Mechanics are well understood.

- High degree of predictability of the energy source.

- Utilises skills from offshore oil, gas and wind power.

- Wave farms are not visually intrusive for the public.

- Significant commitments from energy utilities.

- Long-term support mechanisms from government.

- Large populations live near coastal zones.

Bear points

- Problems of reliability and survivability in open seas.

- Bottlenecks in grid connections.

- Multiple unit arrays will require more maintenance.

- Dependence on government subsidies.

- Too many prototypes of differing designs.

Investment summary

As an investor, you want to make sure that your funds do not sink as quickly as the next bright idea in marine power. Even though there are several companies now delivering power to the grid and the industry is expanding at a rapid rate, marine energy still has many pitfalls.

The good news is that the first 1MW devices are now in place; two UK companies, Marine Current Turbines of Bristol and Pelamis Wave Power of Edinburgh, have become the first in the world to deploy megawatt-scale wave and tidal technologies and supply energy to the grid, with both companies achieving this in 2008. Indeed, Marine Current Turbines' machines have generated more electricity than expected. The company says that its twin rotor devices now generate 5MWh each from the ebb and the flow of each tide – that makes 20MWh per day, enough to power 1500 homes.

However, this is a very high risk area – there are other devices that have ended up at the bottom of the sea. For instance the Canadian company Finavera Renewables put its test machine, the $2.5m Aquabuoy, into the waters off central Oregon on September 2006. The machine unfortunately sank a month later, just one day before it was due to be taken out of the water. The company's shares plunged.

A company called WavePlane Solutions also lost a prototype in rough seas off the coast of Norway just days after deployment in March 2009 and Trident Energy had an unfortunate mishap when its 20kW wave generator overturned in September 2009 as it was being towed out to sea and became grounded 5km off the Essex coastline.

But these setbacks haven't deterred the ocean visionaries; the International Energy Agency estimates that there are at least 200 devices currently under development for wave, tidal, or ocean thermal energy conversion, with machines ranging from floating attenuators and point absorbers to oscillating hydrofoils and vertical axis turbines. They claim that the marine sector needs to undergo a dramatic convergence before it can effectively become commercial, with the market being narrowed down to a few successful technologies in much the same way that it took a period of time for wind turbines to evolve into their present shape.

Some expert investors agree that this process is already happening. "I think we're at the beginning phase of that consolidation," says James Vaccaro, Head of Investment Banking at Triodos, "because you've now got modules which are working at commercial scale, so I believe we will see rapid consolidation in the next two or three years."

Triodos are an investor in Marine Current Turbines (MCT), the first productive tidal energy developer. "We've got a lot of confidence in the future of tidal energy not least because MCT's SeaGen module at Strangford Lough has been successful and it is connected to the grid and delivering electricity," says Vaccaro. "It has got there with a commercial unit at this time, which is probably well ahead of most commentator's estimations of when it was going to get there, is good news for the industry."

Chris Goodall, author of *Ten Technologies to Save the Planet*, believes that there eventually will be marine devices producing electricity at a cost which is competitive with fossils fuels:

> "We do not have to challenge the laws of physics and thermodynamics
> as we have to do with some other technologies. The crucial problems
> are those of mechanical engineering and these are more susceptible to
> eventual solution, probably by continuing to improve strength and
> robustness."[69]

Marine technology and companies

Pure-play marine companies

For individual investors there are currently just two publicly listed pure-play marine energy companies to choose from.

The largest of these is Perth-based **Carnegie Wave Energy,** which has won significant tranches of government funding, both on its home territory in Australia and overseas. Carnegie is also hoping to accelerate development of its technology in the northern hemisphere through a licensing agreement with EDF Energies Nouvelles. The second largest is **Ocean Power Technologies**, who are working on their second-generation PowerBuoy, the PB150. The company is planning America's first commercial offshore wave park in Oregon and has other projects underway in Spain, Japan and Australia. OPT is part of a six-member consortium which was awarded €4.5m by the European Commission in March 2010 to develop WavePort, a project off the coast of Spain aimed at providing its PowerBuoy technology with wave prediction capability.

Corporate backing for marine energy

A number of large companies around the world are working with smaller developers in the area of marine renewables:

- In the US, aerospace giant Lockheed Martin (NYSE: LMT) has entered into an agreement with Ocean Power Technologies to jointly develop utility-scale wave farms.

- In Britain, Rolls-Royce (LON: RR) has invested in Tidal Generation Ltd (TGL), a Bristol-based company which is developing a deep water turbine designed to operate in depths of 35 to 100 metres.

- The Inverness-based company Wavegen was bought by Voith Siemens Hydro Power Generation, part of the privately held Voith group, in 2005. Since renamed Voith Hydro Wavegen Limited, the company was the first to build a shoreline energy converter which uses the principle of an oscillating water column. Its first machine has been supplying power to the grid since 2000 on the Scottish island of Islay. Wavegen is now developing projects on the Isle of Lewis (in conjunction with npower renewables) and in Spain's Basque Country.

- Another German company, Robert Bosch, is backing Yorkshire-based *Lunar Energy*, who are developing a tidal turbine in conjunction with the Aberdeen company Rotech Engineering.

- Through its subsidiary Bosch-Rexroth, Bosch is also backing the Finnish company AW-Energy, who have won €3m in funding from the EU to refine its wave-roller machine, currently undergoing testing near Peniche in Portugal.

- The Swedish energy giant Vattenfall is funding a small Irish company called Wavebob to build a series of demonstration generators off the coast of Ireland. Vattenfall is putting €1m into the joint venture, Tonn Energy.

- Vattenfall is also investing in a joint venture with *Pelamis Wave Power*, whose sea snake was one of the first to be deployed in multiple arrays.

Leaders in wave power

There are four companies who are leading the wave power sector:

- *Pelamis Wave Power* unveiled the world's first commercial wave farm in 2008 – the €9m Aguçadoura wave-power project in Portugal. It featured three Pelamis P1 machines, each generating 750kW.

- Another company at the forefront of the race to commercialise wave energy is *Aquamarine Power*, whose prototype 500kW Oyster was connected to the grid at EMEC in November 2009. The company was awarded over £1m by the Scottish government to develop the Oyster 2, which is designed to have three times the generating capacity of its predecessor. Unveiled in May 2010, the Oyster 2 has fewer moving parts than its predecessor and lower maintenance costs.

- The Swedish company Seabased Industries has developed a system of piston-driven generators which are designed to be deployed on the seabed in depths of between 20 and 100 metres. The company has been running a pilot project off Sweden's west coast since 2006, and in early 2010 announced that the Swedish Energy Agency is providing a grant for a full-scale wave plant off the coast of Smogen which will consist of 400-500 units connected together, with 10MW of capacity.

- A company called Pure Marine Gen has developed a design for a floating device which aims to harness energy from both the vertical and horizontal motion of the waves. The company has received a grant from the Carbon Trust. Another floating device being promoted by Offshore Wave Energy Ltd of Cornwall traps and compresses air in successive wave troughs. The company has received funding from the Carbon Trust and the South West Regional Development Agency.

Leaders in tidal power

In tidal power, the following companies are at the forefront of the industry:

- *Marine Current Turbines* is the main front-runner in the race to commercialise tidal power. Their first SeaGen device has been exporting power to the grid since 2008, although it wasn't fully operational until early 2009. Siemens took a stake of just below 10% in the company in early 2010.

- One of the world's first successful attempts at harnessing tidal power was a horizontal axis turbine mounted on the seabed by Hammerfest Strøm (owned by a consortium which includes StatoilHydro and ScottishPower Renewables), which installed its 300kW prototype at a depth of 50 metres off northern Norway in 2003. It was designed for a three year test period but ran for around four years without maintenance before being pulled out of the water. The original turbine, with some new components, was reinstalled for further research in July 2009. Hammerfest Strøm now plan to install a 1MW prototype at EMEC and a further device in the Sound of Islay to power whisky distilleries on Islay, as well as providing electricity for the island's 3500 inhabitants. Both projects are due to come online in 2011.

- *OpenHydro*, based in Dublin, is further down the road to commercialisation than most. It has developed an open-centred 1MW turbine which is designed to be as simple and robust as possible: its slow-moving rotor and lubricant-free operation also minimise risk to marine life.

- A small Scottish start-up, Scotrenewables, is planning to develop floating turbines which are anchored to the seabed by cables. The company claims that this will lower production costs because expensive seabed foundations won't be needed. However, there are considerable problems to be overcome – not the least of which is how a floating turbine will survive in a storm. Fred Olsen Renewables and the oil company Total are reported to have backed the plan with £6.2m in cash.

Companies to watch

Aquamarine Power (UK) is the developer of the Oyster. The Oyster is designed with a peak power output of 300-600kW per machine. The company, backed by investors including Sigma Capital Group and Scottish & Southern Energy, raised an additional £10m from investors in September 2009. They estimate that they need to raise another £40m to take Oyster through to commercialisation. The company is planning to have a full-scale commercial wave farm in place by 2014, with around 20 devices generating 15MW of power. Aquamarine has an agreement with Airtricity (the renewables arm of Scottish and Southern Energy) to develop up to 1GW of marine energy by 2020. www.aquamarinepower.com

Lunar Energy (UK) is developing a simple horizontal axis turbine, which uses a ducted design to maximise the currents flowing through it. Lunar are planning their first commercial deployment of eight units off the Welsh coast in 2011 in a joint development with E.ON. Lunar has also signed an agreement with Korean Midland Power Co to create a giant 300-turbine tidal farm off the coast of South Korea. www.lunarenergy.co.uk

Marine Current Turbines (UK) installed the world's first tidal current turbine off the coast of England in 2003. From this they developed the SeaGen, which was first installed in Strangford Lough in Northern Ireland in 2008. Since the machine became fully operational in 2009 it has been producing more power than anticipated, due to the currents being stronger than predicted, and is now producing 20MWh per day. The company is now developing a tidal farm off the coast of Wales in conjunction with RWE npower renewables, another in Scotland, and two further projects in Canada. Marine Current Turbines has since raised £3.5m towards the deployment of further SeaGen devices; principal investors include BankInvest, High Tide, ESB International, EDF Energy, the Carbon Trust, Guernsey Electricity and Triodos Bank. www.marineturbines.com

Open Hydro (Ireland) was founded in 2005 and was the first company to plug a tidal device into the grid at EMEC and installed the first tidal turbine in Canadian waters in the Bay of Fundy in November 2009. The company has since won contracts from Électricité de France (EDF) to develop a tidal farm in Brittany (expected to come online in 2011) and from a public utility in Washington State for three turbines in the Puget Sound. It has also acquired an interest in Alderney Renewable Energy Ltd, located in the Channel Islands. The waters around Alderney are estimated to contain one of the largest resources of tidal energy in the world, with a potential capacity of some 3GW. The potential is huge – when fully developed, the tidal farm could comprise around 3000 machines. The company has designed and built its own delivery barge, the Open Hydro Installer, to make it easier and more economical to put the devices on the seabed. www.openhydro.com

Pelamis Wave Power (UK) is working on second generation P2 machines that are longer (at 180 metres) than its P1 prototypes. The company says that the P2 will offer major improvements in efficiency, survivability, operability, maintainability and overall cost effectiveness. The first P2, built for E.On, was unveiled in May 2010 and is capable of generating 750kW. Pelamis has contracts with E.ON and Vattenfall for further wave farms, including one off the Shetland islands with a capacity of 20MW. www.pelamiswave.com

Tidal Generation Ltd (UK) includes engineers who worked on the UK's first successful tidal turbine, the Seaflow project, which was installed in the Bristol Channel in 2003. TGL claims that the turbine's 80 tonne support structure is cheap to construct, easy to install and uses readily available vessels for maintenance. Backers include Rolls-Royce, Garrad Hassan, EDF Energy, E.ON and Plymouth Marine Laboratories. The project has received funding from the Energy Technologies Institute. www.tidalgeneration.co.uk

GEOTHERMAL 4

"Utilities and independent developers have been researching and testing methods of producing electricity from geothermal energy for more than four decades. After languishing for decades, geothermal power is once again catching fire, thanks to the twin challenges of peak oil and global warming."

Investing in Renewable Energy: Making Money on Green Chip Stocks[70]

Introduction

Planet Earth is essentially comprised of a thin crust on top of a huge nuclear reactor that reaches temperatures of 7000°F at its core. The crust itself increases in temperature by 30 degrees for every kilometre of depth. Tapping this heat from the earth's core could turn out to be one of the most abundant sources of low carbon, zero-emission renewable energy we have available. The potential for geothermal power is vast.

Most geothermal power around the world today is drawn from areas where the planet's crust is thin enough to allow engineers to tap into naturally heated underground reservoirs of steam or water to generate electricity. Indeed, the geothermal potential of places like Iceland, Hawaii and New Zealand is well known. But pioneering new technologies are being developed that mean there could soon be a massive expansion of geothermal power, with the possibility of being able to drill down in many other areas – not just those on volcanic fault lines – to harness the heat of the Earth's core. Geothermal is also the power behind ground source heat pumps, which are used to provide heating and cooling for industrial and residential buildings.

There are great advantages to geothermal power. Geothermal plants run continuously and are therefore ideal for providing base-load utility generation. Also, since new generation plants are emission and pollution-free they can be sited anywhere. The technology is well known, electricity generating costs are low once plants have been built and the sustainability of geothermal has been demonstrated by power plants being around for over a hundred years in commercial form: the first geothermal plant was built in

Larderello, Italy, in 1904 and it is still generating electricity. Other plants have been running since 1958 at Wairakei, New Zealand, and since 1960 at The Geysers, California.

Most of the world's current capacity of around 9GW is generated in countries and regions around the Pacific rim with high levels of volcanic activity such as New Zealand, Indonesia, the Philippines and California. The US is the world's largest producer of geothermal power (3.1GW) and the second largest producer is the Philippines (1.9GW), where geothermal provides around 20% of the country's electricity needs. Indonesia currently has about the same capacity as the Philippines but has enormous untapped geothermal potential, with an estimated 27GW that could be exploited.

The geothermal resource

Traditional geothermal plants rely on either dry steam technology (where active steam vents are run through a turbine) or flash steam (where hot water from a vent is vaporised to produce steam to run the turbine). The problem is that the areas of the world with underground aquifers of super-heated water or steam that are within a reasonable drilling distance of the surface are limited.

New technologies are set to change that. One recently developed technique, for instance, is the binary cycle system, which uses water at much lower temperatures than a flash steam plant. The water is passed through a heat exchanger that transfers the heat to a working liquid with a much lower boiling point than water – this fluid is then vaporised to run a turbine. These plants are incredibly efficient and produce no pollutants or emissions.

The potential for the use of the binary cycle system is huge. In the US, for example, geothermal surveys traditionally ignored any reserves which registered at less than 350°C, but binary cycle plants can produce electricity from sources that are anywhere between 150 and 300°C.

Enhanced geothermal

The enhanced or engineered geothermal system (EGS) is another new geothermal technology. It involves drilling two wells some distance apart into a hot rock mass (usually granite) some 3-5km below the surface. In practice it has proved difficult to execute, but if the technical hurdles can be overcome and with a reasonable investment in R&D, "EGS could provide 100GW or more of cost-competitive generating capacity in the next 50 years," according to the Massachusetts Institute of Technology.[71]

Europe already has two EGS plants up and running: one is an EU-backed demonstration project at Soultz-sous-Foret in eastern France and the other is a commercial plant in Landau, Germany, which has been producing around 20GW a year since it was completed in 2007.

"There is a lot of interest worldwide in re-assessing the resources available," said Dr Jonathan Busby of the British Geological Survey. "The technology has come a long way in the last 20 years and that's opened up a huge volume of extra rock at depths that can now be exploited on a worldwide basis." Europe, Russia, China, the US and India all have substantial thermal resources accessible by EGS. Even the Gulf states are taking an interest, with the Masdar project (p.69) exploring a potential heat reservoir beneath the city.

One big drawback with EGS is the potential to cause earthquakes. An EGS project in Basel was shut down in 2006 after it caused a series of tremors in the Swiss city, leading to $9m worth of damage to housing. In addition, stories of well blow-outs, lost drills and dead-ends are not uncommon – but this is normal in a new industry. The majority of drilling expertise in the world over the last 30 to 40 years has focused on drilling through sedimentary rock to get oil and gas, not drilling through granite.

A new technique called single-well geothermal, which is said to resolve many of the problems caused by EGS, is being investigated by America's Electric Power Institute.

Apart from EGS, other techniques are still under development. One of these involves pumping supercritical carbon dioxide (a pressurised form that is part gas, part liquid) underground instead of water, bringing the heat back to the surface in order to generate electricity. This eliminates the need to fracture the rocks and has the added advantage of leaving some of the carbon dioxide underground (so helping to sequester GHGs). Hydro-geologists at the Lawrence Berkeley National Laboratory in the US estimate it could produce 50% more heat than water-driven EGS.[72]

Growth of the geothermal sector

Geothermal is undergoing a renaissance globally, with the number of countries exploiting its potential set to rise to nearly fifty in 2010.[73]

The US continues to lead in installed capacity (3.1GW), although there are now nearly 150 projects underway which could see this capacity increased to as much as 7GW in the near future, according to the Geothermal Energy Association.[74] The sector has been boosted by over $338m in ARRA funding, with nearly $100m going towards exploratory projects and another $80m towards EGS.[75] Geothermal was one of the early beneficiaries of increased federal funding following the Gulf of Mexico oil spill, with loan guarantees of nearly $200 million pledged to projects in Nevada and Oregon by the Department of Energy in June 2010.

South and Central America are just starting to open up to geothermal, with new licences recently granted in Chile, Nicaragua, Peru, Argentina and Guatemala.

Africa's Rift Valley, which runs from Djibouti in the north to Mozambique in the south, is a potential geothermal hotspot. Test drillings in Kenya have "exceeded all expectations" according to a pilot programme run by the United Nations Environment Programme (UNEP) and the Global Environment Facility. They estimate that the Rift Valley could generate around 4GW, with the potential for Africa as a whole as high as 7GW.[76]

In Australia the focus is on EGS technology, particularly in the huge Cooper Basin (which extends from South Australia to south-west Queensland). Some of the hottest rocks in the world at economic drilling depths are found here, with the entire zone capable of supplying up to 10GW – enough to supplant the country's coal and gas generating capacity.

In the Caribbean, the tiny island of Nevis is about to become the first island in the world not only to be self-sufficient in geothermal power but also to earn an export income from the electricity generated. The discovery of several large geothermal reservoirs has led to the construction of a new plant, part-funded by the Caribbean Community (CARICOM), which will eventually provide 50MW of power – five times more than the two-island nation of Saint Kitts and Nevis needs. It is estimated that 200MW could be eventually obtainable.

Investing in geothermal

Overview

Bull points

- Considerable government support.

- Available constantly, it is the only source of renewable power able to provide base-load electricity for utilities.

- Cost-competitive with fossil fuel energy.

- There are no fuel costs, so no exposure to commodity price risk.

- Maintenance costs are predictable and largely fixed.

- New technologies will vastly extend the range of the resource.

Bear points

- Capital costs are high and plant can take years to generate revenue.

- Obtaining permits and finance is a potential obstacle.

- Geothermal reservoirs can become depleted if not properly managed.

- There is a predominance of smaller companies in this field, with inherently higher risk and less liquidity for investors.

- EGS involves drilling into granite, which is a comparatively new technique.

- EGS has caused earthquakes.

Investment summary

Although the high capital cost of building geothermal plants is currently a drawback, as the industry develops further these should fall. "Geothermal will continue to be a strong growth industry over the coming years," says Jon Forster of Impax Asset Management (who have holdings in Ormat). In the US, the stimulus funding and an extension to the current Production Tax Credit (PTC) are making a difference. "Projects need to be in the ground by 2011 in order to qualify for the PTC benefits, so if credit markets ease – which they seem to be doing – and once there is more clarity around the stimulus money in the US, then geothermal companies could see a ramp-up in their business over the next two to three years," says Forster.

Finance and planning issues are clearly major hurdles but because of its capacity to produce continuous power, geothermal is in a different category to other sources of renewable energy. Bozena Jankowska, manager of the Allianz RCM Global EcoTrends Fund, believes it should be considered as more of a utility-type investment. "It is a very interesting alternative technology, it is very well-established and certainly more mature than the wind sector," she comments.

Geothermal technology and companies

> "Today's geothermal is a bit like gold mining; wide open for small operators willing to devote time and capital to discovering and bringing to market a viable resources. Many will succeed, since there is so much geothermal potential out there. Some will turn a single, well-run property into a nice earnings stream. Others will roll up less well-capitalised 'juniors' and build major producers, just as mining firms do today."
>
> **Clean Money: Picking Winners in the Green-Tech Boom**[77]

There are three broad geographical regions that investors looking at geothermal energy should pay attention to: North America, Australia and the UK. We will now take a look at each of these in turn.

North America

The world's largest producer of geothermal power is the US oil giant Chevron (NYSE: CVX). Their geothermal operations started more than 30 years ago when they discovered Darajat, a major field in Indonesia. The company's other important sites are Gunung Salak in Indonesia and Tiwi and Mak-Ban in the Philippines. Combined, the four Pacific Rim sites generate 1.27GW of geothermal energy.

Most of the publicly listed pure-play geothermal companies are based in North America, with the Toronto Stock Exchange currently the favoured exchange for a listing.

The most significant event in 2009 was the IPO of **Magma Energy**. The company's only plant currently generating power is Soda Lake, in Nevada, but Magma has four further sites under development in the US and five in

South America. It has also taken a stake in H S Okra, the largest privately owned geothermal company in Iceland.

There has been some recent consolidation in this sector, with four smaller geothermal companies merging into one. Three Canadian-listed companies (GTO Resources, Polaris Geothermal and Western GeoPower) combined with Nevada-based **Ram Power** in 2009. The new consortium has a portfolio of projects underway in California, Nicaragua and Canada, with a potential capacity over 500MW.

The largest pure-play geothermal energy company is **Ormat Technologies Inc**, which develops and builds its own plant and also supplies equipment and turn-key plants to other developers.

Binary cycle plants

Ormat is a world leader in binary cycle plants but it faces competition from large corporations who have recently moved into this space. For instance Pratt & Whitney, a division of United Technologies (NYSE: UTX), recently bought the Italian manufacturer Turboden, who make high efficiency turbogenerator systems. Smaller companies developing similar systems include Exorka International, a German company which is owned by *Geysir Green Energy.*

One of North America's leading geothermal producers is the Calpine Corporation (NYSE: CPN), which operates 15 geothermal power plants in northern California, with 725MW of capacity. However, Calpine's main business is power from natural gas, with around 40 plants in the US.

Smaller developers of geothermal in America include **US Geothermal**, who have operational plants in Idaho and Nevada. The company has won over $7m in ARRA funding towards the $10m cost of developing an EGS plant in Idaho, and a further $4m towards the cost of new technologies at its Nevada site. Another company with interests in the south and western US is **Raser Technologies**, who have licences in Nevada, Utah, New Mexico and Oregon.

Also operating in the south-western US is **Nevada Geothermal Power**, who recently commissioned their first plant in northern Nevada. This is currently producing 27MW, although the company has already started work to expand its capacity to 40MW.

Search giant Google is backing EGS in America with investments of up to $11m in start-ups such as AltaRock Energy and *Potter Drilling*. It has also awarded a grant to a university geothermal laboratory to update the Geothermal Map of North America. This is seen as a crucial step in providing a more comprehensive picture of the country's EGS potential.

Australia

In Australia, there are a large number of companies looking at EGS in the Cooper Basin – around 20 have applied for drilling licences. The biggest of these is **Geodynamics**, which has licences covering 2500 square km in the region. Geodynamics has received over AU$90m in grants from the federal government for the development of its 25MW demonstration plant.

The second most advanced EGS operator in Australia is **Petratherm**, which is developing a plant at Paralana in the Flinders Range, some 600km north of Adelaide. The site contains some of the best heat-producing rocks found anywhere in the world, and the company has won nearly AUS$70m in government grants towards this 30MW demonstration project.

One of the problems being faced in Australia is transmission, since the hot rocks are a long way from population centres. This is a familiar issue around renewable power.

United Kingdom

In the UK the hottest rocks at the most accessible depths are found in Cornwall. The Department of Energy and Climate Change (DECC) is funding exploratory work by two new companies in this area. EGS Energy have teamed up with the Eden Project to develop a 3MW pilot plant that would supply electricity to the Eden Project and district heating to a nearby town. Another new company, Geothermal Engineering, is developing a 10MW pilot plant to supply heating to nearby homes.

Companies to watch

Geysir Green Energy (Iceland) wholly owns Iceland Drilling Ltd and has a share in the Icelandic geothermal company HS Orka. It has operations in China, the Philippines and the US. Its German subsidiary Exorka is developing geothermal projects in Bavaria using binary cycle technologies. www.geysirgreenenergy.com

Potter Drilling (US) is currently developing a drill that they say will make drilling faster, deeper and cheaper. Using hydrothermal spallation (a process of shooting hot water at rock in order to exploit flaws in the rock's construction) there is no contact between drill bit and rock, so the drill bits last longer. The company, which is still at the test stage, won $5m from the US Department of Energy in 2009. Investors include the Massachusetts Institute of Technology and Google.org. www.potterdrilling.com

POWER STORAGE | 5

Introduction

Energy storage is a key component in the low carbon revolution, slotting into the matrix in partnership with renewables, smart grids, electric cars and energy efficiency. Advanced battery technologies that address these needs are forecast to grow to a market worth $60bn by 2013.[78]

Finding cost-effective and efficient ways of storing energy from renewable sources will contribute to a more widespread adoption of wind, wave and solar power techniques because it will also change the economics of renewables. For example, wind often blows hardest at night, and may produce more power than required at this time of day. If the electricity produced during off-peak periods could be stored and then sold during peak periods when prices are higher, it would generate better returns. Similarly, power storage can help smooth out the peaks and troughs of supply and demand on smart grids.

Another factor propelling this market is the growth in distributed generation – that is, vast numbers of people are expected to start installing renewable systems in their homes as the price of wind, solar and other technologies falls to grids parity. This poses another problem for the utilities that they will have to manage as they build out the smart grid. Clusters of solar power, for instance, are likely to develop in certain neighbourhoods, towns and commercial districts. When the sun is shining, these houses will be exporting energy to the grid – but when the clouds come over, they may switch very quickly to net importers of electricity.

Solar systems will need to be linked to household batteries, or electric car batteries, to smooth out the fluctuations. There will also be opportunities for local storage facilities to help with load balancing – community energy storage parks are already being proposed.

The two broad categories of power storage are battery storage and non-battery storage.

Investing in power storage

Overview

Bull points

- The electrification of transport has begun.

- Renewables will make grid storage a necessity.

- Distributed generation will open up new markets.

- Steady improvements in safety, cost and energy storage capacity.

- Secondary markets will improve the economics of battery production.

Bear points

- Cost of raw materials and processing (li-ion).

- Potential scarcity of lithium.

- The need for much higher energy densities (li-ion).

- Life span of li-ion products.

- High costs (sodium-sulfur).

- Lack of manufacturing capacity (sodium-sulfur).

- China has a 95% monopoly on some raw materials.

Investment summary

The year 2009 was good for battery technologies, with established manufacturers performing well on stock markets and start-ups succeeding in attracting venture capital.

The headline-grabbing event for power storage in 2009 was the flotation of A123 Systems, which designs and manufactures rechargeable lithium-ion batteries. Founded by engineers from the Massachusetts Institute of Technology, the company is currently developing batteries for BMW, Chrysler, GM, Delphi, Chinese automaker SAIC and others. A123 made its market debut on 24 September 2009 and leapt almost 50% by close on the first day – even though the company had posted increasingly large losses for the previous three years.

Although A123's IPO was the most eye-catching event in the cleantech sector it wasn't the only power-storage related story. Equally compelling was Warren Buffet's investment into China's BYD Co, a car and battery manufacturer. Based in Shenzhen, BYD has risen over a short time-scale to become the world's biggest producer of rechargeable batteries for cellular handsets. It also makes cars and car parts, but the division which is said to have caught Buffet's attention is making lithium-ion batteries and hybrid and all-electric vehicles. Warren Buffet's MidAmerican Energy Holdings (a subsidiary of the Berkshire Hathaway Group) first invested in BYD in September 2008, with BYD agreeing to sell a 10% stake for $230m.

Buffett's investment provided BYD with a solid endorsement and the capital necessary to follow its ambitions of launching hybrids onto the market and it made headlines again in July 2009 when it became clear that Buffet had made an incredible $1bn dollar paper profit from his stake. MidAmerican Energy has since been looking to add to that stake, according to press reports. BYD's plans to enter the US market are accelerating, with its e6 electric car being launched there a year earlier than originally planned.

The growth of interest in the power storage sector has been mirrored by the scramble amongst US battery companies for federal stimulus funding and to establish a domestic US battery industry to compete with Asian manufacturers.

To this end, 14 US energy storage companies have joined forces to create the National Alliance for Advanced Transportation Battery Cell Manufacture. The US Department of Energy's Argonne National Laboratory, a leading developer of new battery technologies, has been active in encouraging the alliance and will serve in an advisory role. The alliance hopes to replicate the success of Sematech, a collaboration of semiconductor manufacturers formed in the 1980s that raised millions in government grants and private investment to help US manufacturers recapture their lead in semiconductor technology from Asia.

This is a parallel not lost on Sanford L Kane, a former director of Sematech and one of the founders of the battery alliance. "Semiconductors and battery cells are both strategic elements of their ultimate end products," said Kane. "Batteries will be to automobiles what semiconductors were to computers."[79] Whoever builds the batteries, in other words, will build the cars.

Such is the importance of this market that over $2.4bn was awarded to battery and electric drive manufacturers under Obama's 2009 federal stimulus plan. Amongst the winners were A123 Systems, who were awarded $249m; the company plans to spend this, along with a similar amount of its own cash, on a new manufacturing plant. Johnson Controls was another winner, with $299m in grant aid.

A recent report from *Cleantech Investor* on battery technologies profiled over 100 companies directly or indirectly involved in energy storage technologies.[80] The list included over 30 companies funded by venture capital investors and a host of other privately owned companies, as well as more than 40 stock-market quoted companies. The companies are predominantly listed in the US, with over 50% traded on the NYSE, NASDAQ or OTC Bulletin Board. Almost 20% are quoted in Tokyo and close to 15% in China. Europe is notable by its absence from this list, the exception being the French company Saft. In terms of the technologies the authors note that lithium-ion is the predominant technology, with over 50 companies listed as working in this field.

As well as the pure-play companies discussed here, large multinationals such as General Electric, LG Chem, Toshiba and Panasonic are moving to establish or increase their market share. Toshiba is building a new plant in Japan to manufacture a new super charge ion battery (SCiB), which it says will charge more quickly than li-ion and retain its charge for longer. These batteries are already in use in Schwinn's Tailwind electric bicycle, and Toshiba is scaling up production for the electric car market and large-scale solar installations. Panasonic, which bought Sanyo (then the world's largest lithium-ion battery maker) in 2008, is supplying batteries to Tesla for its Roadster and Model S cars. South Korea's LG Chem Ltd, another industry leader, has developed li-ion polymer batteries specifically for the electric vehicle market.

Power storage technology and companies

Battery storage

> *"Sales of advanced batteries and hybrid vehicles are likely to be significantly stronger than the market expects in coming years. Companies that are at the forefront of battery and electric vehicle technology are likely to thrive in coming years and decades."*
>
> **Profiting From Clean Energy**[81]

Lead-acid batteries

Lead-acid batteries are the oldest type of rechargeable battery. Although they have a low energy-to-weight ratio and corresponding low energy-to-volume ratio, they can supply high surge currents. This, along with their low cost, has made them popular for kick-starting car starter motors. About 90% of batteries sold today are traditional lead-acid, however they need regular maintenance.

Advanced lead-acid batteries share much of the same chemistry and packaging but use different electrodes. The manufacturers claim that these new units require less lead and yet have higher power delivery rates, faster recharge times and longer life cycles than conventional lead acid batteries. They also look much the same and can be made on the same production lines as conventional lead-acid batteries.

Amongst the companies working on advanced lead-acid are **Axion Power International**, **C&D Technologies Inc**, **EnerSys**, and **Exide Technologies**.

One promising start-up in advanced lead-acid batteries is *Firefly*, based in Illinois, which was spun-out from heavy vehicle manufacturer Caterpillar.

Lithium-ion

Lithium-ion (li-ion) batteries are currently one of the most common types of battery found in consumer electronics such as cameras and laptop computers. They have a very high energy-to-weight ratio, there is no memory loss and they have a very slow self-discharge when not in use. Thanks to their high energy density, they are increasingly being used in defence and aerospace applications. Li-ion is hitting the mainstream on a much larger scale with the growth in electric vehicles and grid storage.

Although the development of electric vehicles is the main impetus behind these batteries, it is utilities that will benefit in the long run. Cleantech analyst Pike Research forecasts that li-ion batteries will be the fastest growing category for utility-scale applications, expanding to a $1.1bn worldwide business by 2018. "Utilities will be the downstream beneficiaries of innovation and investment in lithium ion batteries for the transportation sector," says senior analyst David Link. "While li-ion was once limited to consumer electronics devices, it is quickly becoming the battery of choice for electric vehicle manufacturers. Improved storage capacity and economics will lead the utility sector to adopt li-ion, as well – we anticipate that 2011 will be the inflection point for growth in this category." Pike Research forecasts that revenues from li-ion batteries will represent 26% of the $4.1bn global stationary energy storage business by 2018 (www.pikeresearch.com/newsroom/energy-storage-market-to-reach-41-billion-in-10-years).

One problem to date has been the high cost of li-ion batteries. However, major car manufacturers are hoping that creating secondary markets for these batteries once they can no longer be used in electric vehicles will help bring the cost down. After ten years of use (or 150,000 miles) their performance drops below what is required for electric vehicles – but they still keep as much as 70% of their storage capacity. Car makers such as Nissan and General Motors are now looking to recycle these batteries for use as power storage on wind farms, or emergency back-up power.

Lithium – will there be enough?

Demand for lithium is soaring as battery-makers worldwide rush to produce lithium-ion power packs for electric vehicles. There is a debate over exactly how much of this commodity is available and how the world is going to meet its needs for electric cars.

Around half of the world's reserves of lithium are found in Bolivia (notably in the vast Salar de Uyuni salt flats). The Bolivian Government is well aware of the strategic value of this resource and is playing hardball with mining consortiums who want to extract it. They are aiming to become the 'Saudi Arabia of lithium' and insisting that tenders must include a commitment to develop battery manufacturing in the country.

Other countries with significant reserves include Chile, Argentina, Brazil and China. Prices of lithium have been increasing steadily over the past few years as demand has increased. Like any other commodity, this trend is likely to continue. You can gain some exposure through the Sociedad Química y Minera de Chile (NYSE: SQM), a world leader in the production of lithium carbonate. However, although SQM supplies around 30% of the world's lithium, the business only represents 10% of the company's gross margin.

Listed companies in the area of lithium-ion batteries include:

- **A123 Systems**, which plans to supply 5m li-on batteries for electric vehicles by 2013 from the manufacturing facility they are building in Michigan.

- **Ener1**, which is working on both utility scale li-ion and car batteries. Their clients include Volvo, Fisker and bus manufacturer AC Transit.

- **Altair Nanotechnologies**, which is taking a different tack to some of the main li-ion developers. It has replaced the traditional graphite materials used in conventional li-ion batteries with lithium titanate. The lithium-titanate batteries are being tested in a new electric hybrid bus in California that will make it possible for the bus to be charged in 5-10 minutes.

- Ontario-based **Electrovaya**, which produces li-ion polymer batteries that are claimed to be smaller, lighter and more powerful than competing batteries. The company is working with car, bus and truck manufacturers in China, Norway, US and India.

- **China BAK Battery Inc**, which is one of the largest manufacturers of lithium-based battery cells in the world. The company began trading on NASDAQ in 2006 and they are currently working with a number of car makers to incorporate lithium-phosphate cells in electric vehicles.

- Texas-based **Valence Technologies Inc**, whose third generation lithium batteries are specifically designed for electric vehicles. In early 2010 Valence won a $3m order from the Tanfield Group, owner of Smith Electric Vehicles, to deliver advanced battery modules for their commercial vans. Valence is also developing smart grid applications for these batteries.

- French battery group **Saft Batteries**, which is a major player in the lithium-ion arena, especially since a recent tie-up with Johnson Controls gives it access to US federal funding and the North American markets.

- In the UK, the defence technology company QinetiQ (LON: QQ) has developed a new low-cost lithium-ion cell chemistry and associated flexible battery management system for hybrid electric in conjunction with the technology company Ricardo, with part-funding from the Department for Transport under the UK Energy Saving Trust Low Carbon R&D programme.

Sodium-sulphur batteries

Sodium-sulfur batteries are similar in concept to traditional lead-acid batteries except that they use liquid sodium, so they are built quite differently. They have high energy densities (three times greater per volume than lead-acid cells) and high power levels, however they need to be maintained at temperatures of 250-350°C. Sodium-sulfur batteries have been installed in conjunction with renewable sources of power in Japan, Germany and the US. Barriers to widespread adoption include the high costs involved and the lack of manufacturing capacity – the sole mass producer of these systems on a large scale, **NGK Insulators** of Japan, has a waiting list of two years for orders. GE has also been working on smaller-scale sodium batteries (for more information see the box on General Electric's dual battery system on p.125).

Grid-scale applications of sodium-sulfur batteries have been developed since the 1980s by a partnership between the Tokyo Electric Power Co and NGK Insulators, with NGK now established as the world's leading supplier.

Flow batteries

The first chlorine flow battery was developed by Charles Renard and used to power his airship *La France* in 1884, but these days are mostly used for stationary energy storage and load levelling applications. The key characteristic is that the active material (the electrolyte) is stored outside the battery stack and pumped through the cell stack as required. The advantage of flow batteries is that they can react very quickly and can be rapidly recharged by replacing the electrolyte liquid. The disadvantage is that they are complicated (requiring pumps, sensors, control units and secondary containment vessels) and their efficiencies are relatively low (around 75-80%). However, flow batteries are gaining ground in large-scale energy storage because of their relatively low price compared to other grid storage batteries such as sodium-sulfur. The different types available include the redox (reduction-oxidation) flow battery, the hybrid flow battery and the redox fuel cell battery (which are in some ways similar to fuel cells, as the name suggests).

The main players are **ZBB Energy Corporation** and the privately held Premium Power Corporation. Both of these companies make zinc-bromine flow batteries. Premium Power Corporation maintains that their Zinc-Flow system is "lower in cost than lead acid batteries up front and roughly equivalent to pumped hydro, at under 2 cents/kWh, on a long-term basis."[82] A promising company in this field is California-based *Deeya Energy*.

Ultracapacitors

Ultracapacitors (sometimes also called supercapacitors) store energy as an electrical field, rather than chemically as batteries do, which means that they can charge and discharge much more quickly than batteries – the drawback is that they store much less energy than batteries. With an extremely high energy density thousands of times greater than standard capacitors, ultracapacitors provide an independent, instantly available source of power unaffected by temperature, shock or overcharging. They can also be charged and discharged an almost unlimited number of times without any deterioration in their performance.

Ultracapacitors are increasingly being used in a wide range of energy applications, either on their own or in conjunction with batteries. For instance, ultracapacitors are being fitted to subway trains and buses (vehicles with a lot of stop-start operations) in regenerative braking systems, which capture the energy used during braking and use it during acceleration. This makes these vehicles much more fuel efficient and less polluting. They are also used in electronic applications such as flash units in cameras. Smart grid applications include uninterruptible power supply (UPS) and voltage regulation and smart metering – the ultracapacitor will keep transmitting information from the meter even if power is shut down.

Another application for ultracapacitors is in hybrid and electric vehicles, where they can provide a quick boost of energy. This means that you can have a smaller battery pack, thus cutting down on costs. It also prolongs battery life, by cutting down repeated cycling of the battery.

The ideal set-up is said to be for vehicles to have one-third of their storage capacity in capacitors and two-thirds in batteries.

We're only just at the beginning of the commercialisation of ultracapacitors. The market is expected to expand from $208m in 2008 to $877m in 2014, according to Lux Research, signifying a compound annual growth rate of 27%. Lux expects that transportation will drive large supercapacitor applications, with an expected expansion from $86m in 2008 to over $320m in 2014. "As volumes increase, we expect large players including Panasonic, NEC Tokin and Maxwell Technologies to benefit most from economies of scale," said lead author Jacob Grose. "As that trend unfolds, the market may see more diversification as large companies bolster their portfolios through acquisitions of smaller firms."[83]

One of the more established pure-play companies in this field is San Diego-based **Maxwell Technologies**, who have been producing their Boostcap ultracapacitors since 2004 (the company also produces microelectronics for the space and satellite industry).

Another long-established company is the Korean manufacturer Nesscap, who are targeting heavy-duty transport and industrial energy storage. Japanese companies involved in ultracapacitors include Panasonic and NEC Tokin.

Early-stage companies working on ultracapacitors include the Ukrainian company APowerCap Technologies, whose ultracapacitors can be used for a wide range of applications, including consumer electronics, power quality systems and vehicles. American start-ups include EEStor, Ioxus (owned by Custom Electronics Inc) and Seattle-based EnerG2.

Nanomaterials

Considerable advances are being made in battery sciences in nearly all of the chemistries discussed here. Breakthroughs are also being made in nanomaterials – a nanomaterial called graphene, for instance, is being used to develop more efficient power storage devices.

Graphene is a one-atom thick sheet of carbon atoms tightly packed into a honeycomb lattice – like an atomic-scale chicken wire, made up of carbon atoms and their bonds. It is an extremely low density material that is said to be between 50 and 200 times stronger than steel, and due to its incredibly high surface area to mass ratio, it is also a very efficient conductor of electricity (it has up to five times the conductivity of copper with only 25% of the density).

Adding graphene to li-ion batteries has been shown to increase the usable charge and prolong battery life. Graphene can also be used to produce ultracapacitors with a greater energy storage density than is currently available – possibly doubling their current capacities.

Two companies producing commercial products in this field are Ohio-based company *Angstron* and the Texas-based company *Graphene Energy*. Expect to see a lot of interest in this new carbon material in the years ahead.

General Electric's dual battery system

General Electric is developing numerous applications under their 'Ecomagination' programme. The company has already developed sodium metal halide batteries for a hybrid locomotive and they have also got a research partnership with li-ion specialist A123 Systems (GE is a significant investor, with a $70m stake). Now GE is creating a dual battery system which combines li-ion with sodium, and they are hoping that this new hybrid will achieve an optimal balance of acceleration and electric range, while minimising the size and cost of the battery and maximising its life.

The company is investing $100m in a new manufacturing facility in upstate New York, with production expected to begin mid-2011; they say that the new hybrid battery will work in anything from trains to heavy trucks, buses and cars. Grid storage is another big market for the sodium/li-ion battery.

Non-battery storage

Pumped hydro storage

The most cost-effective means of storing large amounts of electricity is pumped hydro, which uses two water reservoirs, separated vertically. During off-peak hours, water is pumped from the lower reservoir to the upper reservoir. When electricity is needed, the water flow is reversed to generate electricity. There is over 90GW of pumped storage in operation worldwide, which is about 3% of global generation capacity.[84] Factors limiting the expansion of pumped hydro include capital costs and the appropriate geography.

Some utilities find pumped hydro a convenient option. Iberdrola, for instance, is currently expanding its existing 635MW La Muela plant in Valencia, Spain, with the addition of a second powerhouse, the 852MW La Muela 2. When completed in 2012, it will be Europe's largest pumped hydro scheme. Iberdrola is also involved in the development of several other plants that will help firm up the variability of their extensive wind capacity and eventually add nearly 1750MW of capacity to the grid system of Spain and Portugal by 2018.

A variation on pumped hydro is being proposed by New York-based Riverbank Power, who want to create massive caverns some 600 metres underground beneath a body of water such as a flooded quarry. The water would flow downwards to create electricity during peak periods and be pumped back up again at off-peak rates. As the caverns have to be mined the costs are very high – around $2bn for 1GW of capacity.

Compressed air storage

Compressed air energy storage (CAES) is another utility scale storage system that is relatively straightforward in engineering terms. In CAES systems, off-peak electricity is used to pump air into airtight chambers underground. At peak times, the air is released to drive compressors.

CAES plants are large infrastructure projects which take up to five years to build. However, they could well be the most cost-effective form of energy storage invented yet, according to America's Electric Power Research Institute.[85] Researchers claim that CAES wins on cost grounds because of the relative technical simplicity and the potential volumes for storage. Not only are 3bn cubic meters of underground salt caverns available, but you can increase the volume of existing caverns through simple solution mining techniques. If the underground cavern can't be expanded, the air can be stored at a higher pressure. Compressed air can also be stored at depleted oil fields.

There are so far only two operational CAES plants in the world: a 290MW plant in Huntorf, Germany, built in 1978, and a 110MW plant in Alabama built in 1991. Dr. Michael Nakhamkin, who developed the Alabama plant, has since founded a new company, New Jersey-based Energy Storage and Power, who are working on second generation CAES technology backed by $20m from utility group PSEG Global.

Other proposals under development in the US include the Iowa Stored Energy Park (which is a joint project by municipalities in Iowa and several nearby states) and a facility being proposed by Pacific Gas & Electric (PG&E). The Californian utility has applied for $25m of federal stimulus funding to develop a large-scale, 300MW CAES plant which they estimate will cost $356m.

Irish power group Gaelectric Developments Ltd is looking at developing salt caverns near Larne in Country Antrim, a £200m project which could provide between 136 and 300MW of back-up capacity. The company is also investigating the suitability of potential underground sites in Montana, and has identified two candidate reservoirs. One of these sites is conveniently co-located in a high wind resource area, and Gaelectric is pursuing research funding to confirm the storage capability of this reservoir.

Sirius Exploration is another company looking at salt caverns. The AIM-listed mining group has invested in an American company, Dakota Salts, which holds a lease on 5000 acres of salt pan in North Dakota.

Another AIM-listed company exploring back-up power using compressed air is Energetix (LON:EGX) which is marketing its Pnu Power system to utilities and telecoms companies.

A New Hampshire-based company, *SustainX*, is taking a different approach to CAES technology by combining it with hydraulic systems. The company says that this means that it generates electricity directly from the expansion of the compressed air itself, doing away with a secondary heat source. There is also no need for storage to be underground.

Liquid storage

An entirely new kind of battery has been invented by Massachusetts Institute of Technology (MIT) professor Donald Sadoway. Its key components are kept at high temperature so that they stay entirely in liquid form. The materials being used are highly secret, but Sardoway has been awarded $7m by the American federal agency ARPA-E (Advanced Research Projects Agency-Energy) to pursue it further. Within days of this award being made in November 2009, the French oil giant Total announced a $4m, five-year joint venture with MIT to develop a smaller-scale version of the same technology, suitable for use in individual homes and other buildings.

The battery is based on low-cost, domestically available liquid metals that have the potential to shatter the cost barrier to large-scale energy storage. ARPA-E said the battery technology "could revolutionise the way electricity is used and produced on the grid, enabling round-the-clock power from America's wind and solar power resources, increasing the stability of the grid, and making blackouts a thing of the past."[86]

Flywheels

Energy can also be stored as kinetic energy, for instance in a flywheel system. A basic flywheel system consists of a rotor suspended by bearings inside a vacuum chamber (to reduce friction), connected to an electric motor/generator. The rotor (or flywheel) is accelerated to a very high speed and the energy is maintained in the system until it is needed, at which time it is converted back by slowing down the flywheel.

There are already some examples of flywheel systems being used for grid stabilisation or UPS applications. They are expensive to build but they are very low maintenance and have long lifecycles.

Flywheels are also now starting to be used in electric vehicles. The early development work on flywheels in cars has taken place in motor sports, where they were permitted in Formula One racing cars for the first time in 2009. The idea is to make motor racing more exciting (not a particularly green goal), however once these technologies have been refined in the very demanding world of track racing they will start to be deployed in the wider world, specifically in hybrid and EVs.

One of the world's leading developers of stationary flywheel systems is Los Angeles-based Pentadyne Power, who shipped their first commercial production flywheel in 2004. The privately held company has sold more than 500 flywheel systems since then and their clients include Emerson Network Power, Toshiba, Socomec and defence contractors.

Two publicly listed companies work in this field. The first is **Beacon Power Corporation**, based in Massachusetts. The second company is Texas-based **Active Power**, who have shipped more than 2000 flywheels and clocked up over 50m hours of field operations in 40 countries since the company commercialised its technology in 1996.

Another leading flywheel manufacturer is the privately held Pentadyne Power, who have shipped more than 400 flywheels. A fast-growing start-up in stationary flywheel technologies is California-based *Vycon*, which closed an additional fund round in early 2010 on the back of increased sales of its storage systems.

Two UK companies working at the cutting edge of mobile flywheel systems are Northamptonshire-based *Flybrid* systems and *Williams Hybrid Power* in Oxfordshire. Both companies have developed devices for Formula One racing cars.

Motor sports are one of the main testing grounds for flywheel systems. Porsche showed off the first flywheel-powered Porsche 911 hybrid at the Geneva Motor Show in March 2010. The company said that further testing the prototype at the *24 Hours Nürburgring* would provide know-how for the subsequent use of flywheel/hybrid technologies in their road-going sports cars.

Companies to watch

Angstron (US) is the first advanced materials company to offer commercial quantities of nano-graphene platelets, which boost the storage capabilities of batteries. The company was awarded $1.5m by the US Commerce Department's National Institute of Standards and Technology in 2009. www.angstronmaterials.com

Deeya Energy (US) is developing a new redox flow battery, the L-Cell, which is said to give significant advantages over traditional designs. Originally developed by NASA as an energy source for long-term space flights, Deeya's L Cell is now finding applications in telecommunications and renewable energy storage. In 2009 Deeya completed an oversubscribed $30m series C financing, led by new investor Technology Partners alongside existing investors BlueRun Ventures, DFJ, Element Partners and New Enterprise Associates. This financing brings Deeya's total VC investment to $53m. www.deeyaenergy.com

Firefly (US) has replaced traditional lead metal electrodes with a carbon microcell foam material that is said to improve the performance of lead-acid batteries dramatically. Firefly has won $10.3m in military contracts and established a partnership with C&D Technologies to manufacture their new Oasis battery, which is capable of almost double the run time and life of traditional lead-acid batteries. www.fireflyenergy.ca

Flybrid Systems (UK) has developed a high-speed (60,000rpm) flywheel-based energy storage system made of steel and carbon fibre that is powerful, small and light. The speed of rotation means that the flywheel can be very much smaller and lighter than has previously been possible. The systems are very efficient, with up to 70% of braking energy being returned to the wheels to drive the vehicle back up to speed. The devices are readily recycled and relatively inexpensive to make, as they are manufactured entirely from conventional materials. Their first application was in Formula One racing.

This technology is now being applied to a range of applications outside motor sport, including road, rail and off-highway vehicles. Flybrid won both the Start up of the Year and the top Grand Prix prize at the 2009 British Engineering Excellence Awards. www.flybridsystems.com

Graphene Energy (US) is leading the development of next generation graphene-based ultracapacitors. Backed by the Quercus Trust, Graphene is expected to move out of the research stage and raise funds for a manufacturing facility in 2010. www.grapheneenergy.net

Pentadyne Power (US) was founded in 1998 and has sold more than 800 of its low maintenance, lightweight units since it shipped its first commercial production flywheel in 2004. This award-winning company is backed by venture capital investors including Nth Power, DTE Energy and the Energy Innovations Portfolio. www.pentadyne.com

SustainX (US) is developing CAES technology which generates electricity directly from the expansion of the compressed air itself. It also utilises above-ground storage in the form of normal gas cylinders. The company has received $5.39m from the US DOE for a full-scale demonstration model. Backers include Polaris Venture Partners, Rockport Capital and the US National Science Foundation. www.sustainx.com

Williams Hybrid Power (UK) was founded in 2006 and has developed a novel flywheel which integrates the magnets of the electric motor into the composite structure of the flywheel itself, by mixing magnetic powder into the resin. This means that they can deliver much smaller, lighter flywheels which run at very high efficiencies. The company is building on its Formula One experience to transfer this technology to a variety of other applications, including hybrid electric vehicles (HEVs). www.williamshybridpower.com

Vycon (US) was established in 2002 and is a manufacturer of flywheel systems to provide UPS and other power services. The company closed a $13.7m funding round led by BankInvest of Denmark in January 2010 and plans to use the cash to expand its manufacturing capacity. www.vyconenergy.com

Glossary

CAES: compressed air energy storage

EV: electric vehicle

GW: gigawatt

HEV: hybrid electric vehicle

KWh: kilowatt hour

Li-ion: lithium-ion

MW: megawatt

NaS: sodium-sulfur battery

NGP: nano-graphene platelet

NiMH: nickel-metal hydride

NYCE: New York Cash Exchange

OTC: over-the-counter

PCS: power conversion system

R&D: research and development

SCiB: super charge ion battery

TPPL: thin plate pure lead batteries

UPS: uninterruptible power supply

SMART GRIDS 6

Introduction

"Most of the world's power grids will be upgraded in the coming decade. That means millions of smart meters and related gear, and numerous openings for new technologies, services and business models. The market they are creating is vastly more interesting than the old dumb grid, and should spawn some great growth stocks."

Clean Money: Picking Winners in the Green-Tech Boom[87]

The world's electricity grids are in need of modernisation. Most national power grids use technology invented in the 19th century and the whole infrastructure is hugely inefficient, with up to 20% of all electricity generated lost in transmission.

The shortcomings of the old-fashioned, largely electromechanical electricity grids currently in use have become increasingly obvious. Prone to power failures and blackouts, they are vulnerable to natural disasters and accidents. Additionally, they are mostly built around an outdated model of a central power plant sending energy in one direction to the consumer.

The solution to these problems is the smart grid.

At its simplest, the essence of a smart grid is to add intelligence – or information technology – to the electricity networks. But it is also much more complex than this, giving rise to a radically different approach to power distribution.

One major benefit is that smart grids can take variable supplies of power from multiple sources – such as would be provided by renewables – and distribute it efficiently. When the wind is blowing hard in Norway or the sun is at its peak in Spain, surplus electrons will be more easily distributed to the rest of Europe, for instance. The old grids just cannot cope with the intermittent nature of renewables.

Smart grids will not only handle multiple new sources of energy at the utility scale, they will also encourage the growth of microgeneration by householders; this will change the network model from one of top-down distribution to a two-way flow of energy and communications. This trend is already supported by FITs in many countries.

Another major stimulus for smart grids is the rapid development of EVs and plug-in hybrid electric vehicles (PHEVs) (see Green Transport, p.173).

The European super grid

Europe is moving ahead slowly but surely with plans for a green super grid that would link sources of renewable energy all the way from Norway to Morocco into one highly efficient system. There are already high voltage links connecting many European countries but numerous others are now being proposed and built.

The European super grid would include links across the North Sea, the Irish Sea, the Baltic and the Mediterranean to enable the free flow of electricity from a huge diversity of wind and solar farms.

Work has already begun on the North Sea network; the longest and most powerful subsea high voltage cable in the world, which connects Norway and the Netherlands, was opened in 2008. The 580km link exports cheap Norwegian hydro electricity southwards to the Netherlands during the day, with Dutch off-peak electricity going northwards by night.

Another major cable, connecting the Netherlands and Britain, is expected to be completed by early 2011. A key link between Britain and Ireland, due for completion in 2012, is expected to kick off a huge boom in wind power from Ireland being exported to Britain.

National Grid is planning two major links down the east and west coasts of Britain in order to enable the transfer of power from renewables in Scotland (wind, marine and hydroelectric) to England and Wales. These links will form part of a network that could completely encircle Britain, creating a high-powered ring main which would effectively bypass public objections to new pylons because it will be completely underwater. Coastal wave and tidal schemes could link directly into the high-powered lines.

The east coast link will benefit the massive wind farms currently being built in the North Sea, whilst the west coast link will similarly benefit wind farms being planned for the Irish Sea. The North Sea and Irish Sea networks will eventually connect over a hundred wind farms containing some 30,000 turbines.

The Mediterranean network would draw energy from many sources, including strong summer winds in Morocco and Egypt, and year-round solar power in sunny North African countries (for more information see Desertec: CSP from the Sahara on p.35).

The development of these networks presents huge opportunities for providers of cabling, cable-laying services and infrastructure works.

Investing in smart grids

Overview

Bull points

- Driven by government regulations.

- In regulated markets, utilities will be allowed to increase their infrastructure spend and returns.

- Huge market potential.

- Consumer acceptance increased by being able to earn money from micro-generation.

Bear points

- Who pays? The upfront costs are high and new networks are going to be expensive.

- There are competing techniques for the transmission of information collected from meters: unless common standards are agreed, development of a unified network will be impaired.

- Gap between technology and expectations.

- Technological glitches may hinder consumer acceptance.

- Customer resistance to variable pricing.

Smart grid index

A new smart grid index was launched in September 2009. The NASDAQ OMX Clean Edge Smart Grid Infrastructure Index (NASDAQ: QGRD) tracks companies that are primarily involved in the electric grid, smart meters, devices and networks, energy storage and management and software for the smart grid and electric infrastructure.

Investment summary

A whole new industry is emerging to meet the challenges of creating smart grids for the 21st century, with fresh investment opportunities in everything from smart metering to transmission technology, energy management software and demand-response networks.

There are some conflicting ideas of how much the smart grid is going to cost:

- Estimates for the European super-grid come in at around €128bn.

- In America the Electric Power Research Institute believes that it will cost the US $165bn, or roughly $8bn a year for 20 years.

- Al Gore's Repower America campaign has stated that the overall cost of developing the smart grid in the US is $400bn over a ten-year period (although this includes transmission upgrades as well as smart meters).

- Cisco, outlining its own smart grid strategy, said that the market is projected to $20bn annually in five years.[88]

- Lux Research maintain that the market for the smart grid will reach $65bn in 2013.[89]

Whichever figure you choose, there is going to be a lot of investment in this area and numerous different companies will need to work together over a number of years to modernise and automate the world's electricity systems. It will involve an intensive and broad collaboration between utilities, telecommunication companies, device manufacturers, consultants, software publishers, system integrators and more.

But do not expect instant returns on investments in smart grids – these are big infrastructure projects that require considerable resources to roll out as well as lengthy approval processes. Bozena Jankowska, fund manager of the Allianz RCM Global EcoTrends fund, believes that smart grids are for those with long investment horizons. "I think it is very interesting long term, driven by very long-term structure drivers," she says, but is cautious about which way the market is going to go. "There are a lot of decisions to be made by the utilities which are actually going to be installing this technology," she says. "It is probably going to be a mixture of different solutions from different technology providers." Jankowska advises patience: "It is not something that's going to suddenly start growing overnight. It is going to be a drip-feed process."

Spending on smart grids by country

In the US, President Obama's administration has provided $3.4bn in federal grants to accelerate the transition to smart grids, which is expected to be matched by a further $4.6bn in funding from the private sector. The programme was described as the largest single energy grid modernisation in US history.

South Korea has rolled out one of the most comprehensive smart grid programmes to date, with a $24bn scheme which will involve installing everything from advanced metering infrastructure to 30,000 quick-charging stations for electric vehicles. The government has selected eight consortia to build demonstration-scale networks.

Taiwan's Industrial Technology Research Institute said that they expect some five million meters to be installed within the next five years, at a cost of around $1.5bn.

In China, the government has announced a massive $7.3bn investment toward the smart grid and related technologies.

As well as the listed companies detailed below, there are dozens of private start-ups competing for market share in smart grids. In North America these include *Silver Springs Networks*, *Tendril Networks* and *Trilliant*. Others not profiled here include Agilewaves, GridPoint, Grid Net, Positive Energy, SmartSynch, OpenPeak and Tantalus Systems. Only time will tell which are going to survive.

In the UK, small companies such as *AlertMe, Intelligent Sustainable Energy* and *RLTec* are already up and running. In Germany, the Mannheim-based company Power Plus Communications is a start-up which has so far connected 300,000 households into its broadband over power line (BPL) smart metering software.

Smart grid technology and companies

Smart cities

The world's first smart grid network was developed by Italy's largest power utility, Enel, which fitted smart meters for all 30m of their customers between 2000 and 2005. Although the cost was around €2.5bn, Enel estimates annual savings of €500m a year – in other words, payback on their investment in five years. However, Enel's system (which was installed before anyone coined the phrase 'smart grid') is fairly basic. Homeowners do not have access to in-home displays or options based on the price of electricity. The savings have been made through utility-side improvements such as better voltage and frequency control.

The most comprehensive smart grid network created to date is the SmartGridCity network developed in Boulder, Colorado, by Xcel Energy. Construction of the network backbone and software installation on this $100m project was completed in 2009. Xcel have since launched a web-based portal that gives customers the ability to design and personalise their own energy consumption strategies.

The city of Austin, Texas, is also developing a smart grid. Austin Energy completed the installation of smart meters for all its 400,000 customers in late 2009. As part of the programme, the utility is also partnering on a community-wide initiative to test the integration of roof-top solar and other forms of micro-generation into the grid network.

These are just some of the pioneers in what will soon become a global avalanche of opportunities for developers, manufacturers, installers and software designers.

Grid alliances

Since the smart grid is all about networking and communications, it was only a matter of time before large computing conglomerates stepped in. Recently major players such as IBM, Siemens, Cisco Systems and General Electric have all made bids to grab market share in this area.

IBM, for instance, has developed its gridSMART programme, which will be rolled out to all 5m customers of utility American Electric Power by 2015. The company is also working with the French utility EDF on smart grid solutions. Computer giant Cisco Systems has launched its own smart grid ecosystem involving more than 25 partners including utilities, hardware companies and software firms. Cisco and IBM have teamed up on a pilot with the Dutch utility Nuon to make Amsterdam a smart city.

General Electric is developing a number of smart grid initiatives, including wireless communications, energy distribution, metering, support EVs and more. GE claim that they have one of the broadest portfolios of smart grid solutions available, backed up by their Smart Grid Lab in New York. GE is an investor in Tendril Networks and Grid Net, who will provide management systems for GE's Worldwide Interoperability for Microwave Access, Inc (WIMAX) smart meters.

The company has elbowed its way into smart grids in China, with a demonstration project in the city of Yangzhou for urban smart grid solutions, which could eventually be rolled out elsewhere in the country. Other Western companies looking for business in China and taking similar steps to GE include Cisco, Accenture, Hewlett-Packard, ABB, Westinghouse, and Oracle. IBM alone is said to be expecting at least $400m in smart-grid revenues in China over the next four years.[90] GE has joined forces with Google to work on technology and policy issues around the smart grid, and it is collaborating with the search giant on finding solutions to enable the large-scale integration of EVs into the grid. Google has launched its own application, called PowerMeter, which displays home energy consumption on a PC or smart phone. The energy-tracking software was first made available to consumers in Britain in 2009.

The German company Siemens predicts revenues of €6bn over the next five years from smart grids. The company acquired meter specialist Energy4U GmbH in 2009 and is also partnering with the world's leading meter supplier Landis+Gyr.

Security is a prime concern with the smart grid – once IT is added to the network, it is open to hacking. The potential for economic disruption or cyber terrorism is considerable: whole cities, airports or traffic systems could be shut down by hackers attacking substations. Defence contractors have been quick to identify a lucrative market for cyber security, with big names such as Lockheed Martin, Raytheon, Boeing and British defence contractor BAE Systems keen to bring their expertise to smart grid communications.

Grid efficiencies

A major area for green investing is sophisticated grid management systems known as *demand response networks*. These work on an industrial scale in much the same way as a smart meter can tell a domestic dishwasher or refrigerator not to power up during a peak pricing period. Demand-response companies sign up commercial and industrial customers who are willing to cut down their non-essential power usage on demand, usually in response to some sort of disruption elsewhere on the electricity grid, for instance record heat waves (leading to higher than normal demand for air-conditioning), fires under transmission lines or plant failures. The utility calls the demand-response aggregator, who in turn immediately notifies all their participating customers – or, in some cases, automatically makes remotely controlled adjustments in heating, ventilation, and air condition (HVAC) settings, lighting and other equipment.

The reduction in demand provides the relief the utility requested, ensuring that service on the grid carries on as usual. When the event is over, normal operations are resumed at customers' premises. The network can also be called into action when wholesale electricity prices are peaking (hence the expression 'peak shaving' for reducing demand). It is a form of energy efficiency which enables utilities not to have to build extra power plants that would only be used in periods of peak demand.

"[The move towards] smart grids is recognising that a transmission grid is sized around peak load," says Richard Postance, a partner at Ernst & Young LLP. "Power loads vary throughout the day and the opportunity in smart grids is primarily the ability to move demand around that peak." He gives an example of half-time during a football match, when demand can rapidly rise by 10% or more on the electricity grid. "So suppose it is half-time and everyone turns their kettle on – what if all the fridges in the country stopped for half-an-hour because they had plenty of heat capacity left in them?" asks Postance. "That's the vision – by using smart meters to move demand, a smart grid is able to be smaller, or have less of a safety margin, because the utilities understand what's going on."

Bruno Derungs of Climate Change Capital believes that shifting energy usage patterns will make a big difference. "In Europe research shows that between 20% and 50% of the electricity being used by private consumers can be moved," he says. "That's a substantial part."

In North America a market leader in this field is Boston-based **EnerNOC**, which manages a demand-response network of over 2500 commercial, institutional and industrial customers. EnerNOC sees continuing expansion in this area, particularly as utilities step up their involvement in wind energy.

The second largest player in demand-response is **Comverge**, which currently manages 3GW of capacity. Comverge is also moving into demand-response in domestic premises through collaborations with smart metering companies such as Itron and Digi International.

Another major player in this area is the New York company Cpower (backers include Bessemer Venture Partners, Schneider Electric Ventures and Intel Capital), which has around 2.5GW of demand response under management.

Amongst the larger US 'old economy' companies that stand to benefit from smart grids are Honeywell International (NYSE: HON), which has over 50% of its $37bn portfolio focused on energy systems and smart controls (although this does include everything from turbochargers to biofuel technologies). The company was a pioneer in the demand-response field and has installed over 950,000 load control devices, which makes it one of the largest demand response partners in the US.

To date, demand-response capabilities of this nature are only being built up on the North American grid network. Watch out for any fast movers starting to offer this kind of service elsewhere in the world. "There is no one trying to roll out that business model specifically," says Edward Guinness, co-manager of the Guinness Alternative Energy fund, "but I wouldn't be surprised to see one of those two [EnerNOC and Comverge] start taking an even more active role in Europe."

Steven Mahon of Low Carbon Accelerator agrees. "I think we will see bigger US companies coming into Europe and looking for acquisitions to get access to the European market," he says. "Although the US marketplace is probably the most attractive market in the world at the moment for smart grid, the European one is not far behind. It represents an opportunity every bit as big so I think we'll see US companies, whether tech start-ups or the more established players, looking to be active in Europe."

Guinness believes that demand-response is a high growth area but warns that the long-term future has pitfalls. "Our view is that if they are really successful then the utilities will just start doing it themselves, because the utilities know the end-users better and are better placed to manage it then a middle-man." The cost of the technology that they are putting in on site is low, he says, so there are low barriers to entry. "Either you are going to see the utilities coming in or the margins are not going to be sustainable at the high levels they are right now," says Guinness.

Smart metering

> "It is going to be tremendous, the market is going to be really huge not just in terms of smart metering but management control, load control, personal electricity control … this is the big picture, to connect all these applications through a smart grid and impact your personal power consumption."
>
> **Bruno Derungs, Climate Change Capital (CCC) Private Equity**

Smart meters are a key technology for the smart grid; they are digital meters that allow electricity users to monitor their usage in real time through in-home displays and hopefully alter their behaviour accordingly. Utilities can vary the price of electricity according to demand and the time of day, so consumers will be able to choose to power low-priority appliances or charge their electric vehicles when prices are cheapest. This more efficient use of power will reduce the need for new generating capacity to be provided in the future.

Smart meters are already being rolled out in their millions in countries all over the world. "Smart meters are the vanguard of smart grid deployments," according to Pike Research.[91] Household appliances are also currently being developed that will link into home networks and make use of two-way communications with utilities. Manufacturers such as GE, Miele and Whirlpool are all starting to produce smart appliances of this nature.

The EU requires member states to equip 80% of consumers with smart meters by 2020 and 100% by 2022. In fact many countries have already adopted regulations that put them ahead of this timetable. Sweden became the first country in the world to achieve 100% uptake of smart meters in July 2009 and Italy is forecast to be at this stage by 2011. Major roll-outs are expected in Spain and Ireland from 2011 onwards, in France and Portugal from 2012, and in the Netherlands, Finland and Norway from 2013.[92]

In Britain the government has outlined plans for smart meters to be installed in all homes in the country (approximately 26m) by 2020. The total cost is expected to be around £8.5bn, with energy suppliers responsible for picking up the tab. The Department of Energy and Climate Change (DECC) said that the scheme would save an estimated £14.5bn over a 20-year period. The government has also unveiled a £12m investment programme to encourage schools to install smart meters. Supplied by British Gas, the meters will feature dashboard-style displays to help teachers and pupils to learn about energy efficiency whilst also allowing schools to manage and reduce their energy costs.

Worldwide there are estimated to be around 1bn of the old-style, electromechanical electricity meters that will need to be replaced with new smart meters. In the US, around 15% of households (about 20m) are estimated to already have new-style smart meters. That leaves 110m households which need new meters. Another estimate is that the world will need 30m smart meters a year for the next 30 years, with each meter costing between $50 and $100.[93]

Europe is currently the top region for smart meter adoption but North America is tipped to lead the market from 2010 onwards.

Metering companies

The world's largest metering company is Landis+Gyr, which has been making meters since 1896. The Swiss company was bought by Bayard Capital of Australia in 2004 (Bayard has since changed its name to Landis+Gyr Holdings) and today has operations spanning more than 30 countries with an installed base of more than 300 million meters and annualised sales of more than US$1.25bn.

The global market leader amongst publicly listed meter companies is **Itron**, which was founded in 1977 and with its headquarters in Liberty Lake, Washington. Other US companies in this space include **Badger Meter** and

ESCO Technologies. The Toronto-based **RuggedCom** has been operating secure networks for communications with electricity sub-stations for some time, and is now poised to capitalise on this with smart grid contracts.

In the UK, **Bglobal plc** is a leading provider to the energy market. The company reported an acceleration of activity in 2009, with their workforce installing nearly 4000 meters in a month for customers such as Scottish & Southern Energy, npower, and British Gas. Another listed UK company, **Spice**, is working in partnership with a large number of utilities and commercial organisations on smart metering and energy efficiency.

An early mover in smart grids is California-based **Echelon**, who were responsible for installing the first smart city network for Enel SpA in Italy.

Grid operators

Transmission networks aren't pure plays in smart grid, but there is certainly a case to be made for green investments in this sector.

Take **National Grid**, for instance, which has electricity and gas networks in the UK and the US. The company is actively pursuing more energy-efficient, smart grid solutions and is involved in smart metering trials on both sides of the Atlantic. The case for green investment in the company is reinforced by their wholesale and enthusiastic adoption of climate change policies, which must rank amongst the most enlightened and far-reaching of any FTSE100 company.

Another transmission operator with a significant green brief is **ITC Holdings**, the largest independent electric transmission company in the US.

Components and ancillary services

In terms of the infrastructure of the smart grid, billions will need to be spent on new transmission lines. **General Cable** is a major player in the design and manufacture of cables and fibre optics and may benefit considerably from grid upgrades globally. One of the largest cable manufacturers globally is the French company **Nexans**.

Another global player is the Italian company **Prysmian**. The group focuses especially on high-value-added markets such as underground and submarine power transmission cables and systems, cables and systems for industrial applications, and optical cables for voice, video and data transmission.

Advances in cable technology, and the development of new types of more efficient cables, will also create opportunities in this area. For instance, the vast majority of overhead power lines are made from heavy steel and aluminum cable. This design, known as aluminum conductor steel reinforced wire, is over 100 years old. A Californian company, **CTC Cable Corporation** has now developed an alternative to this based on carbon fibre hybrid composites from the aerospace industry.

Most of the world's transmission grids currently use alternating current (AC) but the new generation of super grids will be constructed using either high voltage direct current (HVDC) or superconducting cables (see the superconductor revolution feature below).

The benefit of HVDC is that it can transmit large amounts of power over long distances with lower losses and lower capital costs than AC. This is particularly true with long underwater cables, which suffer even greater losses when AC is used.

The two leading players in this sector are **ABB** and Siemens. The new generation of inter-continental links all use HVDC. It is also indispensable for offshore renewables, although because variations in wind speed can cause severe voltage fluctuations this has led to the development of a new kind of HVDC that works at much lower voltages and is capable of stabilising the AC voltage at the output end. ABB call this HVDC Light, whereas Siemens' version is known as HVDC Plus. These systems can be above ground, buried underground, or under motorways or freeways – there are plenty of options that help to bypass public objections to new pylons.

Companies offering utility infrastructure services in North America include **PowerSecure**, **Power-One** and **Quanta Services**.

The superconductor revolution

The race is on to capitalise on what could become the biggest infrastructure revolution since the creation of the internet – the commercialisation of superconductors. Although superconductors have been known about for some time, it's only now that they're being commercialised.

Superconducting is a phenomenon whereby when certain metals and ceramic materials are cooled to very low temperatures, they have no electrical resistance. Superconducting wires are near perfect conductors of electricity – they can carry up to 150 times as much power as a comparable copper wire with close to zero electrical losses.

The US Department of Energy is in no doubt as to the significance of superconductivity. "It has the potential for bringing a more fundamental change to electric power technologies than has occurred since electricity use became widespread nearly a century ago," the department states. "High-temperature superconductivity (HTS) power equipment has the potential to become a key 21st century technology for improving the capacity, efficiency, and reliability of the electric system."[94]

Another huge advantage of superconductors is that they are much smaller than comparable copper wires, with a smaller ground footprint – so extra capacity can be added alongside existing power lines without having to build unsightly new pylons. They can also be buried underground, with no loss of electrical capacity (which is not the case with normal power lines).

Superconductors also have the ability to prevent current surges from damaging the grid, since some superconductors turn from conductors into resistors when the current exceeds a certain level. Another application is therefore in fault current limiters (FCLs), devices which have the potential to make the smart grid more efficient by protecting equipment from power surges.

As well as their use in transmission grids, superconductors provide fundamentally new opportunities in energy efficiency. The size and weight of motors, generators, transformers and other equipment can be reduced by 50% and more, while the systems' capacity is increased at the same time. This has implications for wind power, hydro power and most other types of power generating systems.

The two companies currently at the forefront of commercialising superconductors are **American Superconductor Corporation (AMSC)** and **Zenergy Power**.

AMSC was the first company to install a working HTS transmission cable in a power grid and has now signed contracts for other installations. Zenergy's first commercial product is an industrial induction heater.

The two companies are now racing to develop second generation HTS wires. These technologies will have major implications in the renewables field, particularly wind power (see Super turbines, p.75).

Both companies are also working on fault current limiters and marine propulsion. AMSC has built a superconductor ship's motor for the US Navy and Zenergy has received funding from the EU to develop motor and generators for marine electric drive systems.

Companies to watch

AlertMe (UK) has developed a system that consists of a meter reader, a hub connecting in-home accessories to the AlertMe service on the web and a dashboard. The software is integrated with Google's PowerMeter, making it easy to track energy consumption live from an iGoogle homepage. To date the company has raised £8m through Index Ventures and hopes to sign-up 2m customers in the next two years. www.alertme.com

Intelligent Sustainable Energy (UK) provide real-time energy displays for all their appliances via their energy management software. The system has a user-friendly display; secure communications; credit, pre-payment and pay-as-you-go applications; the ability to handle complex tariffs; and is easy and low cost to install. www.ise-oxford.com

RLtec (UK) supplies software that can be incorporated into the control unit of electrical appliances such as fridges, electrical heaters and air conditioning units. The company has received a total of £2.1m in funding from the Low Carbon Accelerator, which is their biggest shareholder. www.rltec.com

Silver Springs Networks (US) has caught the attention of numerous utilities with their radio frequency mesh; internet protocol (IP)-enabled networking technology that is embedded in other companies' meters. The company has so far raised around $170m and plans an IPO at an unspecified future date. Clients include American Electric Power, Pacific Gas & Electric, Florida Power & Light and Pepco, as well as utilities in Australia. www.silverspringnet.com

Tendril Networks' (US) ZigBee standard software allows users to see their energy consumption on their own computers or a web portal, and programme their home network as required – telling the washing machine only to run at night, for instance. Major investors include GE, Access Venture Partners, Appian Ventures, RRE Ventures and Vista Ventures. www.tendrilinc.com

Trilliant's (US) multi-tier architecture provides secure two-way communications that enable distribution automation, advanced metering and consumer demand-side management applications. With the acquisition of broadband wireless provider SkyPilot in 2009, Trilliant now offers a secure end-to-end smart grid solution with true broadband capacity and complete coverage, all based on open industry standards. Investors include zouk ventures and MissionPoint Partners. www.trilliantinc.com

Glossary

AC: alternating current

AMI: advanced metering infrastructure

AMR: automated meter reading

BPL: broadband over power line

DC: direct current

DECC: Department of Energy and Climate Change (UK)

DRSG: Demand Response and Smart Grid Coalition

FCL: fault current limiter

FIT: feed-in-tariff

GmbH: Gesellschaft mit beschrankter Haftung (company with limited liability)

HTS: high-temperature superconductor

HVAC: heating, ventilation, and air conditioning

HVARC: heating, ventilation, refrigeration, and air conditioning

HVDC: high voltage direct current

IP: internet protocol

V2G: vehicle-to-grid

WiMAX: Worldwide Interoperability for Microwave Access, Inc

HYDROGEN & FUEL CELLS

7

Introduction

Before the low-carbon economy, there was the hydrogen economy. In fact, supporters have been predicting the arrival of the hydrogen economy for decades, with its promise of clean, green power from hydrogen-powered fuel cells. But it always seems to be just over the horizon, tantalisingly out of reach. Even large companies that have poured millions into R&D have failed to come up with a commercially viable product.

Take Rolls-Royce, for instance. The engineering group, better known for its turbines and aircraft engines, has been researching fuel cells since 1992. At some point they announced that they would produce a prototype hybrid power plant by 2004, but that didn't happen. The company pumped $100m into a joint venture with a Singapore-based consortium in 2005, still with no result. From 2006 to 2009 Rolls-Royce made further investments in America, buying up an Ohio-based developer of fuel cells and spending $3m upgrading their R&D facilities. Currently, Rolls-Royce is planning to complete the design of its utility-scale fuel cell in 2012. No date has been given for a commercial launch.

Sceptics say that the hydrogen economy is a distant fantasy, claiming that producing hydrogen and building the infrastructure is just too expensive, so fuel cells will never make it onto the mass market. Even so, there are signs that the balance has now shifted in favour of hydrogen's proponents. The same drivers that are propelling other clean technologies – climate change, peak oil, and energy security – are having an impact, and the logic behind hydrogen energy looks increasingly compelling.

Investing in fuel cells

Overview

Bull points

- Rising energy prices.

- Synergies with the growth in renewables.

- New low-cost production techniques.

Bear points

- High cash burn rates in some companies.

- Cost of raw materials (catalysts such as platinum).

- Cost of hydrogen infrastructure.

- Cost of the finished products.

Investment summary

Media headlines over the past couple of years are indicative of the general feeling about the fuel cell sector. They include: "Fuel Cell Fervour Goes Flat", "Fuel Cells a Damp Squib", "Fuel Cell Uncertainties", and "Fuel Cell Maker Closes Shop". The last of these headlines refers to PolyFuel, a California-based developer of methanol fuel cells which launched on AIM in 2005. Despite injections of more than $40m in venture capital and winning $5m in US federal funding, the company went bust in 2009.

Part of the problem is simply the cost of fuel cells. Current system costs are still too high by a factor of at least ten for widespread uses, according to the Carbon Trust. These costs could be brought down in the future through volume production, but projections show that even then, with today's technology, costs would remain too high for most markets by 30-40%. For instance, the projected cost of residential micro-CHP (combined heat and power) is said to be around £5500-£6500 per unit, which is £2000 more than a condensing boiler.[95] The fact that it gives you electricity as well as heat is of course the justification for this premium.

Analysis from the Carbon Trust shows that if substantial cuts can be achieved, the global market could be worth over $26bn in 2020 and over $180bn in 2050.[96] The UK share of this market could be $1bn in 2020 rising to $19bn in 2050, they say.

Fuel cell companies had a good year in 2009, with firms including AFC Energy, Acta, Ceramic Fuel Cells and Ceres Power showing strong gains. "All of these companies are nearing the point when they should have commercial products," noted Andrew Hoare in *Quoted Cleantech* in January 2010. "After years of cash outflows, they will need to show that these products are successful and generating revenues and profits."[97]

Finance and investment specialist David Stevenson is less positive about the sector. "My brutally honest assessment of fuel cells is that I've given up waiting. I will believe it when I see it – it always seems to be just around the corner ... and then is not. It may all work out but my suspicion is that when that day comes investors will have lost patience and run away". He counsels extreme caution for private investors.

Government support

The European Union is investing over €1bn in a programme involving 64 companies and 54 universities with the aim of speeding up the commercialisation of fuel cells and hydrogen technologies in the next decade.

The UK is one of the leading fuel cell research hubs in the world, drawing on the country's strong materials science and chemistry research. The government's Technology Strategy Board has invested around £9m in projects designed to lower the cost of fuel cells and improve their reliability, durability and performance. The Department of Energy and Climate Change has launched a separate £7.2m Hydrogen and Fuel Cell Demonstration programme and the Carbon Trust has weighed in with its Polymer Fuel Cells Challenge, which aims to make polymer fuel cells an everyday commercial reality.

Speaking about the Carbon Trust's programme, Dr Robert Trezona of the organisation said:

> "Fuel cells have been ten years away from a real breakthrough for the past 20 years. This is a critical moment for UK fuel cell technology as emerging markets combine with technology cost breakthroughs to create a golden opportunity to launch world-beating products onto a

massive global market. Our initiative aims to drive forward the commercialisation of the UK's unique fuel cell expertise."[98]

The programme aims to deliver breakthroughs which will bring costs down by a factor of around 35% in order to make producing fuel cell systems more attractive for mass markets.

Germany is running a national programme to test residential fuel cells. In Japan, the government's Hydrogen and Fuel Cell Demonstration Project has been running since 2002 and a consortium of companies has installed around 2000 residential fuel cell units for testing.

Fuel cell technology and companies

How fuel cells work

A fuel cell is an electromechanical device that uses the chemical properties of a fuel (often hydrogen) and oxygen to directly create electrical current. There is no combustion involved. A fuel cell is technically similar to a battery although it doesn't store energy, but produces electricity as required from an external fuel source. There are a number of types of fuel cell which are normally distinguished by the electrolyte they contain (see Fuel cell types box on p.157).

Fuel cells have been used as power sources in remote locations or in applications such as submarines or spacecraft very successfully. They are compact, lightweight and reliable, and they operate silently with no emissions. The problem in using them for mobile applications such as cars is not just the storage required for hydrogen onboard the vehicle, but also the storage and distribution network which would be needed on the roads.

A stationary fuel cell is effectively a combined heat and power (CHP) system and can be used in residential or commercial buildings to replace conventional boilers. As well as generating electricity they produce heat that can be used for hot water or space heating.

Stationary fuel cell systems like this have been used in commercial buildings for some time. United Technologies Corporation (NYSE: UTX) is the first company to make large, stationary fuel cell systems for CHP use and install them in hospitals, universities and large office buildings. The company is also installing one of the largest fuel cell systems in the world with a 4.8MW installation at the Freedom Tower and three other new towers under construction at the former World Trade Center site in lower Manhattan. In London, several new office blocks have recently been constructed with power supplied by UTC fuel cells.

The privately held California start-up Bloom Energy caused a stir in early 2010 with the unveiling of their Energy Server, the *Bloom Box*, which they claim will "change the way the world generates and consumes energy". Powered by solid oxide fuel cells, each device provides 100kW of power, enough to meet the energy needs of 100 average homes or a small office building.

Building large and expensive fuel cell systems is comparatively easy. Building systems small enough to fit into the average home (micro-CHP), and cheaply enough to be affordable, is a different proposition. The prize is a system which would provide all the electricity and heat a household requires, at double or treble the efficiency of the electricity you buy from a utility. Despite the obstacles, mass production of micro-CHP units is now underway, with the first commercial units expected to be on the market in Britain during 2010-2011.

Fuel cell types

Proton exchange membrane or polymer electrolyte (PEM) fuel cells: one of the most common types, based around a plastic or polymer membrane. PEM cells are lightweight, powerful and increasingly durable, and can be used in applications ranging from vehicles to CHP. Currently very expensive.

Alkaline fuel cells (AFC): used in the US space programme for decades; currently being developed for more large-scale applications.

Solid oxide fuel cells (SOFC): can use normal fuels such as natural gas, propane or LPG as well as hydrogen. Challenges include scaling down the technology to domestic size.

Direct methanol fuel cells (DMFC): popular for very small scale applications such as powering mobile phones and laptops. Also in use for forklift trucks and other material handling vehicles.

Molten carbonate fuel cells (MCFC): mostly used for large stationary applications, can also be run on other fuels.

Fuel cell companies

"Unlike some analysts who predict that fuel cell technology will never take off, my perspective is that it is a very promising technology, but will just take much longer to mature than many of its proponents estimate."

Green Investing: A Guide to Making Money through Environment-Friendly Stocks[99]

The history of fuel cell investment is typified by the story of the Canadian company **Ballard Power Systems**, which has struggled for nearly three decades to commercialise its products. The company was founded by Geoffrey Ballard, widely acknowledged to be the father of the fuel cell industry. Ballard began developing PEM fuel cells in 1983 and built his first fuel cell bus in 1993. Daimler and Ford invested $750m to buy a one-third stake in the company in the 1990s.

By the end of the decade the future was looking rosy for Ballard, who was elected a "hero of the planet" by *Time* in 1999. He told the magazine that fuel-cell cars should become economical by 2010 and that "the internal combustion engine will go the way of the horse. It will be a curiosity to my grandchildren."[100]

However, after pouring millions into R&D the company gave up the fight to make vehicle fuel cells profitable in 2007 and sold these assets to Daimler and Ford. It is now simply a supplier to the joint company they set up and the new, slimmer Ballard Power Corporation has agreements with companies in Denmark, Germany and the US to continue working on other fuel cell developments.

As well as Rolls-Royce, which has already been mentioned, another UK company with a significant involvement in fuel cells is Johnson Matthey (LON: JMAT). The company's business revolves around catalysis, precious metals, fuel cells, fine chemicals and process technology. However, the company won't disclose what percentage of the business comes from fuel cells.

Major Japanese corporations are also pouring money into this field, amongst them Toshiba, Sharp and Sony.

Other fuel cell companies of note include:

- **Ceramic Fuel Cells** is a front-runner in the race to market for residential systems. It is developing technology to provide electricity from natural gas.

- **Ceres Power** has developed a wall-mountable CHP unit that fits into the same space as a normal boiler and uses all the same gas, water and electricity connections.

- **Hydrogenics** has supplied fuel cells systems for mobile and stationary applications.

- **IdaTech** is working with PEM fuel cells, principally for telecoms and UPS applications.

- **Intelligent Energy** is involved in a joint venture with Scottish & Southern Energy PLC to commercialise mini-CHP systems.

- **Plug Power** is one of the first companies to market commercially viable fuel cell products.

- **Protonex** is one of the only fuel cell companies operating in both PEM and SOFC technologies.

- **Proton Power Systems** is the holding company for Munich-based Proton Motor and whose targets include mobile applications for fork-lift trucks and buses.

- **SFC Smart Fuel Cell** is a market leader in DMFC technologies. Their JENNY fuel cell provides portable power for troops and provides sufficient energy for a 72-hour mission.

- *Acal Energy* claims to have achieved a breakthrough in costs on DMFC units, having replaced expensive platinum with low-cost, proprietary liquids. Acal Energy was a finalist in the 2009 Carbon Trust Innovation Awards and is planning a full-scale field trial during 2010.

- *Oorja Protonics* is now on its fifth generation DMFC designs – it has a proven track record in power systems for forklift trucks and similar applications. The company is currently developing uses for their fuel cells as range-extenders in EVs and PHEVs.

Hydrogen technology and companies

The hydrogen cycle

Although hydrogen is the most abundant element in the universe, it doesn't exist in nature in a useful, pure form (unlike conventional hydrocarbon fuels such as oil or coal). Consequently, it needs to be produced using energy from another source. Like electricity, hydrogen is therefore an energy carrier rather than a fuel – however, it has a significant advantage over electricity in that it can easily be stored for later use.

The most common way of producing hydrogen is through steam-reforming of natural gas or methane. Around 95% of hydrogen is produced in this way. The drawback is that using fossil fuels such as natural gas to produce hydrogen is not desirable in terms of sustainability or GHGEs – even though manufacturers claim that the higher efficiencies achieved in a mini-CHP unit mean that, overall, householders will be reducing their carbon footprint.

Another way of producing hydrogen is through the gasification of coal. The world's first such plant is being planned in Kern County, California, by Hydrogen Energy International, a 50-50 joint venture between BP and the global mining company Rio Tinto. The proposed 250MW plant would produce hydrogen from petroleum coke (a by-product of oil refining). It would also capture 90% of the carbon dioxide produced in the process and pump it into nearby oil fields to enhance oil recovery. The consortium is also building a natural gas-fired hydrogen plant in Abu Dhabi (see 'Masdar City: the renewables powerhouse' on p.69).

A further option is to take advantage of the large amounts of waste hydrogen currently produced in chemical and industrial facilities (particularly chlorine plants) and use the hydrogen to generate electricity. There are several companies targeting industries that produce hydrogen as a by-product from their operations and seek to add economic value to the waste by turning this into electricity. Hydrogen is a by-product of the production of chlorine and caustic soda, for instance. **AFC Energy** is developing alkaline fuel cells for this market.

Hydrogen can also be produced through electrolysis, where an electric current is passed through water to split it into its constituent atoms (hydrogen and oxygen). Although this is an expensive means of producing hydrogen, if the electricity used comes from renewable sources then it is totally carbon-free.

Electrolysis has major advantages if combined with renewable energy. Excess energy produced by wind turbines at night, for instance, can be converted into hydrogen via electrolysis and used to generate electricity during the daytime. An electrolyser is basically a fuel cell working in reverse, so the cycle is this: renewable energy generates electricity, which is used to split water into oxygen and hydrogen. The hydrogen is stored and then combined in a fuel cell with oxygen (from the air) to create electricity.

Several prototype systems have already been built along these lines, such as the hydrogen mini-grid system in Yorkshire (see the hydrogen mini-grid box below). The problem is that this is not yet a cost-competitive alternative to conventional fuels.

The hydrogen mini-grid

In South Yorkshire an experimental hydrogen mini-grid has been up and running since 2009, providing power to the Environmental Energy Technology Centre in Rotherham. This flagship project is the first building in Europe to be powered solely by renewables and hydrogen. Power comes initially from their on-site Vestas turbine. This is either consumed directly, or used to create hydrogen through electrolysis. The stored hydrogen can then either be used in a Fuel Cell Vehicle (FCV), or used in a fuel cell to generate electricity.

Surplus electricity (from either the wind turbine or the fuel cell) can also be exported to the national grid. This hydrogen mini-grid system is the only wind-to-hydrogen installation in Europe, and the first to have both the ability to dispense hydrogen for FCVs as well as use it in a fuel cell to generate electricity. www.hydrogen-yorkshire.co.uk

---

The hydrogen highway

Fuel cell vehicles are already in use in many countries. The first generation of fuel cell buses was tested in an EU-sponsored programme called Clean Urban Transport for Europe during the early 2000s. The programme covered nine cities including London, where the buses delivered 'outstanding results' according to Transport for London.

The mayor of London, Boris Johnson, is planning to boost this sector by building six hydrogen filling stations in the capital in time for the 2012 Olympics. Through the London Hydrogen Partnership, the mayor hopes to deploy 70 hydrogen vehicles in the city, which will include hydrogen buses as well as other vehicles such as black taxis, motorbikes and cars.

Hydrogen-powered buses are now being rolled out in many other countries. Daimler has recently launched its second-generation fuel cell buses, which are running on routes through Hamburg. The new hybrid buses (which also have lithium-ion batteries) use 50% less hydrogen than earlier models thanks to an improved fuel cell design.

Honda's FCX Clarity went into production in 2009, with around 200 vehicles currently on the road in the US and Japan. GM's Chevrolet Equinox, of which it has produced around a hundred, passed its one millionth mile in test drives in 2009. Other manufacturers (including Toyota and BMW) are also working on FCVs.

In Germany the government is investing €500m into a network of hydrogen filling stations. "Germany ... is to become the market leader for modern drive technologies," said the Minister for Transport, Wolfgang Tiefensee. "Our aim is to continue consistent and systematic promotion of electromobility based on batteries and fuel cells. Today we can see that Germany is setting the pace when it comes to hydrogen and fuel cell technology."[101]

The Nordic countries are working together through the Scandinavian Hydrogen Highway Project, which aims to have 100 buses, 500 cars and 500 speciality vehicles on the roads and up to 45 refuelling stations in place by 2015. In South Korea the government has pledged to have 12 hydrogen filling stations and 500 hydrogen vehicles (including 20 buses) operational by 2012.

The main barrier to the more widespread adoption of FCVs is the enormous cost involved in building a re-fuelling infrastructure. For this reason, critics claim that FCVs will never become mainstream. And whilst governments in Europe and Asia have launched numerous initiatives to prime the hydrogen economy for vehicles, America has shunned it.

In the States, proponents of FCVs faced a setback when Energy Secretary Steven Chu said that he was slamming the brakes on research for mobile fuel cells (surprisingly, the Bush administration had been bullish on hydrogen and rolled out a $1.5bn research programme in 2003) citing the cost and durability of vehicle fuel cells, the inability to store large volumes of hydrogen fuel, the absence of a carbon-free way of generating the hydrogen and the need to build a nationwide re-fuelling infrastructure as reasons for his decision. The issue came down to a simple question, said Chu: "Is it likely in the next 10 or 15 or even 20 years that we will convert to a hydrogen-car economy? The answer, we felt, was no."[102]

Many energy experts voiced concerns that the US shouldn't be shutting the door on this route. Chu responded that the DOE will continue to support stationary fuel cells, as well as funding basic research to improve the catalysts and other system components.

Whilst mobile applications can be dependent on a distribution system being put into place for hydrogen, stationary applications do not have this drawback. Stationary fuel cell plants can also be constructed on a much larger scale: **FuelCell Energy**, based in Connecticut, builds high-temperature MCFC units and has installed over 60 systems worldwide. The company has recently received federal support to develop hybrid fuel cell/turbine generators and advanced SOFC applications.

The hydrogen network

So far, there are less than 100 public hydrogen filling stations in the entire world. North America has the most, with around 60-70 operational stations in the US and Canada. However, the majority are in California (about 24 are in a cluster around Los Angeles). Japan has 12. In Europe, Germany has the most, with around 30 stations. Belgium and Italy have just one each. Norway has four stations along a hydrogen highway between Oslo and the North Sea oil hub of Stavanger. In Sweden, one station is open in Malmo, with three others planned. In Denmark, one public station has opened in West Denmark with five other Danish cities due to follow.

In Britain, London has one private fuelling station, with several public stations planned in time for the 2012 Olympics. The Welsh Assembly has decided to make the M4 motorway a hydrogen highway, with a range of fuelling points installed by 2015. The scheme will be linked to a new £6m hydrogen engine test facility at Port Talbot (just off the M4) being built by the University of Glamorgan.

Low-cost hydrogen

Production and distribution of hydrogen is one of the main barriers to the adoption of the hydrogen economy. The target that everyone is working towards is a cheaper way of producing hydrogen.

The privately held Linde Group, which is the world's largest manufacturer of hydrogen plants (almost all the filling stations in the world that supply liquid hydrogen have been built by Linde) is developing a process for the sustainable production of hydrogen from biogenic raw materials. The company has built a plant in Germany that produces hydrogen from glycerine, a by-product of biodiesel production.

A Sheffield-based company, **ITM Power**, has developed a low-cost unit for making hydrogen that is small enough to be used in the average home or business. The company is planning to install a prototype in a zero carbon home in South Tyneside.

The Italian company **Acta** is developing an electrolyser designed for domestic or light industrial use, with the potential to provide power for a range of FCVs, outboard motors and other transport applications.

Cutting-edge work in this field is currently taking place in America, where companies such as *Sun Catalytix* and the *Nanoptek Corporation* are working on different processes to achieve low-cost hydrogen.

The most controversial claims around hydrogen generation come from a New Jersey company called BlackLight Power, who say they have invented a new process that will generate 200 times more hydrogen than if electrolysis is used. Sceptics have poured cold water on the science behind it, but the company's founder remains optimistic. "It represents a boundless form of new primary energy," Randell Mills told Reuters. "I think it is going to replace all forms of fuel in the world."[103]

Companies to watch

Acal Energy (UK) is developing low-cost PEM fuel cells, which replace expensive platinum with a proprietary, low-cost liquid – a system they claim will cut the cost of fuel cells by 40%. The company is currently developing a prototype with support from the Technology Strategy Board and hope to have a commercial product by 2012. Investors include RisingStars Growth Fund, the Carbon Trust, Synergis Technologies and NorthStar Equity Investors. www.acalenergy.co.uk

Sun Catalytix (US) is a start-up looking at ways to make hydrogen with only sunlight and water – essentially duplicating the water-splitting reaction that occurs during photosynthesis. Backed by Polaris Venture Partners, the company was awarded $4m of federal grants in 2009. www.suncatalytix.com

Nanoptek Corporation (US) is backed by the Quercus Trust and is working on what they call a solar hydrogen generator, which uses a proprietary photocatalyst in a process known as photoelectrochemical (PEC) water dissociation, or photolysis. Nanoptek say that they have improved the PEC process by developing a titania photocatalyst that absorbs significantly more sunlight than normal titania. www.nanoptek.com

Oorja Protonics (US) makes DMFCs that provide battery charging for forklifts, pallet loaders and other vehicles. They are now moving into EVs and PHEVs. Investors include McKenna Management, Spring Ventures, Sequoia Capital and DAG Ventures. www.oorjaprotonics.com

GREEN TRANSPORT | 8

"Electric vehicles and related technologies form a potentially huge sector, with correspondingly huge returns for investors who back the winning manufacturers and technology developers at an early stage. In the race to develop a mass market for electric vehicles, we're barely off the starting grid."

Cleantech Investor[104]

Introduction

About a century ago you could buy an electric car which ran for 200 miles between charges. Using a battery designed by Thomas Edison, the Detroit Electric went on sale in 1911. Unfortunately, its top speed was 20mph – which is one of the reasons why the electric cars championed by Edison were overtaken (literally) by the gasoline-powered internal combustion engine (ICE), starting with Henry Ford's Model T.

But after a hundred years of refinement, the internal combustion engine is now demonised as a major source of urban pollution, congestion and increasing GHGEs. Added to this, peak oil and global warming are increasing the appeal of the electric vehicle (EV) once more. "We can start from the premise that there is nothing that can save the internal combustion engine over the long haul," wrote one analyst, "regardless of the fuel being burned."[105]

The decade from 2010 is set to be a period when the nascent EV industry starts scaling up to much more significant proportions; a growing percentage of vehicles on the roads will soon be electric, or hybrid electric. In North America, the forecast is for 250,000 on the road by 2011 and China is aiming for double that, with a production target of 500,000 in the same time frame.[106] Japan and South Korea are gearing up for over 1m vehicles a year by 2011. European manufacturers are also jockeying for position in this fast-expanding market.

There wouldn't be any point to this switch-over if these new generation vehicles were powered by electricity derived from fossil fuels. In reality, green transport is just one part of the low-carbon jigsaw alongside smart grids, new battery technologies, the distributed generation of renewable power and smart houses.

Green transport also covers fuel cell vehicles (FCVs) powered by hydrogen (see the chapter on Hydrogen & Fuel Cells) shipping and aviation, public transport and green fuels. There are opportunities in some of these areas for investors.

Investing in green transport

> *"Demand for efficient, clean vehicles and related gear and infrastructure is almost incalculable (certainly worth north of $1trn in the coming decade). So to the winners in this race will go massive spoils."*
>
> **Clean Money: Picking Winners in the Greentech Boom**[107]

Overview

Bull points

- Long-term prospects for EVs are strong.
- Developing range of component suppliers.
- Technological acceleration might happen suddenly.
- Strong government support.
- Costs will start to fall.
- Urban drivers will stimulate demand.

Bear points

- Development risks with competing technologies.
- Slow consumer acceptance.
- Lack of charging infrastructure.
- Scarcity of stocks, with potential for a bubble.
- Valuations contorted by subsidies.
- Lack of range will hinder uptake.
- Costs are still too high.

Investment summary

The electric and hybrid vehicle industry is still in its early stages and there are many hurdles to be overcome. Principle among these hurdles are the following three issues:

1. The cost of batteries, electric motors and other components needs to fall if the cost of the cars themselves is going to compete with conventional cars. The high density li-ion batteries which are needed to provide acceptable driving ranges add at least 30-50% to the cost of a vehicle. The market for people who are prepared to pay over the odds for the green option is limited.

2. The drive to reduce energy use and curb GHGEs has also spurred manufacturers to develop much better and cleaner conventional cars – good in itself, but they are still dependent on finite fossil fuels.

3. The range limit for BEVs is currently around 100 miles, which is fine for urban runs and short commutes, but it won't be high enough for the whole market. The initial market for EVs is also partly dependent on government subsidies and incentives and these won't continue forever.

Despite these caveats, manufacturers are bullish on the prospects for greener vehicles. Ford expects 10-20% of its fleet to be electric (hybrids, PHEVs and pure EVs) by 2025. Standard hybrids will make up 70% of that total, they claim.[108]

The advent of more affordable batteries, longer driving ranges and more widespread charging infrastructure (including home charging points) would all help to expand the EV market. If more cars become visible on the roads, this will send a signal to consumers and drive up demand. As more models become available, there will be a wider range of suppliers for batteries, motors or other components, which will bring down production costs.

The first cities in Europe which are likely to see widespread adoption of low-carbon vehicles are Oslo, Copenhagen and Amsterdam, according to Th!nk, who analysed a range of factors including infrastructure support, market fit and hybrid sales. In America, their estimate is that the top four cities will be Los Angeles, San Francisco, Chicago and New York.

Investors who want to gain exposure to EV stocks do not have a huge amount of choice, given that investing in the major car manufacturers can hardly be considered a green option.

Most of the opportunities related to this sector lie with battery and supercapacitor technologies; however, there are some niche companies supplying motors, components or charging devices which are of interest.

There will be some forthcoming floatations amongst the new breed of carmakers, such as Th!nk, Fisker Automotive, Coda Automotive or Tesla Motors. But these companies face a tough time in the highly competitive and capital intensive world of car manufacturing. They are having to start from scratch in building their distribution networks.

Indeed, there is even the hint of a bubble in the electric car sector as green money chases too few offerings. For instance Tesla revealed in its IPO filing that it lost $32m in the first nine months of 2009 (other calculations put its losses at nearly $237m since its 2003 launch). Despite these negative signals, demand for shares is expected to be high.

Government incentives

In Europe the EU has outlined a €5bn green car initiative which includes loans from the European Investment Bank and support for both EVs and FCVs. Nissan is building a new plant to produce the Leaf EV in Sunderland, England, which is partly funded by EU grants.

In the UK, the government has allocated around £140m to the Technology Strategy Board's Low Carbon Vehicle programme to help accelerate investment. They have also set up a £25m ultra-low carbon vehicles competition, with more than 340 electric vehicles taking part in trials all over the country.

The British government has created a new Office of Low Emission Vehicles (OLEV), which will bring together key departments within Whitehall to work together on low-emission vehicles. It has set up a £20m Low Carbon Vehicle Procurement Programme to supply electric vans to the public sector, and allocated £30m as seed money to the 'Plugged In Places' EV charging scheme. Tax breaks are also now available for individual or commercial buyers of EVs.

In the US, the DOE is providing up to $25bn in loans through its Advanced Technology Vehicles Manufacturing programme. Recipients so far include Nissan ($1.4bn for plant to build the Leaf EV), Ford ($5.9bn), and Tesla ($465m for plant to build their EV sedan). The government also offers tax rebates (from $2500 to $7500) to individuals who buy low-carbon vehicles.

In an attempt to position itself as America's first green transport city, San Francisco has adopted building codes requiring all new homes and offices to be wired for EV charging points.

On his visit to China in November 2009, President Barack Obama announced the launch of a US-China Electric Vehicles Initiative in conjunction with President Hu Jintao. The initiative will include joint standards development, demonstration projects in more than 12 cities, technical road-mapping and public education. The two leaders emphasised their countries' strong shared interest in accelerating the deployment of EVs in order to reduce oil dependence, cut GHGEs and promote economic growth.

Green transport technology and companies

The electric vehicle revolution

Although FCVs might be on the horizon later in the decade, at present it is EVs which are stealing the show. This wouldn't be happening were it not for major advances in power storage capabilities, including the development of much better batteries delivering more energy than previously possible (see Power Storage).

Battery electric vehicles (BEVs)

This is the most basic concept, with the car powered just by its battery. One of the first BEVs on the road was produced by the Norwegian company Th!nk in the 1990s. Ford was an early supporter, investing $150m over a four-year period, but when Ford pulled out of EVs in 2003 it left Th!nk floundering. The company went into court-protected bankruptcy but was re-invigorated in 2009 with $47m in cash from a new round of backers including Swedish car maker Valmet Automotive, the American company Ener1 and the Norwegian government's investment fund Investinor. The biggest shareholder is Ener1, the parent company of li-ion battery maker EnerDel. Th!nk has now moved production to Finland.

Mitsubishi Motors was an early developer of BEVs, and its iMiEV is the first mass-market model from a mainstream car maker. With a top speed of 87mph, the mini-size car has a range of around 100 miles. The budget-priced G-Wiz, made in India, is another early BEV.

These first generation vehicles are about to be joined by the next generation from the big auto-makers, most of which are due on the streets during 2010-2011.

Ford has unveiled its new Transit Connect EV, which has a top speed of 75mph and a range of around 80 miles on a single charge. Ford is targeting delivery rounds where owners use the same general routes and return to a home base on a daily basis for re-charging. Ford is producing another four types of EV, including the Ford Focus saloon car in 2011.

Nissan launches the Leaf EV (a four-door with a 100-mile range) in the US in 2010. In Britain, Nissan is building the Leaf at a new plant in Sunderland and plans to have them on the market in 2011. To keep the cost down, Nissan plans to lease the cars' batteries to owners rather than sell them.

But the EV market has been really revved up with the arrival of high-profile sports cars such as the Tesla Roadster and the Fisker Karma. These electric supercars, with top speeds in excess of 100mph and a range of over 200 miles, have become the new vehicle of choice for the eco-rich, with waiting lists running into months. Fisker is hoping to achieve production of 15,000 vehicles annually by 2011. Tesla Motors, which is planning an IPO in 2010, must be hoping that its share price will accelerate as fast as the Roadster, which goes from 0-60mph in just four seconds. In a demonstration of faith in the company, motor giant Toyota took an equity stake in Tesla in May 2010 and announced that they intend to cooperate on the development of electric vehicles. Audi is also planning an EV sports car in 2011.

Hybrid electric vehicles (HEVs)

An HEV combines an internal combustion engine with an electric motor/battery system which is intended to supplement the ICE for urban driving and better fuel economy. The battery is charged by the ICE.

The first and most famous HEV is the Toyota Prius, beloved (until recently) by Hollywood stars and urban greenies alike. First produced in 1997, it had achieved cumulative sales of around 1.5m by 2009. The second best-selling hybrid to date has been Honda's Insight.

Plug-in hybrid electric vehicles (PHEVs)

A PHEV is a hybrid with a normal size engine but a bigger battery, which gives it a longer electric-only range. The battery is charged either by the engine or from mains electricity. Ford is planning to launch its first PHEV in

2012. Chinese car maker BYD has launched a PHEV on its home territory and plans to export them to Europe and the US in the near future. The new Prius will also be a plug-in version.

Extended-range electric

This version uses a smaller ICE but a much bigger battery, which becomes the main power source. The ICE acts as a generator to top up the main battery. The most eagerly awaited extended-range vehicle is GM's Chevrolet Volt, due for release in 2012 (in Britain this will be launched as the Vauxhall Ampera). The car will provide the equivalent of 230 miles to the gallon in city driving. Jaguar Land Rover is also developing its extended range Limo Green, said to give a comparable performance to the Jaguar XJ but with low carbon dioxide emissions and fuel consumption.

Range extenders can come in many forms, either as a small ICE, fuel cell or even a microturbine.

Electric vehicle makers

Three California-based companies are slugging it out at the cutting edge of electric vehicles (two of them aiming initially for the high end of the market and one the middle):

1. The first is Tesla, who have already sold over 1000 of their first EV Roadster model in America. They claim that this sports car accelerates faster than virtually any other car on the road and is twice as energy efficient as Toyota's Prius. The Roadster recently set a world distance record for EVs with 313 miles on a single charge. The company has launched a right-hand drive version for Britain, with a price tag of £87,000 (but there is no tax and no congestion charge payable). However, Tesla plans to stop production on its signature Roadster and concentrate on the Model S, a four-door sedan which will retail for a more affordable $57,400. The company expects the vehicle to be on the road by 2012 and say that 2000 people have paid a deposit.

2. Next up is Fisker Automotive, who are planning to launch their $90,000 Fisker Karma in late 2010 (it was originally due in 2009). Fisker, who reportedly have a waiting list of around 1400 people for their PHEV, raised a further $115m in January 2010 from investors including A123 Systems (who will supply the batteries). The company has also applied for a federal loan.

3.   The third contender is Santa Monica-based Coda Automotive, who are developing a four-seater EV with a range of 90-120 miles. No firm launch date or price have been set for the vehicle, which will be assembled in China using batteries made by Tianjin Lishen Joint Stock Co, a leading li-ion battery manufacturer.

The world's largest manufacturer of commercial EVs is the UK company **Tanfield Group**, whose vans are marketed as Smith Electric Vehicles. Tanfield's fleet vans are used by many well-known corporations in the UK (including the Royal Mail, Sainsbury's, Parcelforce, DHL, TNT and British Telecom) and they now also have a US division, with early customers including Coca-Cola, Frito-Lay, AT&T and Staples.

The other main supplier of commercial vehicles in the UK is the privately-owned company Modec, based in Coventry. Modec has been extremely successful with its chassis cab, drop-side and box van models, which have a payload of two tonnes, 50mph top speed and a range of 60-100 miles.

Yorkshire-based **Eco City Vehicles** is mainly a distributor of London taxis, however the company has recently diversified into electric trucks and launched an electric taxi, the Mercedes eVito.

In California, the **ZAP** (zero air pollution) company began as an assembler of electric bicycles and has since grown to become a leading distributor of low-carbon vehicles. It launched its first own-manufactured vehicle in 2006.

Another US vehicle conversion company is **Li-ion Motors** (previously known as EV Innovations) based in Las Vegas. The company supplies electric scooters, bicycles, motorcycles, cars and trucks.

EV components

Detroit-based **Azure Dynamics** makes drivetrains and other components for electric, PHEV and hybrids. **Enova Systems**, based in California, is a leading supplier of electric motors and power management systems for EVs, PHEVs, and FCVs.

Also in California, **Quantum Technologies** works across a range of services which include powertrain engineering, system integration and control systems. Quantum's most high profile role is as a co-founder of Fisker Automotive: all Fisker models will feature Quantum's Q-Drive powertrain.

An alternative to conventional electric powertrains is being developed by *Atria Controls*, who have developed a modular EV architecture which reduces mechanical complexity and enables heavy vehicles such as buses to travel much farther in pure electric mode.

The Colorado-based company **UQM Technologies** is a developer of propulsion systems for EVs and FCVs.

The Canadian company **ZENN Motor Company** (zero emission no noise) was one of the first to mass produce a short-range EV with their three-door hatchback which launched in 2006. The company is now focusing efforts on the commercialisation of its ZENNergy drivetrain, which is powered by EEStor's ultracapacitors.

A UK company, *Evo Electric*, is developing high-torque electric motors and generators designed to reduce the cost, weight, size, complexity and power requirements of electric powertrains for EVs. Evo's motors are being used in the new Radical SRZero electric supercar, a new all-electric boat, and various commercial and military vehicles.

The global business-to-business services company **Ricardo** has developed a leading position in consultancy and process engineering for advanced clean diesel technology, hybrid and EV systems, fuel efficient gasoline engines, efficient transmission systems and vehicle electronic systems integration.

Greener ICEs

The Buckinghamshire-based company **Clean Air Power** has pioneered the use of natural gas to power vehicles using its Dual-Fuel system.

Offering a technology which is similar to Azure Dynamics, **Clean Power Technologies** in East Sussex has developed a heat recovery system which uses excess ICE heat to generate auxiliary power. The system has a number of applications in transport (including road vehicles and ships) as well as the power generation sector.

The San Diego-based company *Achates Power* is developing a new diesel engine which they claim offers a combination of fuel efficiency and power density at significantly lower cost.

EV infrastructure

The big buzz on EV infrastructure has been around the California-based start-up Better Place, who are proposing a network of battery-swap stations. The idea is that you pull into the station and a robot changes the battery for you from underneath the EV, replacing the depleted battery with a fully-charged one. Better Place pulled in $350m in second-round financing in early 2010, valuing the company at $1.25bn. They have agreements in some regions (including Denmark, Israel, Hawaii and Australia) to build battery swap stations and hope to launch the first network in Israel in 2011.

However, Better Place faces massive obstacles, not the least of which is that it has only signed up one car maker, Renault. Others, including Toyota and Volkswagen, have dismissed the scheme as unworkable. It would need car manufacturers to co-operate on designs which allow for the removal of batteries of all shapes and sizes from beneath every car. The evolution of higher capacity, smaller, and cheaper batteries may also put a dent in their plans.

Other companies are getting on with more basic EV charging systems. Amongst the forerunners in America is **ECOtality**, who are leading on a major trial of EV charging through their subsidiary eTec with the aid of a $100m federal grant. The project involves installing charging points to support 1000 Nissan Leaf EVs in each of five US states (Arizona, California, Oregon, Tennessee, and Washington).

A major competitor is the California-based company *Coulomb Technologies*, who are rolling out their network-connected charge stations in North America, Europe and elsewhere.

Another company involved in car charging is Ricardo, who have unveiled a new EV charging station in conjunction with PEP Stations in America. Similar to a standard fuel pump, the PEP Station allows drivers to charge their EVs using bank cards.

In Europe the market leader for EV chargers is the Brighton-based company *Elektromotive*, who installed their first Elektrobay kerb-side recharging unit in Westminster in central London in 2006. Elektromotive has since installed units in 16 countries around the world and its state-of-the-art chargers have become a benchmark for others to follow.

Electric vehicles and solar power

Solar power and electric vehicles are very much tied to one another. One of America's best-known solar installers, SolarCity, has expanded into EV charging with the purchase of SolSource Energy (North American distributor of EV vehicle chargers for Toyota Tsusho) and is creating the world's first solar-powered, fast-charge EV corridor between San Francisco and Los Angeles.

SolarCity is the primary installer of EV charging stations for Tesla Motors, with numerous Tesla owners using domestic PV panels to charge their cars. "When you combine solar power and electric vehicles, you are enabling a carbon-free lifestyle," said Lyndon Rive, SolarCity's CEO.

Other US companies such as Solatron, Solar Power Inc and Envision Solar are designing and building solar canopies for car parks. In Britain, Romag Holdings has unveiled its PowerPark design, which uses the company's existing PowerGlaz PV solar technology with electric inverters built into the framework of a slanting canopy.

Vehicle to Grid (V2G)

V2G basically describes a system whereby EV owners can sell power back to the grid when the electric vehicle is not in use. There are many issues still to be resolved here. For instance, consumers will want to charge their cars when they can get the cheapest electricity (if they do not have their own renewable source) and although most will charge them at night, others might not. The utilities are sketching out 'heat maps' of particular urban areas which are at risk from over-loading the grid in a situation where a large number of electric vehicles are charged simultaneously.

Differential pricing (offering people different tariffs for using electricity at different times) is one way of changing behaviour. National Grid is looking at options such as controlling the charging of cars according to when the wind is blowing (which is mostly at night). In Germany, power companies currently pay consumers to take electricity when the wind is blowing hard during off-peak periods: it is cheaper for them to pay householders to absorb a minimum amount of energy than it is to shut down the turbines, so a situation could arise where customers are paid to charge their cars.

Another option is for consumers to draw down power to car batteries when it is cheap, and sell it back during peak hours when it is most needed. This V2G capability is already being piloted by Duke Energy in America.

Ford is pioneering an onboard device with V2G capabilities, allowing the car to be programmed (via an on-board touch screen) as to when and for how long it should be charged. The company says that this might be licensed to third-party suppliers: there will be opportunities for software companies in this niche.

In March 2010 GE announced that it will start developing smart charging stations that communicate with utilities to optimise the economics of EV charging, dovetailing with GE's other smart grid offerings.

Biofuels: the third generation and the rise of oilgae

There are a number of good reasons for the green investor to stay well away from palm oil and other first-generation biofuels, despite headlines proclaiming (for example) that "Profits gush from palm oil" (*Investors Chronicle*).

First generation biofuels are now irrevocably tainted by the fact that their production is damaging and unsustainable. The mass production of ethanol has displaced food production and driven up food prices globally, leading to food shortages and riots in a number of countries. In addition, the clearance of hundreds of hectares of rainforest in Indonesia and Malaysia to make way for palm oil plantations has led to indiscriminate forest clearing, loss of habitat for threatened and endangered species (particularly orangutans), poor air quality from burning forests and peatlands, and disregard for the rights and interests of local communities. The EU's Renewable Energy Directive is part of the problem. It promotes the use of biofuels through a mandatory, binding target: by 2020, 10% of all fuels for road transport of EU member states needs to come from biofuels and although the EU will not recognise feedstocks from wetlands as 'renewable', many other ecosystems are at risk due to very weak criteria for limiting the impacts of biofuel production.

However, there is one area of biofuel production that is starting to look very promising (as well as sustainable) – making transport fuels from algae.

Algae is one of the fastest growing plants in the world and oil makes up about 50% of its weight. Algae can produce 15 times more oil per acre than other plants and it does not need freshwater, which means that it doesn't add to water stress or compete for productive land. Algae are also voracious consumers of carbon dioxide, which means that they can absorb unlimited quantities of waste carbon dioxide injected into the water.

Governments as well as user groups (such as airlines) have suddenly started to take an interest in the humble algae. In January 2010 the US Energy Secretary Steven Chu announced more than $80m in federal funding for advanced biofuels, with most of it going towards algae research. In Britain, the Carbon Trust has created the Algal Biofuels Challenge with a mission to commercialise algae-based biofuels, which they believe could replace over 70bn litres of fossil-derived fuels annually by 2030.

Oil majors are also taking an interest. Royal Dutch Shell are running a pilot plant in Kona, Hawaii, in conjunction with local firm HR BioPetroleum. Other large corporations working in this area include Linde and Dow Chemical (NYSE: DOW). Another Hawaiian test plant is being built by UOP LLC, a division of Honeywell (NYSE: HON), with the help of $25m in ARRA funding. The company has also set up a joint research project in Masdar City to investigate biofuels made from saltwater-tolerant crops grown in the desert.

There is very limited choice for green investors in this space at present, with just two nascent companies quoted on the markets and a handful of unlisted start-ups. Florida-based **PetroAlgae**, which has a prototype algae farm up and running, announced its first commercial revenues in 2010 (a licence for projects in Morocco and Egypt). The company has also signed agreements with Indian Oil, Indian's biggest company, to develop algae farms on the sub-continent and with Asesorias e Inversiones Quilicura (AIQ) to develop large-scale facilities for green fuels in Chile.

Its main rival in the race to commercialise algal fuels is the California-based **OriginOil**, who unveiled their first pilot bioreactor system in early 2010. OriginOil believes that algae production in the future will be localised, and attached to everything from waste-water plants, factories, breweries and any other location that generates carbon dioxide.

Non-listed companies working in this field include *Sapphire Energy* and *Solazyme*:

- Sapphire Energy has developed an algae-based fuel they call green crude. This was used in a test flight on a Boeing aircraft in 2009 and also provided the fuel for a sponsored drive across America by the world's first algae-powered car. The company has been awarded $100m in ARRA funding to build a full-scale plant in New Mexico.

- Solazyme, based in San Francisco, are building their first production plant with US federal funding. It has developed a technology that allows algae to produce oil and other useful by-products in standard fermentation facilities quickly, efficiently and at large scale.

A recent report from GTM Research indicates that the economics of biofuels point to near-term opportunities for cellulosic ethanol (second generation biofuels) and the long-term ascendancy of algae biofuels, with significant growth forecast despite the economic and logistical constraints affecting the commercialisation of these plants.[109]

Green shipping

The shipping industry often slips under the radar when it comes to accounting for GHG emissions – compared to aircraft, they are not so visible and not many of us travel on them. However, the world's 80,000-strong fleet of commercial ships is estimated to account for somewhere between 3% and 5% of global carbon dioxide emissions (more than air travel, which is estimated at around 2%). This has prompted calls for shipping to be included in a global emissions trading scheme. Ships are also responsible for significant emissions of nitrogen oxides (NOX) and particulate matter (soot) from the bunker fuel they burn.

Increasingly stringent international regulations are forcing shipping companies to clean up their act. For instance, the International Maritime Organisation has agreed a series of Emission Control Areas where the maximum sulphur content in fuels must be reduced: these regulations already cover the North Sea, the English Channel and the Baltic, and the coastlines of the US and Canada are due to follow suit.

One way to play this trend is through marine services company Hamworthy (LON: HMY), who provide high technology products, systems and services to the marine, and oil and gas industries globally. Anticipating the new rules on sulphur emissions, Hamworthy recently bought Krystallon, a company which makes seawater scrubbers to remove sulfur and particulates from exhaust gases. As a major supplier of on-board waste-water treatment plants, Hamworthy is also well placed to benefit from new global regulations on the discharge of waste-water effluent from shipping.

An innovative approach to reducing costs and GHG emissions has been adopted by the German company *SkySails*, who have developed a kite sail that can dramatically cut fuel bills. Depending on the prevailing wind, the ship's average annual fuel costs can be reduced by 10 to 35% (up to 50% in optimum conditions).

Another creative approach to reducing shipping emissions comes from the Rotterdam-based DK Group, who have designed a system to push compressed air through cavities in the ship's hull. This reduces drag, therefore cutting fuel consumption. The company claims that its system can deliver fuel savings of up to 15%.

Both these innovations are now entering the mainstream. The shipping company Stena, whose fleet consists of around 80 vessels, has designed a next-generation bulk carrier called the Stena E-MaxAir, which they claim will be the greenest tanker in the world.

Its hull has an air cushion to minimise friction with the water, and the ship is fitted with slow-rotating propellers to help reduce fuel consumption. The ship uses a kite sail and runs on liquified natural gas, considered the cleanest fossil fuel. Stena say that the E-MaxAir uses 32% less fuel than a comparable tanker and produces 35-40% less carbon dioxide and 90% less NOX, amongst other benefits.

Another way for shipping to cut GHG emissions is simply to slow down. Hundreds of ships globally are now practising slow steaming (reducing from 24 or 25 knots to 20 knots) and even super-slow steaming (down to 12 knots) in order to reduce carbon dioxide emissions and save money. Danish shipping giant Maersk estimates that by halving shipping speeds over the last two years, it has cut fuel consumption by up to 30%.

Public transport stocks

One way of investing in green transport is to buy shares in public bus and train operators or companies involved with public transport infrastructure. Passenger numbers on trains and buses in Britain, for instance, have surged in the past few years. However, this doesn't always translate into increased profits for operators. Trains in particular have a complicated business model, with a mix of public and private finance. Profits at bus and train operators are also related to oil prices. This is a complex area and you need to do your research thoroughly. The main public transport operators in Britain are:

- Arriva (LON: ARI)
- First Group (LON: FGP)
- the Go-Ahead group (LON: GOG)

- National Express (LON: NEX)
- Stagecoach (LON: SGC)

Government investment in rail infrastructure is also increasing globally, presenting opportunities for specialised engineering companies. Brazil, France, China, Russia and Japan have all promised massive upgrades to their existing network. In America, the Obama administration has pledged $8bn towards developing a high-speed rail network. Some stocks to consider include:

- Invensys (LON: ISYS)
- Jarvis (LON: JRVS)
- Alstom (EPA: ALO)
- L.B. Foster (NASDAQ: FSTR), a US company which supplies everything from new and used rail to track work and accessories.

Companies to watch

Achates Power (US) was founded in 2004. This start-up is developing new engines which provide fuel efficiency and power density at much lower cost. Achates is currently developing and testing a lightweight, fuel efficient 4.2 litre engine which they claim rivals engines nearly twice its size. The company is backed by leading VC firms including Sequoia Capital, Madrone Capital Partners, Rockport Capital Partners and InterWest Partners. www.achatespower.com

Atria Controls (US), formerly Adura Systems, has designed the Mesa (modular, electric, scalable architecture) powertrain for use in series hybrid, all electric and fuel cell mass transportation buses, large utility vehicles and other automotives. The company validated its powertrain in a prototype vehicle in 2009 and is now in the process of scaling up. It won the Frost & Sullivan 2009 Technology Innovation of the Year award, and also offers a complete package of electronics, software and battery pack technologies for EVs. www.atria-inc.com

Coulomb Technologies (US) is rolling out its EV charging networks in North America and Europe and has plans to expand into Asia and South America. Linked by an RF-based network, the system includes sophisticated management features and web-based applications for car owners, fleet operators and other users. The company raised $14m in a Series B funding round in February 2010 from investors including Voyager Capital, Rho Ventures, Siemens Venture Capital and Hartford Ventures. www.coulombtech.com

Elektromotive (UK) is the developer of the Elektrobay recharging stations. Consumers access the Elektrobay's power socket using a personalised wireless key fob that opens a secure, weather-proof door. Whilst charging the unit locks shut, thus stopping anyone else using it. The company has installed more than 250 units in the UK – Westminster in London has around 60 car-charging bays and Boris Johnson, London's mayor, has promised to install 25,000 charging points by 2015. Other bays are installed in Saudi Arabia and Europe. www.elektromotive.com

Evo Electric (UK) is developing high-torque electric motors and generators based on their proprietary axial flux technology. Demonstration motors have been used in the Radical SRZero electric supercar and the Fast Electric boat designed by Patterson Boatworks. The company is backed by Imperial Innovations. www.evo-electric.com

Sapphire Energy (US) has successfully made 91-octane gasoline out of their green crude made from algae (which is chemically identical to the molecules in crude oil). Investors include Arch Venture Partners, the Wellcome Trust, Cascade Investment (a VC company owned by Bill Gates) and Venrock (the VC arm of the Rockefeller family). www.sapphireenergy.com

SkySails (Germany) developed the world's first practicable kite propulsion system for shipping in 2001, with full-scale prototypes tested from 2007 onwards. SkySails is currently equipping three new cargo ships and a fishing trawler with their latest model, the SKS C 320. This has a towing kite which is 300m^2 larger than the first prototype, generating 16 tons of tractive force in good winds – and thus saving twice as much fuel as the first version. The company is also working on a larger kite with an effective load of 32 tons, which it plans to have available in 2012. www.skysails.info

Solazyme (US) has developed an algae biodiesel that meets US military specifications and renewable jet fuel, as well as by-products which include edible oils, flours, powders, various oleochemicals and consumer products including cosmetics. Investors include Braemar Energy Ventures, Harris & Harris Group, Lightspeed Venture Partners, Roda Group and VantagePoint Venture Partners. The company has won a $21.8m federal grant to build its first biorefinery in Pennsylvania. www.solazyme.com

Glossary

ARRA: American Recovery and Reinvestment Act (stimulus bill)

BEV: battery electric vehicle

EV: electric vehicle

FCV: fuel cell vehicle

FFV: flex-fuel vehicle

GHGE: greenhouse gas emissions

HEV: hybrid electric vehicle

ICE: internal combustion engine

KERS: kinetic energy recovery system

LEV: light electric vehicle

NOX: nitrogen oxides

OLEV: Office of Low Emission Vehicles

PHEV: plug-in hybrid electric vehicle

V2G: vehicle-to-grid

GREEN BUILDINGS | 9

Introduction

Buildings consume a huge amount of energy; some estimates claim that they are responsible for 40% of global energy usage and a similar proportion of carbon emissions, making them the single biggest source of global warming.[110] This clearly means that there is enormous scope globally for green buildings, whether it's retro-fitting old buildings, creating better new buildings, implementing low-carbon communities, or developing ideas and techniques which can ultimately be implemented anywhere. The building sector in many countries is being transformed in line with these possibilities, with increasing energy awareness and policy directives leading to the development of a vast range of techniques and technologies for greener buildings.

Taking Europe as an example, around 2m new buildings are constructed every year and the European Union is committed to a target of all new buildings being zero-carbon-rated by 2020. However, the greatest potential for energy savings lies in retrofitting the existing building stock of some 200m buildings.

In Britain, houses are rated against the Code for Sustainable Homes, launched in 2007. The code sets out minimum standards for energy and water use and a house receives a rating (from one to six stars) depending on how it measures up in nine different categories. The government target is that all new homes built from 2016 must be zero carbon, with industrial and commercial buildings falling into line by 2019.

The move towards green and zero carbon buildings is creating "an unstoppable momentum" according to Paul King, chief executive of the UK Green Building Council, who says that it is generating an "unprecedented amount of innovation" as developers, architects and energy companies work together to find solutions to climate change.[111]

In America, the green buildings sector has received a huge boost under the federal stimulus plan, which included $4bn to rehabilitate and retrofit public housing, $5bn to 'weatherise' (the improvement of insulation to save energy) homes for people with modest incomes, and $3.1bn for local governments to reduce energy use and carbon dioxide emissions.

The US Green Building Council estimates that green building will support nearly 8m jobs and pump $554bn into the American economy between 2009-2013. "Our goal is for the phrase 'green building' to become obsolete, by making all building and retrofits green – and transforming every job in our industry into a green job," said Rick Fedrizzi, chief executive of the organisation.[112]

The introduction of energy codes for new buildings is now federal policy under the American Clean Energy and Security Act of 2009. California adopted the first green building code in 2008, and a number of state and local governments have since adopted green building policies.

The growth in this sector – with many more companies emerging than can be covered in this book – is evident from the enormous success of London's annual Ecobuild exhibition, the world's biggest event for sustainable design, construction and the built environment. Almost doubling in size every year since its launch in 2005, the range and diversity of sustainable solutions on offer at Ecobuild is vast: it encompasses everything from rainwater harvesting to eco-paints, from green roofs to enviroloos, and from natural ventilation and daylight systems to kitchen counters made from recycled glass.

Investing in green buildings

"Green building is being adopted by everyone from architects to builders to appliance makers. But it is less of a revolution than a mass conversion. Upstarts, by and large, are not displacing entrenched interests."

Clean Money: Picking Winners in the Green-tech Boom[113]

Overview

Bull points

- Growth markets with enormous potential.

- Low-carbon buildings are inherently efficient and offer cost savings.

- An ambitious new EU directive (May 2010) stipulates that all new buildings in the EU must be 'nearly zero energy' by 2020.

- The 'green new deal' or Pay-As-You-Save scheme in the UK has the potential to transform microgeneration.

- Some sectors (such as LED lighting) could be poised for explosive growth.

- Innovation in developing materials, systems and other technologies to increase building energy efficiency is being driven by major corporations.

Bear points

- The building industry is inherently conservative.

- High upfront costs.

- Lack of agreed standards internationally.

- Haphazard and inconsistent approach to the application of building codes.

Investment summary

The market for green building services and products is huge. The World Business Council for Sustainable Development estimates that the size of the market of building and efficiency services alone is between US$0.9trn and US$1.3trn.[114]

Energy efficiency is one of the main areas in green building and construction and important within this is building controls. This is a big area, covering everything from heating, ventilation, air conditioning and refrigeration controls (HVACR) to complete building management systems. On an industrial scale, reduced energy usage is also provided by demand-response management systems (see Smart Grids). An up-and-coming area is voltage optimisation, which is applicable to both the residential and commercial sectors.

Building materials represent a very high percentage of embodied carbon. In fact, nearly every type of building material you can imagine is being put under the spotlight and re-examined – so major manufacturers of all descriptions are racing to overhaul their product lines to help builders meet ever-stricter energy efficiency requirements. These include cement manufacturers and development-stage companies trying out cement alternatives. Green bricks and timber substitutes are other growth areas. There is considerable interest in new materials made from fast-growing resources such as industrial hemp or bamboo, but these are not going to replace traditional building materials any time soon.

With lighting considered to be responsible for 20% of all electricity usage worldwide and up to 33% of all electricity used in commercial buildings, it is not surprising that energy efficient lights are an increasingly important part of the agenda. This a huge growth area, with some significant investment opportunities.

The green buildings sector also includes renewable technologies such as BIPV (see Solar Power), micro-CHP, biomass and heat pumps.

There are other areas relating to green building (such as windows and cladding) which are beyond the scope of this book but in general these will tend to be solutions provided by existing mainstream players.

Technology and companies

Corporate moves

Large companies have already indentified the synergies between different branches of their businesses and worked out how these can be brought together into smart buildings, both residential and commercial.

General Electric is promoting a net zero energy home which will incorporate their technologies for generating and storing energy as well as managing it efficiently. This will include everything from smart appliances to energy-efficient lighting and advanced power storage. The company is planning to develop solar PV and small-scale wind products which will fit into this strategy and their new home energy manager system is designed as the central nervous system of the house, controlling appliances and renewable technologies. Smart thermostats will work in conjunction with this system, advising home-owners whether they should be using energy from the grid, using stored energy, or selling energy back to the grid.

The Japanese company Sanyo is taking a slightly different tack, and has launched a range of pre-fabricated, modular green homes which come fully-fitted with geothermal heat pumps, solar PV systems, LED lighting fixtures, and lithium-ion batteries to provide back-up power. The homes qualify for government subsidies in Japan and buyers can also earn income by selling surplus power under Japan's FIT.

Sanyo is now owned by Panasonic, who plan to invest more than $1bn by 2012 in converting their business from the world's biggest plasma-TV maker to a supplier of solar power and energy-saving technologies for buildings. The Osaka-based company's new home energy systems will connect together all the appliances in the house and provide home-owners with savings of between 30% and 50% on their energy bills.[115]

Construction materials company Saint-Gobain (EPA:SGO) has teamed up with the University of Nottingham's Department of the Built Environment to create a zero carbon prototype, called the HOUSE (Home Optimising the Use of Solar Energy). The company says that HOUSE will show how low energy architecture can lend itself to the mass market with a modular design that is so versatile it can be worked into terraces, rows or stacked as apartments.

One of the world's largest construction companies, Skanksa (STO:SKAA) has already shifted in this direction. The company has been working on sustainability issues for the last decade and recently published its own manual on green thinking, which contains details of over 21 major projects on three continents it has been involved with. The company says that it "aims to be a leader in quality, green construction" globally.

Building controls

Large corporations such as Honeywell International (NYSE:HON) dominate the buildings control sector. The company operates in a wide range of other markets (from aerospace to automotive products) as well as buildings.

Johnson Controls (NYSE: JCI) is the other major American corporation involved in this area and is one of the world's leading suppliers of equipment and systems for HVAC, lighting, security and general building management. The company has announced a tie-up with IBM to develop smart building technologies.

There are also some smaller companies working in this area.

Chicago-based **Lime Energy** provides energy efficiency and renewable energy technologies across the United States. The company specialises in energy efficient lighting upgrades, mechanical and electrical retrofit and upgrade services, water conservation, weatherisation and renewable project development and implementation.

A German company, *EnOcean*, has developed an entirely new way of operating building controls which is much more energy-efficient and cost effective than traditional methods. Their system uses switches and sensors linked to devices by low frequency radio waves.

Data centres are extremely power-hungry facilities but many tend to waste energy by over-cooling their IT equipment or otherwise mismanaging these environments. A Californian company, *SynapSense*, specialises in wireless monitoring and network software which can save IT centres up to 20% on their energy bills by improving the efficiency of their facilities management. Another promising start-up, *Adura Technologies*, is focusing on a wireless control system for managing lighting in commercial buildings.

Power conversion devices for appliances of all kinds, from mobile phones to laptops and lighting, are wasteful of energy. This is the target market for a Cambridgeshire company, *CamSemi*, who have developed a range of award-winning power conversion controllers which are lightweight, efficient and have ultra-low power consumption in standby mode.

Voltage optimisation

Voltage optimisation revolves around the fact that a vast range of electrical equipment is designed to work at voltages which are lower than the voltage supplied by the electricity grid. For instance, most equipment made for use in Europe and the UK today is rated at 220V. However, the voltage supplied within Europe is permitted to be anywhere between 207V and 253V: in the UK it is usually supplied at around 245V, and in Europe often at around 238V.

Therefore, it makes sense to lower the voltage being used through voltage optimisation, and save energy. It has been estimated that if every household in the UK used voltage optimisation to reduce its electricity consumption a typical home could save carbon emissions of 270kg every year (the equivalent of taking 2.3m cars off the road). Not only does the use of higher than necessary voltages waste electricity, it also shortens the life of appliances.

There are a number of companies working in this field in the UK. The only quoted company solely devoted to domestic voltage optimisation is **VPhase**, whose first product, the VX1, is already available. The company estimates that the potential market for their units in Britain is 1.4m homes a year, with the continental market around 7m homes and in America 10m a year.

Industrial and commercial users with big electricity bills have long understood the advantages of voltage optimisation. PowerPerfector, a privately held Anglo-Dutch company, has installed its equipment with dozens of clients including Royal palaces, Hilton hotels and supermarkets. Two installations at Asda stores in the UK have saved just over 15% on the supermarkets' electricity bills, they say. Another company aiming at industrial clients is ActiveEnergy, who claim that their VoltageMaster device can save up to 20% on energy bills. The company is 72% owned by gas component supplier Cinpart (AIM: CINP). The privately held Claude Lyons group is another manufacturer of voltage optimisation equipment.

According to *Cleantech Investor*, "with so many companies offering voltage optimisation solutions there is bound to be some consolidation within this sector eventually. But, with voltage optimisation equipment offering a quick recovery of its installation costs through electricity savings, this sector looks like it has plenty of growth ahead of it during the next few years."[116]

Heat pumps

"There is a major growth potential for installers in the domestic [heat pump] market, especially in European markets, particularly those starting from a

low base like the UK. While many players will be small and regionalised, more broadly based installation companies with critical mass, good organisation and a complementary offering in other renewable energy technologies will enjoy substantial market growth."

Investment Opportunities for a Low Carbon World[117]

A ground-source heat pump (GSHP) exploits the fact that whatever kind of climate you live in, the temperature at a certain depth below ground stays fairly consistent all year round, regardless of season. A ground-based system has a loop of pipe buried in the earth, with the flow and return connected to the heat pump. During the heating cycle, heat is extracted from the ground and distributed through a conventional duct system as warm air. The same heat energy can also be used for a radiant floor system or domestic hot water heating. In the cooling mode, the heating process is reversed – creating cool, conditioned air throughout the home. Instead of extracting heat from the ground, heat is extracted from the air in the house and either moved back into the earth loop, or it can be used to preheat the water in a hot water tank. A variation on this is an air-source heat pump, which are cheaper and easier to install compared to ground-source pumps. However, they are much less efficient.

Europe has long been accustomed to the idea of heat pump technologies. The market is valued at around €800m annually and is growing. Britain lags well behind this: there are around 8000 ground source heat pumps operating in the UK but the Environment Agency estimates that the technology is suitable for around 320,000 homes and businesses.

In Europe the majority of manufacturers and installers are private companies (including Calorex, Dimplex, Geothermal International and Worcester Bosch). The exception is the Swedish company **NIBE**, one of Europe's leading manufacturers and distributors of ground-source heat pumps.

In the US the heat pump business is dominated by large, privately owned HVAC companies such as Lennox, Carrier and Trane, who are competing with around 50 other companies in the space heating and cooling business. Heat pump installations have been boosted by new text credits under ARRA.

The only independent pure-play company is **WaterFurnace Renewable Energy Inc**. The company's headquarters in Fort Wayne, Indiana, serve as a model for commercial geothermal installations worldwide: a pond loop and 41 of the company's own geothermal units meet all heating and cooling requirements for the facility.

Insulation

For those investors interested in companies specialising in insulation, there are a number of listed companies worth investigating:

- One of Britain's leading providers of green support services is the Newcastle-based **Eaga**. As well as being one of the principal agents for delivering the government's Warm Front scheme, Eaga also works with utilities and other partners on Carbon Emission Reduction Target (CERT) programmes.

- The **Kingspan Group**, based in Ireland, is recognised as a leading provider of insulation and building envelope products. The company's long-term aim is to deliver building technologies that exceed existing regulations and meet future zero-carbon legislative requirements across global markets. It builds solar thermal systems, air-source heat pumps, solar cooling solutions and thin-film PV systems.

- The largest supplier of insulation products in Europe is **SIG** plc, based in Sheffield. SIG's main business is distributing insulation, dry lining and similar products but the company also manufactures bespoke products for specialist contractors.

- Founded in 1909, the **Rockwool Group** is the world's leading producer of stone wool. This Danish company began production of stone wool in 1935 and has since expanded from Scandinavia to the rest of Europe, North America and the Far East.

- In Britain **Superglass** is a small company which makes mineral wool insulation. The company has made considerable investments in its manufacturing capacity in the last few years and is now able to produce 70,000 tonnes of mineral wool insulation annually. However, the slow-down in the construction industry and competition from other suppliers has damaged its recent performance.

- An innovative UK start-up, *Web Dynamics*, has developed a hi-tech 'space blanket' for buildings which allows them to breathe whilst also retaining heat. A finalist in the Carbon Trust Innovation Awards in 2009, the company's TLX Gold insulation has successfully been put to the test in a wide variety of buildings.

Concrete: the remix

The manufacturing of cement, the crucial ingredient in concrete, is one of the biggest single causes of carbon dioxide emissions globally – cement plants account for 5% of global carbon dioxide emissions (more than double the entire aviation industry). Unfortunately, cement cannot be recycled: each new road or building needs new supplies of the material. Concrete is a key component in housing and infrastructure, with 80% of current production taking place in emerging economies. China alone accounts for 45% of global demand, with production exceeding 1bn metric tons annually.

Manufacturers have invested significantly in programmes such as the Cement Sustainability Initiative, a global effort by 18 leading cement producers coordinated by the World Business Council for Sustainable Development.

Portland cement, which is the most common type, is made by heating limestone and other materials in a kiln to temperatures of 1500°C, which is a very energy-intensive process. An alternative to Portland cement is to use ground granulated blast furnace slag, which is a by-product of the iron-making industry. This process requires one-fifth of the energy required to make Portland cement and produces one-tenth of the carbon dioxide, according to producers Civil and Marine, a division of Heidelberg Cement (ETR:HEI).

Other companies are searching for solutions in different directions. *iCrete*, based in California, has developed a technology that optimises the concrete mix for efficiency and strength while lowering carbon dioxide emissions at the same time.

Whilst manufacturers struggle to reduce the carbon footprint of traditional Portland cement by installing modern kilns, substituting waste products or taking other efficiency measures, their leeway is limited. Meanwhile the next generation of green building companies are pushing the boundaries to create advanced building materials which will offer more radical technological breakthroughs.

These include start-ups such as UK-based *Novacem*, which is developing a 'green cement' which hardens by absorbing atmospheric carbon dioxide, giving the unique potential for a range of 'carbon negative' construction products. Novacem claim that it will transform the cement industry from a significant emitter to a significant absorber of carbon dioxide; they plan to have a pilot plant in operation by 2011 and are said to be in talks with major cement manufacturers.

Building on green bricks

In the US, CalStar Products has created a green brick made from fly ash. The company says that its non-fired brick is easy to build with and has good mortar adhesion: designed specifically for Leadership in Energy and Environmental Design (LEED) commercial projects, the bricks were scheduled to start rolling off a new Wisconsin production line in late 2009. Fly ash is also being used in green building products by Gigacrete, based in Las Vegas, Nevada. As well as its current PlasterMax range of interior finishes, the company is planning to launch panels made with between 70 and 80% recycled ash by volume; the company has received $3.5m in venture capital from Craton Equity Partners.

Another start-up with a high profile in green buildings is California-based *Serious Materials*, which is marketing EcoRock, a green alternative to standard drywall, which they say uses 80% less energy to produce than standard drywall. The company also makes high-performance insulated windows and glass which they claim deliver performance four times higher than major US brands.

Timber substitutes

The demand for timber in the building industry places pressure on hardwood sources such as tropical rainforests. One way of alleviating this is to treat sustainably grown softwoods so that they can be used as substitutes for hardwoods. The UK company **Accsys Technologies** has developed an acetylation process that does just this, turning softwoods such as pines and firs into solid, durable products with similar properties to hardwood.

Another company working on hardwood substitutes is New Jersey-based **Axion International Holdings**. The company has developed a process that blends recycled plastics into structural building components which are stronger than steel.

Two listed companies specialising mostly in decking, exterior finishes and other wood substitute products made from recycled plastics are **Advanced Environmental Recycling Technologies**, based in Arkansas, and **Trex**, based in Virginia.

The future of lighting

Climate change has rendered the incandescent light bulb obsolete, as evidenced by governments worldwide enacting legislation to phase out the use of these inefficient bulbs, which emit just 10% of their energy usage as visible light (the other 90% is lost as heat). In Cuba incandescent light bulbs were banned in 2005 and in Europe the 100W bulb has been banned since September 2009. There are plans for other incandescent bulbs to be banned by 2012. In the US, the phase-out will take place between 2012 and 2014. Other countries are following suit. As the market for all types of lighting is estimated to be around $75bn globally there are clearly opportunities for companies in the production of greener alternatives.[118]

The current standard choice for energy-efficient lighting is the compact fluorescent (CFL) bulb, which has a lifespan between eight to 15 times that of incandescents. Despite their low energy usage, public acceptance of CFLs has been begrudging – largely because of the colour and quality of light, and the fact that they can't be dimmed. They also contain small amounts of mercury, which has to be dealt with as toxic waste.

Although the latest bulbs are much improved, the lighting industry is already looking beyond CFLs to the next generation of lights, known as solid state lighting (SSL) systems.

Light-emitting diodes

Solid-state lighting does away with light bulbs altogether and replaces them with light-emitting diodes, or LEDs. The benefits of LED technology include better optical efficiency (calculated as lumens per watt), greater reliability and longer product life. There are no toxic components either. Not surprisingly, LEDs have made big inroads in places where bulb replacement is difficult or costly – half the traffic lights in the US, for instance, already run on them.

A major initiative to promote LED streetlights in cities worldwide was launched in 2009 by non-profit organisation The Climate Group: their LightSavers programme will test LED lighting and smart controls in outdoor spaces with trials taking place simultaneously in seven cities.

LEDs are also gradually being adopted in commercial and industrial buildings as stricter building regulations are enforced and they will soon proliferate in our homes. Consumer products built with LEDs, from bicycle lights to head torches, are in the shops now. Large-screen outdoor displays are another common application.

According to some estimates, the conversion of most lighting to LED technology would reduce the carbon dioxide emissions associated with the generation of light by half – in other words, the world's carbon dioxide emissions would be reduced by 10%. The main barrier to adoption at present is price, but one of the world's largest LED manufacturers claim that this is falling by 50% every 18 months.[119]

Another barrier to the more widespread adoption of LEDs is an entire infrastructure built around sockets and bulbs. And whilst some large corporations are moving decisively in this direction, they have also got entrenched interests in continuing to supply the global lighting industry with older, less efficient products. Legislation, as ever, is driving change.

The race to commercialise domestic LEDs has been stimulated in America by the launch of the Department of Energy's Bright Tomorrow Lighting Prize (the 'L Prize'), which offers cash rewards of up to $20m and lucrative public sector contracts for the companies which can offer replacements for the two most widely used bulbs today, the 60W incandescent and PAR 38 halogen lamps. The contest also calls for the development of a '21st century lamp' that delivers more than 150 lumens per watt. The DOE says that 60W bulbs account for 50% of all lighting in the US, with 425m sold each year. If all these were replaced with LEDs, carbon emissions would be cut by 5.6m metric tons annually.

LED market

Strategies Unlimited, a California-based research firm, predict that the market for LEDs will reach $14.9bn in 2013.[120] All of the big players in lighting and electronics are aiming to capitalise on this growth. The Dutch electronics conglomerate Philips (NYSE: PHG) acquired no less than eight companies in this field between 2005 and 2008. Philips is the first company to compete in the American L prize challenge, entering an LED bulb that emits the same amount of light as its incandescent equivalent but which uses less than 10W and lasts for 25,000 hours.

General Electric stepped into the arena with the unveiling of its Energy Smart LED bulb in April 2010. Expected to consume just 9 watts, it will produce the same light as a 40-watt incandescent bulb but with a 77% saving in energy and lasting 25 times as long.

Another electronics giant, Panasonic (TYO: 6752), has beefed up its LED division substantially and is planning to offer more than 100 residential and 350 non-residential products on to the market by 2011. The company expects its LED lighting division to generate sales of JPY 100bn (JPY 70bn domestic and JPY 30bn overseas) by March 2016. Other Japanese companies who are global players in LEDs include Toyoda Gosei (TYO: 7282), who also make car parts, and the privately held Nichia group.

Osram, part of the Siemens group, currently gains around 15% of its global sales of €4.0bn from LED products but is hoping to consolidate its position in all stages of the LED value chain with further expansion. One of the two largest lighting manufacturers in the world, Osram claims that LEDs are on the verge of a breakthrough. "We are shaping the lighting market of the future," says Osram CEO Martin Goetzeler. "Osram expects that LED retrofits as replacements for incandescent lamps will take hold on the market and trigger rising demand. Growth will be driven by falling prices, further technical developments, and global political efforts to ban inefficient bulbs," he said.[121]

Listed companies in this area include:

- **Cree**, an independent manufacturer which is one of the largest producers of LED wafers and LED products in the US.

- **Nexxus Lighting**, which markets LEDs for the commercial, retail, hospitality, entertainment and consumer markets.

- **Lighting Science Group** (LSG), based in Florida, which has a strong presence in what it calls 'architainment' installations but also sells into the retail and commercial markets, as well as casinos, where they have a legacy business around slot machines.

- **Carmanah Technologies**, a Canadian company that has been developing LEDs powered by solar panels since 1996. Their niche market is solar-powered marine lanterns, which are used by ports, harbours, coast guards and marine authorities around the world.

- **Nanoco Group**, a British company that is developing a technology which has the potential to dramatically improve LED lighting. The company specialises in fluorescent semi-conducting materials called quantum dots, which have the ability to emit light in a specific colour dependent on the size of the particle.

Development-stage companies to watch in the SSL market include *Bridgelux*, *Luminus Devices* and *Oree*.

Organic light-emitting diodes (OLEDs)

The next step beyond LEDs is organic light-emitting diodes (OLEDs), where the emitting layer of material is an organic compound. The result is a lightweight, thin sheet of polymer or plastic which illuminates when a charge is applied.

OLEDs are currently being used in applications such as TV screens and cell phones, but they operate at lower efficiencies and typically emit less light per area than LEDs so aren't yet suitable for general illumination. The cost, and longevity, are other barriers.

However, several major companies (including Aixtron, Osram, Philips, BASF and Applied Materials) are working together to create high performance white OLED devices which can be used for lighting. GE also has a major research programme to develop roll-to-roll sheets of ultra-thin plastic that will provide a new means of lighting building interiors. The technology is basically the same as that being used to produce thin-film PV.

New applications are being invented all the time for OLEDs. Their malleable properties mean that they can be used as light curtains, self-illuminating walls, or even windows which change from transparent in the daytime to an opaque colour at night.

The only listed company manufacturing OLEDs is the **Universal Display Corporation.** Based in New Jersey, the company's main line of business is flat panel displays for electronic devices but it is developing white lighting for general applications. It was awarded two grants from the DOE to develop very high efficiency white phosphorescent OLEDs. The company says that it considers white lighting as a potentially lucrative second revenue stream for their technology in the near future.

Development stage companies working on OLEDs include the British company *LOMOX*, who have received £450,000 from the Carbon Trust to accelerate their research, and the German company *Novaled*.

Plasma lighting

Another technology which is moving up fast is plasma lighting. Primarily aimed at the commercial lighting market (which accounts for around one-third of all lighting demand), plasma lights are said to reduce energy usage by 50%, require half the number of units compared to other lamps, and have full dimming and fast turn-on capabilities. The only company with a commercial product to date is Milton Keynes-based *Ceravision*.

Electron-stimulated luminescence (ESL)

Another type of technology is being promoted by **Vu1**, who claim that their electron-stimulated luminescence (ESL) process creates the same light quality as an incandescent but is more energy efficient, and has a lifespan of 6000 hours. The company gave its first public demonstration of their bulb in late 2009.

Semiconductor growth

Most LEDs are made from semiconductor wafers manufactured by a process called metal organic chemical vapour deposition (MOCVD). The two biggest producers of MOCVD systems – which are also used in the production of CIGS solar cells – are the US company Veeco (NASDAQ: VECO) and the German company Aixtron (NASDAQ: AIXG). These companies are currently reporting unprecedented demand from LED manufacturers in China, Korea and Taiwan for their thermal processing equipment.

An Australian company called **BluGlass Ltd** is attempting to commercialise a new technology for growing semiconducting materials which they claim will revolutionise the production of both LEDs and solar cells. Their process is said to be a superior means of producing the next generation of semiconducting materials such as indium gallium nitrides (InGaN). For solar cells, the use of InGaN has the potential to increase efficiencies by up to 50% and provide longer durability. For LEDs, it will increase performance and lower production costs.

Lighting glossary

CFL:	compact fluorescent lights
ESL:	electron-stimulated luminescence
LED:	light-emitting diodes
MOCVD:	metal organic chemical vapour deposition
OLED:	organic light-emitting diodes
RPCVD:	remote plasma vapour deposition
SSL:	solid state lighting

Companies to watch

Building controls

Adura Technologies (San Francisco, California, USA) works on technology aimed at reducing lighting costs using wireless mesh networking systems. The core technology communicates with switches, motion sensors, and light sensors to automatically switch off unused lighting; it also tracks and monitors energy use. Backers include VantagePoint Venture Partners and Claremont Creek Ventures. www.aduratech.com

CamSemi (Cambridge, UK) has developed lightweight power conversion controllers that help reduce energy usage in consumer electronic equipment, household appliances and lighting. Most present day power conversion devices are very inefficient, wasting up to 50% of the power fed into them. The company won the Energy in Buildings category in the Carbon Trust Innovation awards 2009. www.camsemi.com

EnOcean (Munich, Germany), a spin-out from Siemens, designs HVACR monitoring and lighting control systems that are completely wireless and operated by sensors and switches which draw their energy from slight changes in motion, pressure, light, temperature or vibration. The system is flexible, cost-efficient and energy-efficient. EnOcean raised a further €8m in December 2009 from existing and new investors to finance international expansion. www.enocean.com

SynapSense (Folsom, California) provides complete wireless instrumentation solutions that offer energy efficiency savings for data centres. Many data centres over-cool their servers, or have badly placed equipment not fulfilling its role: the SynapSense system, with wireless instrumentation linked into network and management software, enables better management of facilities and can achieve energy savings of up to 20%. The company's backers include American River Ventures, Emerald Technology Ventures, Sequoia Capital, DFJ Frontier, Nth Power and Robert Bosch Venture Capital GmbH. www.synapsense.com

Building materials

iCrete (Beverly Hills, California) has developed software that optimises the concrete mix for efficiency and strength through the use of its patented algorithms. The company licenses the software to precast and ready mix producers. iCrete has to date been involved with several prestigious projects including the Freedom Tower at One World Trade Center. www.icrete.com

Novacem (London) has developed an ultra-low-carbon cement which is said to absorb more carbon dioxide over its lifetime than is emitted during production. The recyclable cement system is based on magnesium oxide and special mineral additives. Backers include Imperial Innovations, the Royal Society Enterprise Fund and the London Technology Fund. www.novacem.com

Serious Materials (Sunnyvale, California) develops and manufactures sustainable green building materials including its super-insulating high R-value Serious Windows, which reduce heating and cooling energy costs by up to 40%; SeriousGlass, which is a super-insulating commercial glass; QuietRock soundproof drywall; and EcoRock, a green alternative to standard drywall. Serious Materials' products are manufactured in the company's five factories across North America. www.seriousmaterials.com

Insulation

The flagship product of *Web Dynamics* (Blackrod, Lancashire) is TLX Gold, a combined multi-foil and breather membrane which controls water vapour and air movement, enabling a building to 'breathe' whilst delivering a comfortable and energy efficient environment. It has successfully been put to the test in the refurbishment of a number of historic buildings as well as several public sector, retro-fit social housing, property conversion and new build projects. www.webdynamics.co.uk

Lighting

Bridgelux (Sunnyvale, California) makes LED chips for SSL applications. In addition to LED chips, the company has recently expanded their product portfolio to include a range of SSL light sources that customers can easily integrate into a variety of lighting applications that will open up new markets in interior and exterior application areas such as street lights, track lights and down-lights. www.bridgelux.com

Ceravision (Milton Keynes, UK) is marketing a super-efficient plasma lighting system which uses radio frequencies to create a high intensity plasma discharge. The lamps reduce energy usage by at least 50% and because they provide so much light, the number of fittings required can be halved. The company says that no other lighting product on the market is even close to delivering these levels of efficiency, and is initially targeting the High Intensity Discharge (HID) lights found mostly in commercial or industrial buildings. www.ceravision.com

LOMOX (St. Asaph, North Wales), which received £450,000 from the Carbon Trust in January 2010, plans to use a very high-yield photolithographic process for printing OLED inks onto surfaces including wallpaper or glass screens. Each layer is locked in place using ultraviolet light and their manufacturing technique allows more light to be produced with less voltage, increasing efficiency. www.lomox.co.uk

Luminus Devices (Billerica, MA) develops and manufactures high performance SSLs under the brand name PhlatLights. Its LEDs are used for indoor and outdoor lighting (including street lighting), entertainment, architectural, automotive, medical and dental, avionic and other applications. Luminus has raised $139m in venture capital funds and has manufacturing facilities in Massachusetts, Taiwan and Thailand. www.luminus.com

Oree (Ramat Gan, Israel) is developing a ground-breaking technology that bridges the gap between LED technology and illumination applications. The company says that its next generation planar LED is a flat, thin, highly efficient light source which will allow general lighting companies and back light manufactures to significantly increase system efficiency and dramatically reduce the cost of LED-based systems. www.oree-inc.com

Novaled (Dresden, Germany) was founded in 2003 and started out as an OLED company, but its proprietary technology has applications in many other fields of organic electronics including organic PV and organic thin-film transistors. The company hopes that its OLED PIN (personal identification number) technology will help make laptop, PDA (personal digital assistant) and television screens more efficient as well as reducing power usage in signage and lighting. It has over 400 patents granted or pending and won the Audemars Piguet Cleantech Entrepreneur of the Year Award in 2009. www.novaled.com

WASTE & ENERGY RESOURCES | 10

"This decade will see the birth of waste-to-energy as a viable industry that's both big and, since its energy source – garbage – is free, potentially very profitable."

Clean Money: Picking Winners in the Green-tech Boom[122]

Introduction

The waste sector is attracting an increasing amount of attention as investors are rapidly waking up to the potential profit to be made here. New techniques are being developed in landfill management, recycling and composting to increase efficiencies, reduce emissions and generate more renewable energy. Food waste, for instance, is being used to power the factories it comes from. Capturing methane from landfill and turning it into energy is becoming a profitable business.

Policy targets that are pushing this sector forward include European Union goals requiring member states to keep reducing the amount of waste sent to landfill and increase the amount being recycled. In Britain, the landfill tax will continue to rise from by £8 per tonne each year until 2013, when it will reach £72 per tonne. This creates a huge incentive for local authorities to find other ways of dealing with waste. These challenges are creating new opportunities in the recycling and reprocessing of waste, energy-from-waste (EFW) programmes, industrial-scale composting plants and other areas.

The larger waste management companies have started to re-position themselves as 'energy recovery specialists' rather than just collectors of rubbish in order to capitalise on these trends. The Biffa Group, for instance, has formed a series of strategic alliances with smaller companies across Europe involved in EFW, anaerobic digestion (AD), recycling, biomass and gasification. As well as its massive landfill operations, the company is now also a net provider of energy – generating around 100MW from its UK operations alone. Similarly, the Shanks Group, another major European player, has branched out into a whole range of technologies from composting to CHP. Its organic waste treatment business, Orgaworld, recently won a contract to handle all the food waste from Marks & Spencer until 2012.

The re-branding extends to waste processing facilities, which are no longer called industrial recycling centres but 'resource parks' and 'ecoparks' in an effort to make them sound cleaner and greener to local communities.

According to Catalyst Corporate Finance, there have been around 40 acquisitions or private equity investments made in EFW companies over the last three years, with a value in excess of £300m. The EFW market is expected to be a major growth area in Europe for at least the next ten years, with almost 100 new plants due to come online by 2012. The UK government's Waste Resource Action Programme estimates that 450 new composting plants will be needed by 2020 to satisfy local authority requirements alone.

One example case is provided by the buy out of Monsal, a market leader in building anaerobic digestion plants, by private equity investors Matrix group in 2009. The company has since won a contract to build a massive bio-waste plant in Scotland which will generate 8000MWh of renewable energy per annum. According to Ashley Broomberg of Matrix:

> "This market is still at an early stage of its growth phase. There is a rich pipeline of opportunities from waste management operators, to merchant operators, landfill and composting owners, food processing companies and the utilities. We expect there to be significant interest in the sector from ... the financial community."[123]

Currently Britain's biggest producer of renewable energy from landfill is the Infinis group, owned by private equity group Terra Firma, which has installed capacity of 313MW from over 100 sites. After a prolonged takeover battle, in November 2009 Infinis also acquired renewable energy developer Novera, which owns landfill gas sites, hydro power stations and two operational wind farms.

An important question for investors is which of the competing companies and various technologies within the waste sector are going to succeed.

We will examine this in the following section on investing in waste and resource management.

Investing in waste and resource management

"The waste-to-energy market in Europe is growing and is expected to do so for at least ten years. Europe's waste-to-energy capacity is expected to increase by approximately 13m tons. Almost 100 new plants will come on-line by 2012."

Investing in a Sustainable World[124]

Overview

Bull points

- Growth driven by national and international policy on waste reduction.

- Guaranteed resource streams.

- Security of energy supply.

- Renewable energy targets.

- Carbon emissions quotas.

- Economic incentives including ROCs and FITs for micro-generation.

Bear points

- Uncertainties over planning.

- Difficulties with obtaining finance, especially for very large projects.

- Some technologies are untested.

Investment summary

There should be some good opportunities for business and investors in waste and resource management. As Mark Wilson of Catalyst Capital says:

> "There is a case for good recycling businesses for years to come. There are some cracking businesses out there using some really advanced technology, who have really solid demand."

At present, there are major differences in aims of the large, established waste management companies and the new technology start-ups. Larger companies are focusing on the longer-term PFI (Public Finance Initiative) contracts with local authorities which can last up to 25 years, whilst a whole batch of new entrants are coming forward to offer local authorities contracts of 5-10 years duration. "You've got a bit of a land grab," says Nigel Taunt, waste expert and director of venture capital at Impax. "There is a battlefield between the big players going for the long-term contracts and the new entrants who are mostly the ones bidding for the shorter-term contracts."

Smaller companies are also suffering from a lack of available capital but some are finding ways around this. "These are the ones that will succeed," says Taunt. "We need some big players to come forward and start consolidating, but that is not happening. I find it a vey exciting area – there is everything to play for and we will start to see the winners and losers emerging over the next two to three years."

As well as this division between large and small companies, it should also be borne in mind that there is a technology battle between the different types of waste treatment techniques at the forefront of waste management and waste-to-energy processes. None are without their drawbacks and it is not yet clear which techniques will be the winners over the long term. For instance, there are considerable doubts as to whether or not energy-intensive technologies such as plasma gasification are going to be profitable.

The UK is considered to be one of the fastest growing waste markets in Europe because it has made so little progress to date with recycling targets compared to other European countries. The increasingly harsh levies on landfill, combined with massive fines from the EU if landfill volumes aren't sharply reduced, means that there are huge economic opportunities for well-positioned companies. Rising commodity costs are also contributing to this growth.

The sector will be given a boost in Britain by the new FITs introduced in April 2010, with anaerobic digestion set to be the main beneficiary. A new Renewable Heat Incentive, due to take effect in April 2011, will similarly boost AD, biomass plants (including EFW facilities) and those processing waste wood as feedstock.

In June 2010 the government also announced a wholesale review of waste policy, with the intention of turning Britain into a "zero-waste society" that would go "further and faster" in boosting recycling rates, processing more recyclable rubbish in the UK (rather than sending it abroad), looking at new ways of dealing with commercial waste and turning more biodegradable waste into energy.

Technology and companies

General waste management

Europe's largest listed waste management company is the **Shanks Group**, which operates in the Netherlands, Belgium, UK and Canada. Shanks says that it operates in countries with the highest recycling rates in Europe and has experience of a number of treatment processes capable of producing renewable energy from waste: their goal is to be "Europe's leading sustainable waste management company". At the time of writing Shanks was the subject of takeover speculation.

Other leading companies include Viridor, which owns 241 operational sites including 24 landfill sites and 18 MRFs. Viridor is part of the Pennon Group (LON: PNN).

Another major player is the Paris-based **Veolia Environnement** group, which has operations spanning 42 countries in waste, energy, transport and environmental services. In the UK, the company operates as Veolia Environmental Services with a network of 13 landfill sites, six energy recovery facilities and five composting facilities.

In Europe, one of the largest players is **Suez Environnement**, who have recently launched their 'green cube' programme to target energy recovery and biomass conversion from waste-water treatment.

In the US, the two largest companies are **Republic Services** and **Waste Management**. In 2008 Republic Services bought out the third biggest company, Allied Waste, leaving these two companies with roughly 50% market share each. Both Republic Services and Waste Management are increasingly moving into EFW schemes. Republic Services has also started putting solar panels on top of landfill sites to maximise the energy generating opportunities.

Other US companies involved in this area include **Covanta**, a major operator of incinerators in the US and Asia. Another US company, **Environmental Power Corporation**, is involved in hydropower, EFW and (with the recent acquisition of the Danish firm Microgy) AD processing.

Anaerobic digestion

This is a well-proven technology which breaks down organic matter in an oxygen-free environment to produce biogas (comprising roughly 65% methane and 35% carbon dioxide, which can be converted to energy) and a nutrient-rich residue which can be used as a fertiliser. Advanced anaerobic digestion (AAD) includes a pre-digestion phase which helps to optimise the key processing stages of AD by breaking down the organic materials beforehand. The end result is the same – a far greater conversion of organic matter into biogas once the material reaches the AD process.

Britain produces 100m tonnes of food and other organic waste every year which could be converted to heat and energy – enough to supply over 2m homes. The Department for Environment, Food and Rural Affairs (DEFRA) has handed out over £10m in grants to promote AD, with five major new projects due to come online in 2011. A new national body, the Anaerobic Digestion and Biogas Association, has set out plans to build more than 1000 anaerobic digestion plants across the UK by 2015. The association says that this will cost around £5bn, but points out that this is a proven technology which can deliver good economic returns. The UK market leader is Monsal, who have installed over 200 AD systems and recently completed Scotland's first large-scale plant, which will handle 30,000 tonnes a year of food waste and generate 1MW of power. Another major player is Biogen Greenfinch, a subsidiary of the privately held Bedfordia Group. In the US, a small cap in this field is the Environmental Power Corporation; it is developing facilities on large cattle farms using technology licensed from a Danish company.

Gasification and pyrolysis

These techniques involve heating waste until it breaks down into a flammable mixture of hydrogen and carbon monoxide (known as syngas) and a residual slag or ash. The syngas can be used to power gas turbines to generate electricity or can be converted into other fuels such as methane, ethanol or synthetic diesel. Opponents argue that it is a dirty process which releases emissions, particularly dioxins, into the atmosphere. However, it is also considered less harmful than incineration.

Gasification is very efficient if there is a consistent input stream, but municipal waste – almost by definition – is going to have a highly variable content. This can present challenges for a gasification plant. The leading operator in the UK is Energos, part of the Manchester-based unlisted power company *ENER-G*, which specialises in energy management and EFW. Energos has six operational gasification plants in Norway and Germany and recently completed the first full scale plant in Britain on the Isle of Wight. The £10m facility will generate annually 2.3MW of electricity from 30,000 tonnes of waste annually. Energos is planning another similar plant on Merseyside.

Another leading EFW company is Monmouth-based Cyclamax, who are developing six resource parks in conjunction with SITA UK (a subsidiary of Suez Environnement) at a cost of £220m. The first four resource parks will use batched gasification technology, using equipment provided by the American company Waste2Energy.

One of the more promising companies in this field is the New Earth Group. The company operates a range of facilities combining mechanical biological treatment (MBT), recycling, in-vessel composting (IVC) and gasification or pyrolysis. They currently have three operational facilities and have secured planning permission for a further three, alongside contracts with a number of local authorities. New Earth is targeting a pipeline of projects that will deliver up to 250MW of renewable electricity generating capacity over the next five years.

Plasma gasification

This involves super-heating waste to temperatures of 1300°C or more, creating a flammable mixture of hydrogen and carbon monoxide (known as syngas) and a residual slag or ash. The syngas can be used to power gas turbines to generate electricity or be converted into other fuels such as methane, ethanol or synthetic diesel. Drawbacks include huge capital costs and high running costs

A consortium called Waste2Tricity is hoping to develop a commercial scale plant in Britain. In the US, Startech Environmental (OTC:STHK) promotes plasma gasification systems. Although they opened a demonstration centre in Connecticut in 2001 a fully commercial plant has yet to be built. The Washington, D.C. based Solena Group is planning to use plasma gasification to turn biowastes into aviation fuel, and has reached an agreement with British Airways to build a plant in east London which they say will produce twice the amount of fuel needed to power all British Airways' (BA) flights from London City Airport.

Autoclaving

Steam cleaning or autoclaving is widely used on a small scale to sterilise medical equipment but its application to household waste on a large scale is only just beginning. The process involves loading unsorted municipal waste into rotating sealed drums, where a combination of steam and pressure results in the organic waste being broken down into a fibrous biomass and the non-organics being sterilised and steam cleaned. The organic residue can be used as soil conditioner, biomass fuel, or fibreboard for the construction industry. The non-organics (aluminium and steel cans, glass and plastics) are then ready to be recycled – the system recovers 70-80% of typical household waste for recycling.

Sterecycle has pioneered this technology and built the world's first commercial autoclave plant in South Yorkshire which is processing 100,000 tonnes of waste per annum. The company say that it recovers 80% of household waste for recycling. Sterecycle is also working on a scheme to link an AD plant to the autoclave unit in order to generate gas – either for feeding into the grid or generating power directly. Large-scale autoclaving plants are also being built by Newcastle-based *Graphite Resources* in Gateshead and South Tees.

In-vessel composting (IVC)

IVC treats green and/or food waste in an enclosed but oxygenated (i.e., normal) environment. It produces compost, but not energy. One of the few publicly quoted companies purely concerned with IVC is the **TEG Group**.

A small company called Accelerated Composting is making in-roads into super-efficient composters aimed at the domestic market. The Cheshire-based company has developed a patented 'rocket composter', an insulated steel tube which produces usable compost within just a fortnight. The machines have the capacity to treat up to five tonnes of organic waste per week.

Methane capture

Coal seams generate and trap methane, which can be extracted in two different ways and used to generate power. There are around 1000 disused coal mines in Britain, so the potential is considerable. One method is to obtain it from abandoned coal mines, either by using the existing shafts or by drilling new holes. This technique is known as coal mine methane (CMM) and is favoured by **Alkane Energy**, who have seven mine gas capture plants operating in the UK (with installed capacity of around 17MW).

Another technique to capture methane is to tap into virgin coal beds by drilling horizontally into the seam (this is called coal bed methane, or CBM). The technology is used widely in Australia, Canada and the US (where it accounts for around 10% of all natural gas production). The CBM industry in the UK is in its infancy, with just one company **IGas**, exploring the technology.

The Dutch company *Green Gas International* works with both of these technologies as well as landfill gas. This rapidly growing company, which currently operates around 50 sites in nine countries, was a winner in the Cleantech Connect 2009 awards.

Specialist recycling

Hydrodec (LON:HYR) has developed a specialist service for re-refining waste transformer oils and selling them on again as their own-branded Superfine transformer oil. The company's fortunes have fluctuated with the price of oil. **Mercury Recycling**, which launched on AIM in 2001, is a specialist recycler of fluorescent lamps. Their process prevents toxic metals including mercury from entering landfill.

Companies to watch

ENER-G (UK) was established in the 1980s, and offers a broad range of technologies including CHP, biogas, ground source heat pumps, energy efficiency and lighting, and EFW. The company has operations in nine European countries. www.energ.co.uk

Graphite Resources (UK) recently opened its first autoclaving plant at Derwenthaugh on the River Tyne, having been founded in 2002. The £50m plant is capable of treating 320,000 tonnes of waste a year. A second EcoParc is also to be built at South Tees. The company's backers include Allied Irish Bank and Alliance & Leicester Commercial Bank (part of the Santander Group). www.graphiteresources.com

Green Gas International (Netherlands) is a developer of CMM and landfill gas projects, founded in 2005. The company has subsidiaries in the UK, Germany, the Czech Republic, Switzerland, the US and China. The company offers a complete methane management programme from gas collection to selling heat and power. covers the whole value chain, from mine gas drainage and gas collection to selling the power generated. Backers include RPG Industries, Standard Bank and Demeter Partners. www.greengas.net

Sterecycle (UK) has built the UK's first autoclaving plant in South Yorkshire and is developing a second plant in Cardiff and hopes to have at least six plants operational by 2013 in various locations including Yorkshire, Wales, London and Glasgow. Sterecycle raised £23m in its first round of fund-raising from investors including Goldman Sachs, Fidelity, Impax, and Ailsa3 Ventures. www.sterecycle.com

New Earth Group (UK) operates a range of facilities and has contracts with a number of local authorities (including an £80m agreement with the West of England Partnership to treat 120,000 tonnes of waste per annum). Their sister company New Earth Energy plans to develop a network of gasification facilities, with the first 1MW plant due to be built alongside their current MBT facility at Canford. Investors include the Carbon Trust and the Ludgate Environmental Fund. www.newearthsolutions.co.uk

Glossary

AAD: advanced anaerobic digestion

AD: anaerobic digestion

CBM: coal bed methane

CHP: combined heat and power

CMM: coal mine methane

EFW: energy-from-waste

FIT: feed-in-tariff

IVC: in-vessel composting

MBT: mechanical biological treatment

MRF: materials recycling facility

MW: megawatt

MWh: megawatt hour

RDF: refuse derived fuel

ROC: Renewables Obligation Certificate

SRF: solid recovered fuel

DIRECTORY

This directory is divided into four sections.

1. *Listed companies*: this covers mostly pure-play companies involved in environmental technologies and services that have listings on recognised stock exchanges. The purpose of these profiles is to provide some history and background to the individual companies and their products – they aren't intended to provide detailed financial information or analysis. Instead, you are advised to research individual companies through external sources or through our companion Green Investor website (www.thegreeninvestor.co.uk), which provides links to financial data.

2. *Green funds*: this provides background details on a cross-section of green funds, including comment from fund managers.

3. *Green indices & ETFs*: this covers exchange traded funds and their underlying indices.

4. *Green private equity funds*: this section provides full details on private equity funds.

LISTED COMPANIES 1

Solar power

Abengoa

Seville, Spain
www.abengoa.com
MCE: ABG
Market cap: €1,337m
12-month high/low: €14.02-24.34

Abengoa's activities range across solar energy to industrial waste, information technology and engineering. Its five main business groups are industrial engineering and construction; environmental services; solar energy; bioenergy and IT.

It was the principal contractor on PS10, the world's first commercial solar power tower and is now building a series of five, 50MW parabolic trough plants and is in a race with Acciona to be the first to reach 250MW of parabolic trough capacity.

In solar power the company has considerable experience in parabolic trough, Stirling dish, and power tower construction. They are currently building the vast 300MW Solúcar solar farm near Seville, which will deploy up to five types of solar technology. They are also constructing Helioenergy 1 and 2 (scheduled to come online in 2011 and 2012) which are parabolic trough plants being built in conjunction with E.ON Climate & Renewables.

In the US, the company is building the world's largest solar plant, the enormous 280MW Solana installation near Phoenix, Arizona. In Algeria and Morocco, they are building the world's first two combined cycle hybrid plants. Abengoa Solar New Technologies, their R&D arm, is currently exploring molten-salt storage systems, company-designed Stirling dishes and 2MW power towers.

Abengoa is not a pure play in solar, since it has other divisions involved in IT, industrial waste, and general engineering – however, there is no doubt that solar represents a considerable growth area for the company.

Applied Materials

Santa Clara, California, USA
www.appliedmaterials.com
NASDAQ: AMAT
Market cap: $16,896m
12-month high/low: $8.19-14.94

Founded in 1967, Applied Materials is a global leader in the fabrication of semiconductor chips, flat panel displays, PV cells, flexible electronics and energy efficient glass. Applied Materials entered the solar PV market in 2006 and is now a leader in process technology for both thin film and crystalline silicon module production.

The company's SunFab production line produces the world's largest thin-film PV modules (at 5.7 square metres), which are designed for turning commercial rooftops into solar farms and parking lots into power plants. The company claims that by 2011 its SunFab line will be the leading producer of thin-film modules globally. Applied Materials is also the world's largest supplier of process equipment for crystalline silicon solar production. The company is present at 108 locations in 18 countries, with manufacturing facilities in Asia, Europe and the USA, and claims that it is on target to meet its goal of $1 per watt modules with an energy conversion rate of 10% by 2010.

Ascent Solar Technologies

www.ascentsolartech.com
Littleton, Colorado, USA
NASDAQ: ASTI
Market cap: $118m
12-month high/low: $2.19-8.83

Ascent Solar produces thin-film PV modules aimed at the BIPV and EIPV markets, as well as aerospace and space products such as unmanned aerial vehicles. Ascent produces CIGS modules integrated into a flexible, lightweight, plastic substrate. Norsk Hydro, the Norwegian energy developer and aluminium manufacturer, is the largest shareholder. The company currently has a production capacity of 30MW annually. It is hoping to increase this to 110MW by 2012.

Canadian Solar

Kitchener, Ontario, Canada
www.canadian-solar.com
NASDAQ: CSIQ
Market cap: $1019m
12-month high/low: $3.00-33.68

Canadian Solar produces ingots, wafers, solar cells (both multicrystalline and monocrystalline), and solar modules, and also designs and manufactures complete solar systems. Founded in 2001, with operations in North America, Europe and Asia, Canadian Solar claims to be one of the world's largest vertically integrated solar producers.

The company has six manufacturing centres in China and operates one of the largest silicon recycling centres in the world. Canadian Solar is currently developing a two-axis tracker, which they claim will be more effective but considerably less expensive than other tracker systems. The company is also researching upgraded metallurgical silicon (UMG) and other third generation solar technologies.

China Sunergy

www.chinasunergy.com
Nanjing, China
NASDAQ: CSUN
Market cap: $204m
12-month high/low: $1.36-6.40

China Sunergy produces solar cells (both monocrystalline and multicrystalline cells) and modules. Its current capacity is around 200MW annually. China Sunergy has begun commercial production of a new, highly efficient solar cell which they say has a conversion efficiency of around 19%.

Day4 Energy

Burnaby, British Columbia, Canada
www.Day4energy.com
TSE: DFE
Market cap: $23.88m
12-month high/low: $0.43-1.02

Day4 Energy is Canada's largest manufacturer of high performance PV modules. The company has developed a new technique for building panels with higher performance, longer lifetime, improved aesthetics and at reduced cost. These techniques, which are also applicable to UMG and thin-film materials, are being commercialised with assistance from Canada's National Research Council.

Dyesol

New South Wales, Australia
www.dyesol.com
ASX: DYE
Market cap: A$117m
12-month high/low: A$0.62-1.15

Dyesol is a pioneer in the commercialisation of dye solar cell (DSC) technology, focusing on EIPV and BIPV applications. The company says its DSC technology can operate from either face, which is opening up huge markets in BIPV products. It also has considerable shade tolerance and only a low dependence on the angle of the light.

The company has launched several JVs focusing on different uses of its technology. They are working with the steel manufacturing group Corus (part of Tata Steel) on integrating solar cells into steel roofing products. A joint R&D facility in Wales is being supported by a £5m grant from the Welsh Assembly Government.

In China Dyesol is working with G-Energy, a newly formed Chinese company, in collaboration with Tsinghua University. In Korea, it has formed a JV with Timo Technologies and a prototype production facility opened in 2009. In Italy, the company is manufacturing glass façades for commercial buildings. Its first production facility in Australia opened in 2009; their existing facility in the UK (at St Asaph, Wales) has been expanded to provide a demonstration facility for European clients.

Dyesol won the prestigious Sustainable Small Company of the Year Award in 2009, which recognises best practice in corporate sustainability across Australian Stock Exchange-listed companies.

Energy Conversion Devices (ECD Ovonics)

Rochester Hills, Michigan, USA
www.ovonic.com
NASDAQ: ENER
Market cap: $360m
12-month high/low: $7.45-29.60

ECD works across a range of technologies including thin-film PV, fuel cells, and NiMH batteries. The company is a market leader in BIPV products: their subsidiary, United Solar Ovonics, makes flexible a-Si laminates distributed under the Uni-Solar brand. The company has a marketing agreement with roofing specialists Carlisle Energy Services (part of the giant Carlisle group) to sell BIPV products. Other PV products include the PowerTilt system for rack-mounted solar panels. This lightweight, low-cost panel system is designed for low-load bearing roofs and can be installed without structural roof reinforcements.

ECD has five production plants in Michigan and one in Mexico; its current capacity is 420MW, with plans to raise this to 720MW by 2011. ECD pioneers other technologies, including a new type of fast, cheap non-volatile digital memory technology designed for use in cell phones, digital cameras and personal computers. It also receives fees and royalties from licenses of its NiMH battery technology and materials.

ECD expanded its reach in 2009 with the purchase of Solar Integrated Technologies (SIT) for $16m. The acquisition of SIT, which specialises in BIPV, and has a manufacturing facility in Los Angeles and an outlet in Mainz, Germany, will significantly strengthen ECD's position in the BIPV market in both the US and Europe. Soon after this acquisition, however, ECD announced a restructuring and laid off 20% of its workforce, citing a slow-down in the US construction industry and increasing competition from Dow Chemical.

Entech Solar

Fort Worth, Texas, USA
www.entechsolar.com
OTC: ENSL
Market cap: $36m
12-month high/low: $0.08-0.37

Entech Solar designs and builds a concentrating photovoltaic thermal (CPVT) system called ThermaVolt. The company claims that their ThermaVolt units generate 4-5 times as much energy as stand-alone PV systems, using 95% less silicon, with the same length and width dimensions as industry-standard PV modules. It has not yet announced a launch date for the product. Entech Solar is also marketing a CPV module, SolarVolt II. The company has a 200MW production facility in Fort Worth, Texas.

Evergreen Solar

Marlboro, Massachusetts , USA
www.evergreensolar.com
NASDAQ: ESLR
Market cap: $260m
12-month high/low: $1.00-2.96

Founded in 1994, Evergreen Solar makes solar wafers using its proprietary string ribbon technology. The company says that this uses significantly less polysilicon than conventional processes, giving them an estimated 10% cost advantage over competitors' products. Its new Quad furnaces, which allow production of four ribbons of silicon at the same time (as opposed to two in earlier furnaces), are said to be exceeding expectations. However, the fall in silicon prices means that Evergreen is having difficulty in competing given that its production facilities are located in a high-cost area (Massachusetts). The company is planning to relocate panel assembly to China in 2010.

First Solar

Tempe, Arizona, USA
www.firstsolar.com
NASDAQ: FSLR
Market cap: $10,175m
12-month high/low: $100.90-207.51

First Solar was formed in 1999 and launched its first product in 2002. The company is the first in the world to integrate thin-film PV into high volume manufacturing: the company has developed automated high-throughput production lines that integrate each production step, from semiconductor deposition to final assembly and test, in one continuous process and transform a piece of glass into a complete solar module in less than two-and-a-half hours. First Solar's panels are made using Cadmium Telluride (CdTe), which is a fairly straightforward semiconductor that lends itself to low-cost production. It is made from cadmium and tellurium, both of which are available in abundant quantities. The panels have an efficiency rate of around 11%.

First Solar's panels can be used on residential or commercial rooftops, or in utility-scale solar farms. One of its largest installations to date has been the 53MW Lieberose solar farm in Brandenburg, Germany, which is the largest in the country and the second largest in the world.

First Solar continued its upward trajectory throughout 2009, announcing various major deals including a ten-year project to build a 2GW plant in Inner Mongolia. The company also bought its struggling rival OptiSolar in 2009: valued at $400m, the deal gained First Solar the rights to develop a 550MW solar field for Pacific Gas & Electric as well as a pipeline of 1.3GW of projects with other utilities in the western US, and land rights on a further 19GW of projects. Because these projects are already under development, First Solar will be able to short-circuit the lengthy approvals process.

First Solar has manufacturing plants in Ohio, Frankfurt, and Malaysia. The company is investing $365m to add eight manufacturing lines of 53MW each in Malaysia in 2010, and is also currently building a new factory in France in a joint venture with EDF Energies Nouvelles. The initial capacity of the plant is expected to exceed 100MW, making it the largest manufacturing facility for solar panels in France. EDF Energies Nouvelles will finance half of the €100m capital cost and will benefit from the plant's entire output for the first ten years. It is expected to start production in 2012.

A significant milestone for the solar industry came in October 2009 when First Solar became the first pure-play renewable energy company to be added to the S&P 500 Index.

GT Solar

Merrimack, New Hampshire, USA
www.gtsolar.com
NASDAQ: SOLR
Market cap: $822m
12-month high/low: $3.62-9.04

GT Solar is a market leader in production equipment for wafer and panel makers, particularly chemical vapor deposition (CVD) reactors, which use the standard Siemens-type process technology to manufacture high quality semiconductor grade or solar grade polysilicon. The company has also shipped over 1000 of its Directional Solidification System (DSS) furnaces, which melt polysilicon and cast multi-crystalline ingots: GT Solar's furnaces are the most widely used in the solar industry. The company recently opened a new PV equipment manufacturing facility (nearly doubling their capacity) and new headquarters in Shanghai in order to further capitalise on their leading market position in polysilicon reactors, specialised furnaces, and engineering and integration services for the PV industry in Asia.

JA Solar Holdings

Shanghai, China
www.jasolar.com
NASDAQ: JASO
Market cap: $895m
12-month high/low: $1.77-6.95

JA Solar Holdings Co is a solar manufacturer based in China, making both monocrystalline and multicrystalline cells and modules. Their monocrystalline solar cells have achieved conversion efficiency rates between 16 and 17%. The company is partnering with Innovalight Inc to commercialise a new generation of high-performance thin-film products using silicon inks which they plan to produce from JA Solar's R&D pilot line in Yangzhou in 2010.

Jetion Solar Holdings

Jiangsu Province, China
www.jetion.com.cn
AIM: JHL
Market cap: £56m
12-month high/low: 34.75-79.50p

Jetion is a manufacturer of high quality solar cells and modules. Founded in 2004, Jetion currently operates four 25MW solar cell production lines and has around 50MW of production capacity for solar panels.

LDK Solar

Jiangxi Province, China
www.ldksolar.com
NYSE:LDK
Market cap: $789m
12-month high/low: $3.75-14.27

LDK makes monocrystalline and multicrystalline solar wafers with an annual capacity of around 3.2GW. LDK has a 70% stake in Italian developer Solar Green Technology.

LDK signed several large development agreements in 2009, amongst which was a 500MW deal with Yancheng City, Jiangsu Province, which will include utility-scale solar farms, BIPV systems and rooftop arrays. A further deal with Suqian City, Jiangsu Province, will involve up to 300MW of solar power over a five year period.

MEMC

St. Peters, Missouri, USA
www.memc.com
NYSE: WFR
Market cap: $2,829m
12-month high/low: $11.50-21.36

MEMC is a global leader in the manufacture and sale of wafers and related products to the semiconductor and solar industries; it has been a pioneer in the design and development of wafer technologies over the past four decades. With R&D and manufacturing facilities in the US, Europe and Asia, MEMC has capacity to produce 8000 metric tons of polysilicon and 450,000 wafers per month.

In November 2009 MEMC completed the acquisition of privately held SunEdison LLC, a developer of solar power projects and North America's largest solar energy services provider. MEMC paid $200m for the company, which manages the development, financing, operation and monitoring of solar power plants for commercial customers, including many national retail outlets, government agencies and utilities. The acquisition strengthens MEMC's position in solar markets and SunEdison will benefit from the technological and cost advantages of MEMC's products.

Phoenix Solar AG

Munich, Germany
www.phoenixsolar.com
ETR:PS4
Market cap: €202m
12-month high/low: €22.63-45.20

Phoenix Solar AG developed from the Phönix Solar Initiative, a consumer association set up in 1994 to promote the sale of domestic solar thermal systems. The company became a commercial concern in 2000 and is now a leading international PV systems integrator with a sales network throughout Germany, as well as subsidiaries in Spain, Italy, Greece, France, Singapore and Australia.

The company is currently building 16 solar parks, including the Jocksdorf PV park, which occupies around 20ha of land on a former military base and will deploy over 105,000 solar modules made by First Solar, with a power output of 8MA. The company is developing other solar parks with a total output of more than 30MW, including a recently completed 1.5MW plant near Le Lauzet in France for E.ON Climate & Renewables.

PowerFilm

Ames, Iowa, USA
www.powerfilmsolar.com
AIM: PFLM
Market cap: £7.63m
12-month high/low: 12-35p

PowerFilm Inc, is a developer and manufacturer of thin-film PV. Founded in 1988, the company makes a-Si film on a durable, flexible plastic substrate. The company integrates its film into BIPV products (including metal roofing, single-ply elastomeric membrane roofing, and architectural fabric) and EIPV applications such as consumer electronics and outdoor equipment including field shelters. The company has a technology partnership with Hewlett Packard Corporation for the development of backplane drivers for next generation flat panel displays.

The company announced staff lay-offs in 2009.

PV Crystalox Solar

Abingdon, UK
www.pvcrystalox.com
LSE:PVCS
Market cap: £218m
12-month high/low: 45.24-125.00p

Established in 1982, PV Crystalox Solar was the first company to develop multicrystalline technology on an industrial scale, producing the first ingots in 1996. The group's activities today cover the entire value chain from silicon production to multicrystalline wafers. PV Crystalox sells most of its products in Japan, Germany and China, with 85% of revenues coming from the top 20 global PV companies in these regions.

PV Crystalox makes silicon ingots in Oxfordshire, with parts of its output shipped to Japan, where they are sold as wafers after processing by a sub-contractor. A second part of the production is processed into wafers for European customers at the group's facilities in Erfurt, Germany. The company has recently inaugurated a new production line at its Oxfordshire plant in order to expand its multicrystalline ingot capacity to 350MW.

Its German subsidiary, PV Crystalox Solar Silicon GmbH, has recently started up production at a new solar-grade silicon plant in Bitterfeld, Germany. The company plans to ramp up production to reach a target of 1800 metric tons by 2011.

Q-Cells SE

Bitterfeld-Wolfen, Germany
www.qcells.de
ETR: QCE
Market cap: € 695.61
12-month high/low: € 7.64-22.50

Founded in 1999, Q-Cells is one of the world's largest solar cell manufacturers. Its core business is monocrystalline and multicrystalline cells but it also has interests in thin-film PV, string ribbon processing and other solar technologies. The company recently announced the development of a new high performance, multicrystalline cell which is 15.9% efficient; Q-Cells is planning to bring it to market during 2010.

Q-Cells has a significant involvement in thin-film PV through a 100% ownership of the Swedish company Solibro, whose modules have one of the highest efficiency ratings in the field (around 12%). Q-Cells hopes to develop Solibro into a leading global provider of thin-film technologies and is aiming for a production capacity of 90MW in 2010.

The company's subsidiary Q-Cells International (QCI) specialises in building large-scale solar farms and rooftop arrays. QCI is aiming for around 150MW of solar farms per year and has formed a JV with MEMC to build them using MEMC's wafers, assembled into modules by Q-Cells. The first solar park in Bavaria will cover 125 ha, generating 50MW.

In 2010 Q-Cells announced a strategic change of direction and the company is now planning to focus more on building solar modules and installing mid-sized solar systems.

Q-Cells' headquarters are in Bitterfeld-Wolfen; it has a production facility in Malaysia and branches in Hong Kong, China and Japan.

Renesola

Jiashan, China
www.renesola.com
AIM: SOLA
Market cap: £282m
12-month high/low: 73.25-244.00p

Renesola makes monocrystalline and multicrystalline solar wafers. It recently completed its own polysilicon production facility in Sichuan Province in order to reduce feedstock costs: the $117m plant will produce around 3000 metric tons of polysilicon annually.

It bought two other Chinese solar companies in 2009: Dynamic Green Energy and Wuxi Jiacheng Solar Energy Technology Co (JC Solar). Dynamic Green manufactures products ranging from polysilicon through to ingots and PV modules and JC Solar produces PV cells and modules for customers such as JA Solar, Motech Industries, Solarfun Power Holdings, and Suntech Power.

Renesola is expecting to achieve capacity of around 1GW of wafer production, 360MW of cell production and 375MW of module production during 2010. With the strategic acquisition of JC Solar and the start of polysilicon production, ReneSola has transformed itself into an end-to-end vertically integrated company spanning polysilicon production to module manufacturing.

The company has also moved into the development of solar farms, partnering with the local government in Wuzhong City to build a 150MW capacity solar array starting in 2010.

Renewable Energy Corporation (REC)

Sandvika, Norway
www.scanwafer.com
Oslo: REC
Market cap: Kr16,220
12-month high/low: Kr24.22-68.35

REC is one of the world's largest producers of silicon materials, PV wafers, cells and modules. It is one of the few companies that doesn't use the Siemens process for producing silicon. Instead, they use their own proprietary technology, which they say produces solar grade silicon at significantly lower cost.

The company has two silicon plants in the USA, with wafer and cell production sites in Norway and solar module assembly in Sweden. REC is building the world's largest solar factory in Singapore which, when it reaches full capacity in 2012, will produce 740MW of wafers, 550MW of cells and 590MW of modules annually. The company's goal is to achieve manufacturing costs below €1 per watt in the new plant.

Romag Holdings

Consett, UK
www.romag.co.uk
AIM: ROM
Market cap: £32.5m
12-month high/low: 28-73p

Romag is a leading manufacturer of specialist transparent composites to the security, renewable energy, architectural and specialist transport markets. By combining high quality float and tempered glass, modern plastics technology and specialist inter-layers, Romag produces a range of long-lasting, high performance laminates, including laminated solar panels. Around 50% of its business is considered to be in solar.

The company is a leading participant in the BIPV market through its PowerGlaz technology. Romag has also recently launched its PowerPark solar car-parking canopy, which is designed as a modular system. It has entered into an agreement with British Gas New Energy to market, distribute and install PowerPark modules.

The company's solar training centre in Consett offers accredited training in solar installation for builders, architects and developers.

Romag should benefit from the recently introduced FIT rates in Britain which will boost building-integrated solar.

Roth & Rau AG

Hohenstein-Ernstthal, Germany
www.roth-rau.de
ETR: R8RG
Market cap: €364m
12-month high/low: €10.45-33.91

Roth & Rau AG is one of the world's leading suppliers of production equipment for the PV industry and has installed its state-of-the-art technology at more than 250 plants worldwide. The company also operates a highly profitable maintenance and services division.

The company has moved into thin-film technologies with the acquisition of CTF Solar GmbH, a cadmium telluride (CdTe) PV manufacturing start-up. Roth & Rau plans to offer CdTe production lines as a general contractor as well as aiming to produce coatings.

In another innovation, Roth & Rau has installed the world's first silicon-ink based solar cell production line in conjunction with Innovalight in Sunnyvale, California. The first pilot line has a 10W capacity and can be easily scaled to many hundreds of megawatts.

The company has opened a new €11m solar R&D centre at their head office and claim to have reached efficiency ratios of 20% on hetero-junction solar cells.

In late 2009 the company won several orders for turn-key production lines in China and India.

Singulus Technologies

Kahl, Germany
www.singulus.de
FRA: SNG
Market cap: €158m
12-month high/low: €1.79-4.97

Singulus Technologies is the world market leader for optical disc production lines for CDs, DVDs and Blu-ray discs. In 2008 Singulus acquired a majority stake in Munich-based Stangl SemiConductor, a global leader in the wet-chemical processes for the PV and semi-conductor industries. This acquisition has given Singulus a significant foothold in the solar market. Thin-film manufacturer Ascent Solar is amongst the company's customers, deploying Stangl's Impedio roll-to-roll wet-chemical coating machines to make CIGS cells.

Singulus is working with leading cell manufacturers in the development of new technologies and concepts for improved cell efficiencies and production technologies. For instance, the company worked with Q-Cells to create a fully automated vacuum-coating system for depositing anti-reflective layers on solar wafers – the aim is to increase the efficiency of the wafers whilst reducing production costs.

SMA Solar Technology AG

Niestetal, Germany
www.sma.de
ETR: S92
Market cap: €2675m
12-month high/low: €27.3-106.

Founded in 1981, SMA has sales and service subsidiaries on four continents in twelve countries. It is the world's largest producer of solar inverters and monitoring systems, with an installed base of around 1m units globally. The company claims the world record for inverter efficiency with its Sunny Mini Central unit, which has an efficiency rate of over 98%.

SMA bought the Dutch company OKE-Services, a specialist producer of micro-inverters, in 2009. OKE is a world leader in micro-inverters, which convert the DC to AC separately at each individual PV panel.

The company recently opened the world's largest inverter factory, which has trebled SMA's production capacity to 4GW annually; the plant is entirely powered by renewable energy. SMA is also expanding in the American market with construction of an additional facility in Colorado which will produce the Sunny Boy, Sunny Central and Sunny Island inverters. The plant will have an initial capacity of 1GW annually.

Solar Millennium AG

Cologne, Germany
www.solarmillennium.de
ETR: S2M
Market cap: €389m
12-month high/low: €6.24-45.35

Founded in 1998, Solar Millennium specialises in parabolic trough power plants. The planning, engineering and technical construction of the solar plants is dealt with by its subsidiary Flagsol.

Solar Millennum is the main contractor on the Andasol CSP plants near Granada in Spain. The first two 50MW plants are already generating electricity, with the third scheduled to come on-stream during 2011. Using molten salt for storage, the plants have the capacity to generate electricity for 7.5 hours after the sun has gone down. These plants use Flagsol's SKAL-ET collectors, however the company claims that its next generation model, called Heliotrough, will deliver cost savings of 15-20% compared to the original system.

Solar Millennium is planning various projects with an overall capacity of more than 2GW worldwide, focusing on the US, Spain, China and North Africa.

In Egypt, the company is building parabolic trough facilities for a hybrid power plant that will use both natural gas and solar energy. Located at Kuraymat, 100km south of Cairo, the combined cycle plant will have a power output of 150MW.

In the USA the company is developing two parabolic trough plants of 242MW each (with an option to include a third) in California, plus a further plant in Nevada.

The company is involved in biomass through its subsidiary Blue Tower GmbH. The 'blue tower' uses a sustainable feedstock to manufacture a hydrogen-rich gas which can then be used to produce hydrogen and electricity. The first 'blue tower' is currently under construction in North Rhine-Westphalia, Germany.

The company is also addressing the problem of water usage and developing a plant in conjunction with Nevada Energy which uses advanced air cooling.

Solarfun Power Holdings

Qidong, Jiangsu Province, China
www.solarfun.com.cn
NASDAQ: SOLF
Market cap: $400m
12-month high/low: $2.27-10.78

Solarfun Power Holdings manufactures solar cells (both monocrystalline and multicrystalline) and modules, and provides cell processing and module integration services. The company has recently launched a square-shaped cell, called the SF2, which is said to give 5% more power than previously.

Solarfun's annual capacity is around 500MW. The company is also pursuing utility-size deals, the first of which is to be a 100MW solar farm in Jiayuguan.

SolarWorld AG

Bonn, Germany
www.solarworld.de
ETR: SWV
Market cap: € 1310m
12-month high/low: € 10.66-24.70

SolarWorld AG is a vertically integrated solar producer with activities across the solar industry from silicon production to turn-key solar power systems and silicon recycling.

The company is continuing to invest in production facilities in its core markets of Germany and the USA. Production capacity for PV modules at Freiberg in Saxony will be tripled to 450MW by the end of 2010. In addition, SolarWorld is expanding its capacity in Oregon, with a target of reaching 350MW by 2011. Alongside their existing plant in California, this will provide capacity of 500MW annually in the USA.

The company expects to have a global production capacity of more than 1GW by the year 2011.

Spire Corporation

Bedford, Massachusetts, USA
www.spirecorp.com
NASDAQ: SPIR
Market cap: $40m
12-month high/low: $3.28-9.00

Founded in 1969, Spire Corporation was one of the first PV companies in the world. Today, it makes manufacturing equipment and full turn-key lines for cell and module production. Spire is also working on next-generation solar cells in conjunction with the US Department of Energy's National Renewable Energy Laboratory and has been awarded $3.7m to work on double- and triple-junction gallium arsenide (GaAs) concentrator cells that potentially have efficiency rates of 40% plus. Spire is one of the pioneers in GaAs fabrication and has the capacity for 25MW of production annually. In addition to its cell and module manufacturing, its Spire Semiconductor subsidiary provides semiconductor foundry services.

Spire has also recently expanded into Asia, with new subsidiaries in India and Taiwan. The company says that more than 90% of all solar manufacturing companies use Spire equipment, which has been installed in approximately 190 factories in 46 countries.

SunPower

www.sunpowercorp.com
San Jose, California, USA
NASDAQ: SPWR
Market cap: $1909m
12-month high/low: $18.92-36.05

Founded in 1985, SunPower manufactures cells and panels in the Philippines, and solar panels under contract in China. It is a spin-off from Cypress Semiconductor (still a majority shareholder).

SunPower has built several utility-scale solar farms, starting with the Bavaria Solarpark in Germany, which was the first solar power plant project in the world when it was constructed in 2004. The company is currently completing a solar farm for PG&E which is said to be the world's largest PV plant with a 250MW capacity, set to come online in 2010. It is also under contract to deliver a utility-scale plant for Florida Power & Light Co and another for the Kennedy Space Center. The company has constructed more than 400MW in large-scale solar and power plant installations worldwide, including solar farms in Spain and Italy.

SunPower's latest product is the T20 Tracker system, which is a single axis, ground-mounted tracker. Designed for quick and simple installation, each unit generates up to 3.7kW of power and, by following the sun, delivers up to 30% more energy than a fixed tilt system.

It has also developed a new, full-sized solar panel with a 20.4% efficiency rate, which it expects to make commercially available by 2011.

SunPower recently announced the availability of the SunPower T5 solar roof tile, the first PV roof product to combine a solar panel, frame and mounting system into a single pre-engineered unit. In early 2011 it will also start marketing its Oasis 'power plant in a box', a prepackaged solar module that can be assembled into large solar farms. The company says that Oasis will speed up the construction of solar farms and reduce plant costs by up to 25%.

Suntech Power Holdings

Wuxi, China
www.suntech-power.com
NYSE: STP
Market cap: $2557m
12-month high/low: $5.09-21.38

Suntech makes a range of PV cells and modules, including BIPV products. It has four production sites in China, one in Japan, and one under construction in the US with around 1.4GW of solar production capacity in total. Suntech's factory in Arizona will have an initial capacity of 30MW when completed in late 2010. It will make Suntech the first Chinese solar company to build a solar factory in the USA.

Suntech offers a complete package for solar farm developers called Reliathon, which provides a discounted deal of panels, trackers and inverters.

Trina Solar

Changzhou, China
www.trinasolar.com
NYSE: TSL
Market cap: $3077m
12-month high/low: $2.88-51.00

Trina Solar is a manufacturer of PV ingots, wafers, cells and modules based in Changzhou, China. Trina is expected to achieve cell and module production capacity of between 850MW and 950MW by the end of 2010.

The company is developing a variety of PV products to complement its existing PV monocrystalline and multicrystalline modules, including BIPV products. Trina Solar has a long-term agreement for the supply of polysilicon with Jiangsu Zhongneng Polysilicon Technology Development Co. Ltd, a subsidiary of GCL-Poly. The company places significant emphasis on the diversity of its polysilicon contracts.

XsunX

Aliso Viejo, California, USA
www.xsunx.com
OTCBB: XSNX.OB
Market cap: $28m
12-month high/low: $0.09-0.26

XsunX is combining manufacturing technologies used by the hard disk industry with thin-film PV processes to create new, low-cost CIGS products. The company has teamed up with Intevac (NASDAQ: IVAC) to develop equipment which they plan to market as a turn-key solution to either enable upgrades to existing infrastructure or to establish new large scale solar manufacturing capacity.

Yingli Green Energy

Baoding, China
www.yinglisolar.com/enmain/user/index.asp
NYSE:YGE
Market cap: $1,702m
12-month high/low: $3.32-19.11

Yingli Green Energy is one of the largest solar companies in China. Its products cover the entire value chain from the manufacture of multicrystalline polysilicon ingots and wafers, to PV cells and modules.

The company has recently commissioned an in-house polysilicon manufacturing plant, Fine Silicon, which will help cut costs and increase profitability. The company also undertakes systems installation.

Yingli has continued to invest in R&D, with its latest programme, Project Panda, having achieved its first phase target ahead of schedule, producing next-generation cells with an average conversion efficiency rate of 18% or higher on a pilot production line.

The company is undertaking a series of JVs with state-owned companies in Hainan Province. Hainan, an island off China's south coast, is one of the country's sunniest provinces. Yingli is building manufacturing facilities with an annual production capacity of 100MW in each of polysilicon ingots and wafers, PV cells and PV modules, and developing solar farms. The projects, which are designed to take advantage of the Chinese government's Golden Sun subsidy programme, aim to deliver 300MW of solar to the grid by 2013.

Wind power

American Superconductor

Devens, Massachusetts, USA
www.amsc.com
NASDAQ: AMSC
Market cap: $1422m
52-week range: $11.66-43.95

American Superconductor (AMSC) operates two complementary business units: AMSC Power Systems and AMSC Superconductors. The core product for power systems is their PowerModule, which is sold to other manufacturers or used in AMSC's own turbines' voltage regulation systems. As well as manufacturing its own turbines, AMSC also licences its designs to other manufacturers. AMSC also offers consultancy services through AMSC Windtec.

AMSC is moving into the offshore market through an agreement with Dongfang Turbine Ltd of China to jointly develop a 5MW machine, which they hope to bring to market by 2012. The company expanded into India in 2009 with the launch of AMSC India, with an HQ in Delhi and a service office in Pune to serve both the wind energy and power grid markets.

At the heart of the AMSC Superconductor division is high temperature superconductor (HTS) wire, which is able to transmit 150 times the amount of energy as a copper wire of the same dimensions. Motor and generators using HTS wire have considerable size, weight, efficiency and acoustic benefits compared with traditional copper counterparts. AMSC's superconducting cables are being increasingly used in smart grid applications globally.

Broadwind Energy

Naperville, Illinois, USA
www.broadwindenergy.com
NASDAQ: BWEN
Market cap: $547m
52-week range: $2.60-12.49

Broadwind Energy operates a complete supply chain for the wind energy sector, which includes wind tower manufacturing, precision gear manufacturing, specialised transportation, and the construction, operation and maintenance of wind farms.

Its subsidiaries include Brad Foote Gear Works (precision gearing systems), Tower Tech (wind tower manufacturing), RBA Inc (specialised welding), Energy Maintenance Services (turbine repairs) and Badger Transport (which specialises in moving tower sections, blades, nacelles and other turbine components).

Broadwind employs more than 1000 people and moved up to a NASDAQ listing in April 2009.

Catch The Wind

Manassas, Virginia, USA
www.catchthewindinc.com
CVE: CTW.S
Market cap: CAD$137m
52-week range: CAD$0.51-3.00

Catch The Wind (CTW) has developed a fibre-optic laser wind sensing (LWS) system, which senses the wind that is approaching the wind turbine at various ranges so that the turbine can adjust itself accordingly. Tests on a Vestas turbine in Nebraska in 2009 showed an average of 12.3% power production increase. The company estimates that with an increase of this order, wind farm operators can expect to generate in excess of $600,000 for a typical 2.5MW turbine or $18m for a typical 75MW wind farm, and that the sensors will pay for themselves within two to three years.

It has also carried out field trials for a buoy-mounted system which will help offshore wind farm developers to more accurately determine wind resources.

The company is now carrying out further tests with partners including Gamesa and Canadian Hydro Developers, and has signed an R&D agreement with the US Dept of Energy's National Renewable Energy Laboratory.

The company is also developing a system for fixed and floating platforms in conjunction with the Canadian company AXYS Technologies that is designed to help offshore wind farm developers determine the wind resource at potential sites.

China High Speed Transmission

Nanjing, China
www.chste.com
HK: 0658
Market cap: HK$20,031
52-week range: HK$8.70-21.00

China High Speed Transmission (CHST) is the country's largest producer of gearboxes for wind turbines, with a 90% market share. Founded in 1969 as a manufacturer of machine tools, the company switched to gearboxes for more traditional industries in 1976 but it has moved to take advantage of the growing Chinese wind power market.

CHST makes 1.5MW gearboxes and is currently developing 2.5MW and 3MW products. It has supply agreements with turbine makers including GE, REpower, Vestas, Sinovel and Nordex. The company also has interests in marine transmissions and gearboxes for high speed trains and urban light rail.

Clipper Windpower

Carpinteria, California, USA
www.clipperwind.com
LON: CWP
Market cap: £265m
52-week range: 63.00-182.00p

Founded in 2001, Clipper's main manufacturing facilities are based at Cedar Rapids, Iowa. Clipper's flagship is the 2.5MW Liberty turbine, one of the largest currently being built in the US. However, the company has had setbacks with production of this turbine, including various blade and drivetrain problems. Resolving these issues has been costly for Clipper. This cash drain, combined with other pressures such as deferred orders, left Clipper short of capital and the company was forced to look for outside investors. In December 2009 it agreed to sell a 49.5% stake to industrial conglomerate United Technologies Corporation (NYSE: UTX). UTC has expertise in gearbox and blade technologies and manufacturing processes, which will now help Clipper expand.

One of its biggest current projects is the Titan wind farm in South Dakota, a joint venture with BP Wind Energy. If built out to its full capacity, the Titan Wind Farm has the potential to be the largest wind development in the world, utilising up to 2000 turbines. The project is so large that Clipper is considering building a temporary turbine factory at the wind farm to save on transport costs.

Clipper also has operations in the UK, where it is currently developing a 10MW offshore wind prototype which is amongst the world's largest machines. The fully operational Britannia turbine will stand at 175 metres in height, with each blade more than 70 metres long. Clipper is currently building a new facility on the River Tyne in the North East of England for blade production. The Crown Estate has agreed to purchase the Britannia prototype, which is scheduled for deployment in late 2011.

The company is also working on 10MW turbines.

EDF Energies Nouvelles

Paris, France
www.edf-energies-nouvelles.com
EPA: EEN
Market cap: €2898m
52-week range: €24.26-39.22

EDF Energies Nouvelles, a 50%-owned subsidiary of the EDF group, is involved in several different renewable technologies.

Wind power accounts for 90% of the group's installed capacity, currently around 2.4GW. The group has numerous projects under construction in Europe and America, including a large US west coast wind farm being developed by their subsidiary enXco. In Canada, EDF EN operates through another subsidiary, Saint-Laurent Energies, and has a deal with REpower to supply a massive 477 turbines for five wind energy projects currently being developed in Quebec. These projects are due to be commissioned between 2011 and 2015.

In solar, EDF Energies Nouvelles has just under 30MW installed in Europe and North America. It has a strategic partnership with Nanosolar for the supply of thin-film panels, which was made at the same time as a $50m investment into the solar company in 2008. EDF EN is also building France's largest solar plant, in conjunction with First Solar. First Solar will build and operate the plant, whilst EDF EN is financing half the cost (estimated at €90m) and will benefit from the plant's entire output for the first ten years. Due for completion in 2011, the plant will have a capacity of 100MW annually and is designed to fulfil all the French company's PV needs for a decade.

EDF EN successfully raised €500m in 2008 to finance expansion in the PV sector and has set a target of installing 500MW in PV by 2012, with total renewables capacity of 4GW.

The company is also involved in biomass (with one facility in Andalusia), biofuel (through a stake in Belgian ethanol company Alcofinance), and biogas (through a stake in Belgian landfill-form-gas company Verdesis). In wave energy, it has an agreement with Renewable Energy Holdings to develop Carnegie's CETO wave energy machines and a partnership with the French maritime group DCNS to work on joint wave and tidal projects. Across all of these projects the group has a target of developing a total renewables capacity of 4GW by 2012.

Gamesa

Vitoria, Spain
www.gamesacorp.com
MCE: GAM
Market cap: €2445m
52-week range: €7.74-17.14

Gamesa set up their first wind turbine manufacturing unit in 1994, with the development of wind farms starting in 1996. The company formerly had interests in robotics, microelectronics, composite materials and solar power but it began to withdraw from non-core activities in the 1990s: it completed its exit from aeronautics and services in 2006 and from solar in 2008.

Gamesa is now the market leader in Spain for wind power and is ranked third globally by market cap. The company has installed over 16GW of turbines in over 20 countries and currently has a portfolio of more than 21GW under development globally. The company has production centres located in Spain, Asia and the United States with an international workforce of around 7000 employees. It has a portfolio of more than 21GW under development globally.

Gamesa's new 4.5MW turbine, the G10x, is claimed to be a technological revolution, which has greater power output and lower costs than any available turbine models and yet can be transported and assembled using the same techniques as a 2MW machine. The company expects to start production of the first units in 2010, ramping up to series production in 2011.

For its future growth the company is focusing on areas such as the USA, China and India. It has manufacturing capacity in the US and China and has recently added a new plant in Chennai, India, which will have an annual manufacturing capacity of 200MW.

Hansen Transmissions

Edegem, Belgium
www.hansentransmissions.com
LON: HSN
Market cap: £650m
52-week range: 77.00-172.50p

Hansen is one of the chief independent manufacturers of wind turbine gearboxes and supplies four of the five largest manufacturers of gear-driven wind turbines.

The company has two manufacturing facilities in Belgium and recently completed a new production facility in Coimbatore, India: when at full capacity (which is expected to be in 2011), the factory will employ some 800 people and have a yearly production capacity of 5GW (representing 2500 to 3000 gearboxes annually).

Additionally, the company has started the construction of a gearbox plant in Tianjin, China, which will have an annual capacity of 3GW when completed in 2011. In late 2009 the company won its first order in China from a domestic turbine manufacturer – Hansen believes this contract underlines the increasing awareness in the growing Chinese wind market of the favourability of high quality gearboxes.

These expansion plans will increase Hansen's production capacity from 4.2GW in 2008 to 14.3GW per annum in 2012. The company has a strong R&D operation to maintain its technological leadership and employs over 2400 people worldwide. Hansen was taken over by Suzlon Energy in March 2006.

Helix Wind

San Diego, California, USA
www.helixwind.com
OTC: HLXW
Market cap: $19m
52-week range: $0.29-3.30

Helix Wind designs and makes small wind turbines. The company offers horizontal as well as vertical-axis turbines to fit different needs. Its most distinctive-looking machine is the Savonius turbine, which has a long helical blade designed to catch the wind from all directions, creating a smooth, powerful torque to force it through the turbine.

The 2009 acquisition of Venco Power GmBH, a German producer of vertical axis small wind turbines, added three complementary turbines to Helix's product range. Helix also bought two other small wind companies in 2009: Abundant Renewable Energy (ARE) and Renewable Energy Engineering (REE), both of Newberg, Oregon. The acquisition of ARE and REE adds a line of horizontal axis turbine products to Helix's existing portfolio.

The company is currently running tests on combining its turbines with cell phone masts, in order to reduce the costs of operating remote phone masts. Helix is so confident of the success of these designs that the test will explore the feasibility of selling power back to the electrical grid.

Recent orders have included provision of 90 to 100 wind turbines as part of an estimated $9.5m rural electrification and off-grid generation project in Jujuy, Argentina, being financed by the World Bank.

Iberdrola Renewables

Valencia, Spain
www.iberdrolarenovables.es
MCE: IBR
Market cap: € 13,229m
52-week range: € 2.72-3.59

Iberdrola Renewables (Iberdrola Renovables) is the world's largest owner-operator of wind farms with an installed capacity of around 10GW. Its main operations are in Spain (4.8GW) and the US (3.5GW). The company has an ambitious pipeline of nearly 60GW of projects globally, and is aiming to reach 18GW by 2012. Iberdrola Renewables is expanding aggressively in the US, where it won $577m in grants from the government in 2009 and is expecting a further $430m in 2010. The group has big plans for offshore wind, with projects under development in Spain and the UK.

The company also operates in wave power, biomass, hydro power and several types of solar power (including CSP and CPV). The company began as a business unit of the Spanish Iberdrola group (one of the four largest engineering and power companies in the world) in 2001. This early start in renewables allowed it to expand well ahead of its rivals. It bought Scottish Power in 2006, adding 2GW of wind capacity to its already fast-developing portfolio.

Iberdrola Renovables floated on the Madrid stock exchange in December 2007 in an IPO worth €4.5bn. Now it is one of the fastest growing elements of the Iberdrola group, with operations in 23 countries worldwide.

Iberdrola Renovables has an ambitious pipeline of nearly 60GW of projects globally, and is aiming to increase net capacity to 12.5GW by the end of 2010 and to 18GW by 2012. In offshore wind, the company has applied to build six new wind farms off the coast of Cadiz, Spain, with 3GW of capacity.

In the UK, their subsidiary Scottish Power Renewables plans to construct two offshore wind farms in Scotland and has an agreement with Vattenfall to develop others. Their forecast is to reach 6GW of offshore capacity by 2020.

In solar, the company has kick-started a CSP programme with its first parabolic trough plant (a 50MW unit in Puertollano which came on-stream in May 2009) and now has a pipeline of 11 more 50MW projects under development. The company owns two PV solar farms, one in Spain (Castile-La Mancha) and another in Greece. The company also has an interest in CPV through an investment in Canadian start-up Morgan Solar, who are preparing to bring their potential breakthrough low-cost CPV systems to market.

In small-scale hydro power, Iberdrola Renovables operates 135 installations in Spain, with a total output of 340MW. In biomass, the company is developing several plants to process forest biomass in Spain.

In marine energy, the company has worked with Ocean Power Technologies to deploy one of its PowerBuoys and an underwater electricity sub-station offshore from Santoña (Cantabria), the first development of this kind in Europe. The second phase will see the installation of nine more buoys, giving a total output of 1.35MW. Scottish Power Renewables is developing projects with Pelamis Wave Power in Scotland and is a part-owner of Hammerfest Strom.

Indian Energy

London, UK
www.indian-energy.com
LON: IEL
Market cap: £20m
52-week range: 79.50-86.50p

Founded in 2007, Indian Energy had its debut on AIM on 9 September 2009, bringing in £9.8m. State Bank of India, the country's biggest bank, has invested $18m in the company, which has offices in London and Mumbai.

Indian Energy owns and operates a 25MW wind farm located at Gadag Plains in the State of Karnataka, which came into operation in February 2009. The company has also begun work on a new wind farm at Theni in Tamil Nadu, with a total of 33 turbines generating around 50MW.

Indian Energy plans to use the funds from its IPO to extend its Gadag wind farm by a further 16.5MW. The company is hoping to build a portfolio of 300MW of operating capacity by 2013. It will benefit from both state tariffs payable for renewables and the Indian government's new Generation Based Incentive (GBI) scheme, introduced in early 2010.

Nordex

Norderstedt, Germany
www.nordex-online.com
ETR: NDX1
Market cap: € 607m
52-week range: € 7.28-14.84

Nordex is a supplier of high capacity wind turbines. Founded in 1985, Nordex was the first company to make 1MW turbines when it launched the N54 in 1995. Four years later, the company completed its 1000th installation of the N54. In 2000, they were the first to launch a 2.5MW machine and these high capacity units remain the main focus for both onshore and offshore use.

To date, Nordex has supplied over 3927 Nordex wind turbines with a total rated output of more than 5.3GW to 34 countries worldwide.

Most of Nordex's business is in Europe (accounting for 75% of sales). It has a big presence in Turkey, where it is one of the leading wind players.

Nordex has production facilities in Rostock (Germany) and China. It has representative offices and subsidiaries in 18 countries, employing a workforce of more than 2000 people.

These facilities are being added to with the building of a new production plant in Arkansas in the US, which is intended to drive more sales of the 2.5MW turbine. Construction of the $100m plant will take place in two phases, beginning with the nacelle assembly plant which will be operating at full scale by 2012 with an annual production capacity of 300 turbines, or 750MW. The entire facility, including rotor blade production, will be fully operational by 2014. Nordex has a number of other American wind farm projects in the pipeline, including a joint development with BP.

Renewable Energy Generation (REG)

Guildford, UK
www.renewableenergygeneration.com
AIM: RWE
Market cap: £62m
52-week range: 60.00-63.04p

REG, which listed on AIM in May 2005, operates through two main subsidiary companies. The first is Cornwall Light & Power (CLP), which operates seven wind farms in Cornwall, County Durham, Cumbria, Cambridgeshire and Gwynedd, with a total capacity of 21.3MW.

The company has a development pipeline of around 350MW but has suffered some planning setbacks with applications in Lancashire and the Isle of Wight being rejected. However, it has begun the process of re-powering its original wind farm at Goonhilly, Cornwall by replacing 14 older turbines with six new machines: the upgrade will boost output from 9.4MW to 15MW.

REG's second main subsidiary is REG BioPower, based in Norfolk. The company has recently secured its first major commercial deal: a five-year contract with the port of Dover to supply electricity and heat from a biofuel-fired CHP plant.

In late 2009 REG sold off its loss-making Canadian operations to International Power for £74m.

Renewable Energy Holdings

Douglas, Isle of Man
www.reh-plc.com
AIM: REH
Market cap: £13m
52-week range: £18.00-39.00

Founded in 2004, Renewable Energy Holdings is a developer of wind, landfill gas and marine energy. The company's primary holdings are in wind power, with most of its revenue derived from wind farms in Germany. The company has a 1MW landfill gas project in Wales.

Renewable Energy Holdings is currently developing wind assets in Poland and has permits to build a 30MW wind farm in south-east Poland.

REH has been involved with the development of the CETO wave energy technology being produced by Carnegie Wave Energy in Australia. However, in 2009 REH sold its IP in CETO to Carnegie, in exchange for a major shareholding. REH is continuing to develop CETO in the southern hemisphere through its Perth-based subsidiary Seapower Pacific PTY Ltd, and in the northern hemisphere in conjunction with EDF Energies Nouvelles.

REpower

Hamburg, Germany
www.repower.de
ETR: RPW
Market cap: €1158m
52-week range: €70.61-149.50

REpower was founded in 2001 and has been majority-owned by Suzlon since June 2007. The company has production facilities in Germany and Portugal.

REpower's product range comprises turbines with rated outputs of between 1.5MW and 5MW; the MD 70/77 range has become one of the most successful turbines in its class (1.5-2MW). To date, they have installed over 1400 turbines globally.

Another of REpower's most successful models is its 5MW offshore turbine; the first offshore deployment was in the Beatrice wind testing zone in the North Sea and further 5M turbines have since been deployed offshore in Germany, Belgium and Scotland. The company made some record-breaking deals during 2009 for these turbines, including a €2bn agreement with RWE for 250 units and the sale of 30 units to Vattenfall for the Ormonde offshore farm in the UK. REpower is now working on a 6MW version of this turbine.

REpower UK is one of the biggest subsidiaries of REpower, with its head office in Edinburgh and service locations across Britain. The company is active in 21 wind farm locations across the country and is involved in a number of new sites currently in planning.

SeaEnergy

Westhill, UK
www.seaenergy-plc.com
LON: SEA
Market cap: £32m
52-week range: 34.00-87.00p

SeaEnergy claims to be the first publicly listed pure-play offshore wind energy company in the UK. Its first project was the deployment of two 5MW turbines at the Beatrice wind farm off the east coast of Scotland in the Moray Firth. Now SeaEnergy is looking to expand this up to around 920MW, in a joint venture with Scottish & Southern Energy subsidiary Airtricity. They are also planning on developing the 905MW Inchcape wind farm in the Outer Tay Estuary. SeaEnergy holds a 25% stake in each venture, equivalent to 456MW production capacity. The company is part of a consortium, Moray Offshore Renewables (25% owned by Sea Energy and 75% by EDP Renewables) which won a contract under the Crown Estate's Round Three of offshore awards, with a licence for 1.3GW in the Moray Firth.

The company is also developing projects in Asia and has an agreement with the Taiwan Generations Corporation to develop a 600MW wind farm in depths of up to 30 metres off the west coast of Taiwan. SeaEnergy's five-year goal is to build 1GW of offshore capacity.

Suzlon

Pune, India
www.suzlon.com
NYSE: SUZLON
Market cap: $10,577.99
52-week range: $53.80-145.70

Suzlon is India's first indigenous wind technology company. Suzlon's first project was a 3MW wind farm in Gujarat but since then it has grown to become the fifth largest wind power manufacturer globally.

The company acquired Belgian gearbox maker Hansen Transmissions in 2006 and the German turbine manufacturer REpower Systems in 2007. Suzlon sold 35.2% in Hansen in November 2009, raising $370m.

Suzlon was hit by a series of production problems on its S88 model in 2008 and the company has since had to retrofit 417 turbines which had cracked blades – this programme was completed in 2009, but cost $100m. This expense had only added to the company's $2.5bn debt which it amassed following its acquisition of Hansen and REpower. The company was attempting to re-finance this debt with a consortium of banks at the time of writing.

Suzlon's current product range includes turbines in the 350kW to 2.1MW range. Suzlon has facilities in India, China and the US with a total manufacturing capacity of 2.7GW annually; it continues to expand into new and emerging high-growth markets globally. The company employs over 14,000 people in 21 countries.

Theolia

Aix-en-Provence, France
www.theolia.com
EPA: TEO
Market cap: € 120m
52-week range: € 1.09-5.48

Founded in 1999 and based in Aix-en-Provence, Theolia SA develops and manages wind farms. Its main wind farms are in France, Germany, Italy and Morocco. It also has wind farms under development in Brazil and India, however the company's recent financial performance means that it is now re-considering its presence in these countries. The group owns a solar park in Germany, from which it derives revenues. Theolia had 421MW of installed capacity in 2009, with around 120MW under construction. It also manages 329MW for third parties. The company is undergoing a re-structuring which involves selling off some of its wind farms, with several disposals already having taken place.

Vestas

Randers, Denmark
www.vestas.com
CPH: VWS
Market cap: Kr56,013m
52-week range: Kr215.25-429.50

The Danish company Vestas delivered its first working turbine in 1979 and prospered during the first renewables boom in the 1980s. By 1991 Vestas had erected its 1000th turbine in Denmark and by the time of its floatation on the Copenhagen Stock Exchange in 1998 it was the world's largest supplier of wind turbines, a position it retains today. The turbines have become 100 times more efficient than they were 25 years ago and the company estimates that it installs a new turbine every three hours worldwide, generating more than 60 million MWh a year.

Currently it has production facility in Denmark, China, Norway, Germany, Spain, Sweden, Italy, the UK, India and the US and employs more than 22,000 people worldwide. The company currently monitors about 15,000 turbines (25GW) around the clock.

Vestas' current portfolio consists of ten turbine models with power ratings from 850kW to 3MW. In 2010 the company is due to install the first of its new V112 turbine, a 3MW model aimed at the offshore market, which it says is capable of generating more power than any other turbine in its class. Alongside this, Vestas is also developing a massive 6MW model for offshore use which it hopes will win prime position in this expanding market. The company's main R&D focus is on improved designs that make use of lighter materials, which should also make turbines easier to service. They are also investing significant resources in optimising the location of each turbine in a wind farm in order to make the most of the wind available. Vestas' R&D centre on the Isle of Wight is testing the world's longest rotor blades, which will play a key role in future offshore developments.

The company is currently investing heavily in new capacity in China and the USA, as the long-term goal is to supply North America from the USA, Europe from Europe and Asia from Asia. In China, Vestas has opened a new foundry in Xuzhou near Shanghai – with this facility Vestas has become the only European wind turbine manufacturer with its own foundry in the country.

Western Wind Energy

Vancouver, British Columbia, Canada
www.westernwindenergy.com
CVE: WND
Market cap: CAD$79m
52-week range: CAD$0.50-1.75

Western Wind, based in Vancouver, Canada, is a small scale developer of wind farms. The company currently has over 500 small turbines producing 34.5MW in California. It is currently developing a further 30MW of capacity there and hopes to eventually expand to 80MW. The company owns additional development land for wind power in California and Arizona. One of its subsidiaries, Western Solargenics, is involved in the development of utility scale thermal power plants. It also has a development team working on renewable energy projects in Puerto Rico and India.

Zoltek

St. Louis, Missouri, USA
www.zoltek.com
NASDAQ: ZOLT
Market cap: $303m
52-week range: $5.08-12.63

Zoltek was founded as an industrial services company and moved into the carbon fibre business in 1988. Zoltek serves a variety of industries (including oil exploration and aircraft makers) and has a significant niche as a supplier of carbon fibre to the wind industry: both Gamesa and Vestas have supply contracts for their carbon-reinforced blade programmes. Multi-axial carbon fibres from Zoltek are also used in the production of the Tesla electric sports car.

Zoltek has production facilities in Hungary, Mexico, Texas and Missouri. In September 2009 Zoltek announced an agreement with Global Blade Technology (GBT) of the Netherlands to accelerate the design and manufacture of wind turbine blades utilising Zoltek carbon fibres. The two companies anticipate that the combination of GBT's expertise in rotor blade design and Zoltek's ability to offer reliable low-cost carbon fibre supplies in high volumes will accelerate adoption of carbon fibres as wind turbine blade lengths continue to increase.

Marine energy

Carnegie Wave Energy

Perth, Australia
www.carnegiecorp.com.au
ASX: CWE
Market cap: AU$70.65m
52-week range: AU$0.12-0.26

Carnegie's CETO system is an ocean-based pumping technology, with pump units moored to the sea floor and connected to submerged buoys. Pressurised water is pumped ashore to drive standard turbines (the system can also be used for desalinating seawater). Carnegie is currently on its third generation design, which is being tested off Western Australia. Construction of a full-scale 5MW wave farm (with AUD12.5m in funding from the Western Australia government) is scheduled for 2011.

Carnegie has been awarded consents for further projects in Western Australia, South Australia and Victoria. The company has signed a $250m agreement with Investec Bank to fund a 50MW wave farm.

Elsewhere, Carnegie has been awarded €3m in French government funding for a demonstration project on Reunion Island and a CAD$2m grant through British Columbia's clean energy fund to develop a project off Ucluelet, Canada. The company is also developing a portfolio of projects in the northern hemisphere in conjunction with EDF Energies Nouvelles.

Ocean Power Technologies

Pennington, New Jersey, USA
www.oceanpowertechnologies.com
AIM: OPT
Market cap: £44.84m
52-week high/low: 234.65-637.40p

Founded in 1994, Ocean Power Technologies (OPT) has been refining its PowerBuoy technology since 1997. The buoy is effectively a giant piston, with the resultant mechanical stroking converted via a power take-off to drive an electrical generator. The buoys have a rugged, simple steel construction, utilise conventional mooring systems, and are simple to install using existing marine vessels and infrastructure.

OPT's current models have ratings of 40kW. The next generation 150kW buoys are under development, with 500kW buoys on the drawing board. In April 2010 OPT won a $1.5m grant from the US Department of Energy to help fund the scale-up of power output to 500kW. The company currently has developments taking place with partners in the US, Australia, Spain and the UK.

OPT is developing the first commercial wave park offshore from Reedsport, Oregon, which will initially consist of ten PB150 PowerBuoys. An even more ambitious plan involves developing a 100MW wave park at Coos Bay, Oregon. OPT claim it will be the largest wave energy project in the world when completed, with over 200 devices.

In Europe, OPT is installing a 1.39MW wave farm off the northern coast of Spain at Cantabria, in conjunction with Iberdrola Renovables, Total and other partners. In the UK, the company is installing its PB150 at EMEC, and is aiming to be one of the first developers connected to the Wave Hub, with a 5MW array currently on the cards.

OPT is also working in Australia, having won a $60m grant to build a 19MW wave farm off the coast of Victoria. It has development projects underway in Japan with Mitsui Engineering.

The company is also looking to commercialise its underwater substation pod. The device can aggregate up to ten offshore power generation devices into one common interconnection point in order to transmit offshore power and data to onshore utility grids. The pod is designed for use in depths of up to 50 metres. At present, a 1.5MW pod is being built and tested as part of OPT's Spanish co-production with Iberdrola Renovables.

Geothermal

Geodynamics

Milton, Australia
www.geodynamics.com.au
ASX: GDY
Market Cap: AU$218m
52-week range: AU$0.73-1.29

Founded in 2000, Geodynamics' main focus is the Cooper Basin in Australia. It has drilled five wells to date. Geodynamics has been awarded $AUS90m funding by the federal government towards its 25MW demonstration plant, which it expects to be operational by 2013. The company also has a drilling programme in the Hunter Valley in New South Wales, for which it has won over AUS$17m in grants.

Magma Energy

Vancouver, British Columbia, Canada
www.magmaenergycorp.com
TSX: MXY
Market cap: CAD$402m
52-week range: CAD$1.41-2.10

Magma has ambitions to become the "pre-eminent geothermal energy company in the world". Its IPO in July 2009 raised CAD$100m. Magma's only plant currently generating power is Soda Lake, in Nevada. This plant has averaged 8MW in recent years but the company hopes to increase this to an eventual total of nearly 29MW. The company has seven other sites under development in Nevada and one each in Utah and Oregon. In South America, Magma has five exploration sites in Peru, two in Argentina and two in Chile. In Central America, Magma has won the concession for two geothermal sites in a joint bid with Polaris Geothermal (now a subsidiary of Ram Power). In 2009 Magma bought a 43% stake in Icelandic geothermal company H S Okra, which has 175MW of installed capacity and generates a further 150MW for district heating.

Nevada Geothermal Power

Vancouver, British Columbia, Canada
www.nevadageothermal.com
CVE: NGP
Market cap: CAD$90.47m
52-week range: CAD$0.28-$1.16

Nevada Geothermal is developing projects in Nevada and Oregon. The company currently holds a leasehold interest in three projects in Nevada and one in Oregon with a combined potential of up to 200MW of capacity. The company's flagship project is the Blue Mountain Faulkner I plant in northern Nevada which was completed in October 2009 (built by Ormat). Work has already started to expand the capacity of this plant from 27MW up to its full potential of 40MW, with the assistance of $60m in federal funding.

Ormat Technologies Inc

Reno, Nevada, USA
www.ormat.com
NYSE: ORA
Market cap: $1541.22m
52-week range: $22.84-44.13

Ormat is a world leader in geothermal. It develops, builds, owns and operates geothermal plants and also supplies equipment and complete power plants to other operators.

Ormat is also a major supplier of recovered energy generation (REG) technology, which captures unused waste heat from industrial processes and converts it into electricity. The company has built REG plants worldwide and currently has projects under construction in Italy, Spain, and the USA.

The company has around 520MW of geothermal and REG-based capacity globally, with a further 220MW under development. The majority is in the USA, followed by Guatemala, Kenya, Nicaragua and New Zealand.

Recently Ormat has branched out into solar PV for rooftop installations.

Petratherm

Adelaide, South Australia, Australia
www.petratherm.com.au
ASX: PTR
Market cap: AU$27.66m
52-week range: AU$0.22-0.48

Petratherm is one of two Australian companies leading the pack in the development of EGS. Its flagship project is based at Paralana in South Australia's Flinders Ranges. The proposed 30MW plant has received nearly $AUD70m in federal funding and lies just 11km from a potential client, which is a mining company. Petrathem capped a 3.7km deep well at this site in December 2009.

The company is also developing EGS projects in China, and geothermal and district heating schemes in Spain and the Canary Islands

In Spain, Petratherm is working on district heating schemes in Madrid and Barcelona which have received government funding. The company is also undertaking a major geological survey to assess the geothermal potential in Tenerife.

In China the company has identified several prospective sites for EGS projects south east of the country and signed up key Chinese geological institutions.

Petratherm is also involved in solar technologies through its subsidiary Heliotherm. The company is aiming to reduce the cost of solar thermal by combining solar thermal, geothermal and combustion technologies. The project, which is being supported by the University of Adelaide's Centre for Energy Technology, is aiming for a 40% reduction in the cost of solar thermal technology.

Ram Power

Reno, Nevada, USA
www.ram-power.com
TSE: RPG
Market cap: CAD$495m
52-week range: CAD$2.89-4.08

Founded in 2008, Ram Power recently combined with GTO Resources, Polaris Geothermal and Western GeoPower. The company has a portfolio of projects underway in California, Nicaragua and Canada with a combined estimated capacity of 500MW.

In Nicaragua the company has obtained a geothermal concession with an estimated capacity of over 200MW – one of the largest geothermal resources in the western hemisphere. The power plant is currently on stream with 10MW and work is underway for initial expansion to 72MW.

In California Ram Power is developing various projects in the Imperial Valley with a potential capacity of 22GW. Ram Power's project pipeline also includes four other major geothermal resource areas in Nicaragua, the US and Canada.

Raser Technologies

Provo, Utah, USA
www.rasertech.com
NYSE: RZ
Market cap: $76.06m
52-week range: $0.88-4.80

Founded in 2003, Raser Technologies has geothermal interests in Nevada, Utah, New Mexico and Oregon. The company holds licence rights to several key technologies used in geothermal and other heat-transfer based systems, including technologies for more efficient heat transfer and waste heat recovery.

Raser also makes high performance electric motors using their Symetron technology, which improves the torque density and efficiency of electric motors and drive systems in EVs and HEVs.

US Geothermal

Boise, Idaho, USA
www.usgeothermal.com
AMEX: HTM
Market cap: $92.18m
52-week range: $0.60-2.09

US Geothermal currently has two operating power plants at Raft River, Idaho and at the San Emidio Desert in Nevada. At the company's Raft River site EGS technologies are being investigated, with the DOE providing $7.39m towards the $10.21m cost. The company has also been awarded $3.77m in ARRA funding to develop new seismic and satellite imagery techniques at San Emidio. The aim is to increase productivity in each well and reduce the number of wells that need to be drilled. A third site at Neal Hot Springs in eastern Oregon is also being developed – it is expected to have a capacity of 22MW. In April 2010 the company was awarded a concession in Guatemala, 14 miles (22.5 kilometres) south-west of Guatemala City.

Power storage

A123 Systems

Watertown, Massachusetts, USA
www.a123systems.com
NASDAQ: AONE
Market cap: $1834m
52-week range: $14.31-28.20

Founded in 2001, A123 Systems developed out of MIT's research labs. The company raised $378m for its IPO on the NASDAQ in September 2009 and has quickly risen to become one of the world's leading suppliers of high-power li-ion batteries designed for transportation, smart grid and portable power applications. The company is currently building a li-ion battery facility in Michigan with the help of a $249m grant from the US DOE and plans to supply 5m li-on batteries for electric vehicles by 2013. A123 is also moving into grid-scale batteries in conjunction with GE and is working with Southern California Edison to build the world's biggest li-ion storage battery to iron out the power curve from wind turbines in the Tehachapi Mountains. They have manufacturing facilities in Asia too.

A123's customers include Chrysler, Daimler, GM, Cessna and Volvo Truck.

Active Power

Austin, Texas, USA
www.activepower.com
NASDAQ: ACPW
Market cap: $64.5m
52-week range: $0.46-1.50

Founded in 1992, Active Power makes flywheel UPS systems. The company developed its CleanSource technology in 1996 and since then has shipped more than 2000 flywheels and clocked up over 50m hours of field operations in 40 countries. The company offers two systems: the CleanSource DC energy storage system and CleanSource UPS. Based in Austin, Texas, the company went public in August 2000.

Altair Nanotechnologies

Reno, Nevada, USA
www.altairnano.com
NASDAQ: ALTI
Market cap: $77m
52-week range: $0.60-1.55

Altair Nanotechnologies is a Canadian company with its headquarters in Reno, Nevada, and a manufacturing facility in Anderson, Indiana. Altair Nano is the first company to replace traditional graphite materials used in conventional li-ion batteries with lithium titanate. Positioned between a battery and a super capacitor, Altair Nano's li-ion batteries are said to be three times more powerful than existing batteries with a longer cycle life and faster charge/discharge rates. The battery is also three times more efficient at storing braking energy than conventional li-ion batteries. The batteries are being used in a new electric bus built by Colorado-based Proterra LLC, which is said to be the only electric hybrid bus that meets California's new zero emission rules. The company's other divisions are researching SOFCs; pigment processing; performance materials; and life sciences.

Axion Power International

New Castle, Pennsylvania, USA
www.axionpower.com
OTC: AXPW
Market cap: $90m
52-week range: $0.78-2.75

Axion Power International is a developer of advanced lead-acid batteries in which lead-based electrodes are replaced with activated carbon; they are hoping it can be used for both electric vehicles and grid storage. This is said to provide batteries that deliver higher power delivery rates, faster recharges and longer life cycles than normal. Whereas standard lead-acid batteries can take up to eight hours to fully charge, Axion's battery can be charged in two hours, they say. The batteries are the same dimensions as a normal battery and can be manufactured on the same lines, thereby cutting costs significantly. Axion's PbC technology has been integrated into its PowerCube system, which combines smart grid technology with a vehicle recharging station power by wind or solar. The company has undertaken tests for utility applications in New York and also for wind and solar storage in Toronto. It is currently scaling up its manufacturing with the help of $1.2m in federal support.

Beacon Power Corporation

Tyngsboro, Massachusetts, USA
www.beaconpower.com
NASDAQ: BCON
Market cap: $55m
52-week range: $0.32-1.09

Beacon Power developed its first flywheel systems for telecoms back-up power, but is now applying them to grid-scale storage. Their fourth-generation system, Smart Energy

25, is designed specifically for grid frequency regulation. Beacon Power has 2MW of operational storage at their headquarters and is building a new plant with a production capacity of 20MW annually, which is due for completion in 2011. National Grid is currently assessing their technology and its potential to store wind energy is also being investigated by the California Energy Commission and Southern California Edison. Beacon also owns a manufacturer of solar PV inverters and is developing solar PV power conversion systems.

C&D Technologies Inc

Blue Bell, Pennsylvania, USA
www.cdtechno.com
NYSE: CHP
Market cap: $43m
52-week range: $1.09-3.12

One of the oldest battery companies in the USA, C&D has been making batteries for over a hundred years. They have six manufacturing plants and three R&D facilities. The company provides batteries, electronics and fully integrated power systems which meet UPS needs in the telecoms, utility, switchgear and solar markets. C&D Technologies is manufacturing advanced lead-acid batteries in conjunction with Illinois-based start-up Firefly.

China BAK Battery Inc

Shenzhen, China
www.bak.com.cn
NASDAQ: CBAK
Market cap: $153m
52-week range: $0.86-5.22

China BAK battery is one of the largest manufacturers of lithium-based battery cells in the world. The company began trading on NASDAQ in May 2006 and has manufacturing facilities in Shenzhen and Tianjin, China. The company's main products are cylindrical lithium-ion cells, high power battery cells and lithium polymer cells. China BAK is currently working with a number of car makers to incorporate high-power lithium-phosphate cells in electric vehicles.

Electrovaya

Mississauga, Ontario, Canada
www.electrovaya.com
TSX: EFK
Market cap: CAD$55m
52-week range: CAD$0.19-1.43

Electrovaya produces li-ion polymer batteries for use in laptops, aerospace and defence applications, and EVs. Electrovaya has production deals for electric cars, trucks and manufacturing in China and a partnership with Tata Motors and Milko Grenland/Innovasjon to manufacture batteries and electric cars in Norway. It launched a prototype, the Maya 300, in 2009. Electrovaya's battery also powered the electric Hummer

H3 ReEV range-extended electric SUV launched in 2009. The government of Ontario gave the company a grant of CAD$16.7m to support battery research and pre-commercialisation activities during 2009.

Ener1

New York, New York, USA
www.ener1.com
NASDAQ: HEV
Market cap: $549m
52-week range: $2.35-7.90

Ener1 claim that their li-on batteries come in smaller, lighter formats, but provide twice the available power and energy density of current batteries. Its subsidiary EnerDel has designed battery packs for two prototypes currently being road tested for Volvo's V70 and C30 electric vehicles and it has taken a stake in Th!nk Global, the Norwegian electric vehicle producer. The first cars using EnerDel's products will be the Th!nk City town car and Fisker's Karma, both launched in 2010.

EnerDel's li-ion cells use a prismatic design (as opposed to the conventional cylindrical model) which allows for potentially higher energy density levels and dissipates heat more quickly. They are also easier and quicker to assemble in production. The company is currently doubling their production capacity with the help of $118m in stimulus funding.

A collaboration between EnerDel and Nissan involves an R&D project to develop a new form of electrolyte, in conjunction with the Argonne National Laboratory in Chicago. The company is supplying batteries to AC Transit for its next-generation hybrid fuel cell buses and is working with the US DOE in this sector. The company is also developing utility-scale energy storage systems.

EnerDel also has a $1.29m contract with the US Army to design and test battery systems for a hybrid version of the Humvee truck.

EnerSys

Reading, Pennsylvania, USA
www.enersys.com
NYSE: ENS
Market cap: $1100m
52-week range: $8.60-24.57

EnerSys is the largest industrial battery manufacturer in the world, operating facilities in over 100 countries. The company's products and services are focused on motive power (for forklift trucks and other material handling vehicles) and reserve power (for UPS applications). The company makes nickel and lead-based batteries and claims that its TPPL batteries deliver 20% better performance than competitors. Recently, EnerSys has expanded its li-on capacity.

Exide Technologies

Milton, Georgia, USA
www.exide.com
NASDAQ: XIDE
Market cap: $437m
52-week range: $1.83-8.87

Exide Technologies is one of the world's largest producers of lead-acid batteries with operations in 80 countries. It created a new division to pursue new markets for renewable energy and li-ion battery applications in 2009 after purchasing the assets of Mountain Power organisation – which added high performance, large capacity rechargeable li-ion batteries to Exide's technology portfolio. The new division will focus on large-scale storage for grid-connected renewable energy; off-grid renewable power generation and storage, and new industrial storage applications. The company sells batteries under a wide range of brands (including Centra, DETA, Exide, Exide NASCAR Select, Exide Select Orbital, Fulmen and Tudor).

The company is also working on advanced lead acid batteries with the help of $34.3m of stimulus funding. In addition to its own advanced carbon technology, Exide is also working with Axion Power International on advanced lead-acid products.

Maxwell Technologies

San Diego, California, USA
www.maxwell.com
NASDAQ: MXWL
Market cap: $426m
52-week range: $4.90-21.81

Maxwell is based in San Diego with a European base of operations in Rossens, Switzerland. It is the global leader in ultracapacitors, the world's largest supplier of high-voltage grading and coupling capacitors for electric utility infrastructure, and a leading developer of radiation-hardened microelectronics for space and military applications. In December 2009 the company delivered its one-millionth large cell ultracapacitor.

Maxwell's Boostcap ultracapacitors have been deployed on trains, subways and buses in many countries including Germany, Korea and the USA. In 2009 the company won $13.5m in orders for ultracaps to be fitted to over 850 Chinese buses. Maxwell is working with ISE Corporation to develop hybrid drive systems for heavy vehicles and with the Tianjin Lishen Battery company to develop hybrid ultracapacitor/li-ion battery solutions.

NGK Insulators

Nagoya, Japan
www.ngk.co.jp/english
TSE: 5333
Market cap: ¥653,889
52-week range: ¥1180-2340

NGK is a Japanese ceramics company which works across the energy, environmental, and electronics fields. Amongst other products, it makes ceramic filters for cleaning car exhaust gases, ceramics for semiconductors, and components for inkjet printers and other electronics. In the energy sector, NGK provides insulators for power lines and transformers and builds NAS batteries for renewable energy storage. Developed in conjunction with the Tokyo Electrical Power Company the NAS battery uses beta alumina for its solid electrolyte, which gives it very high efficiencies. To date NGK has supplied over 270MW in some 200 locations, including for solar installations in Germany and wind farms in the US. The company has also supplied American utilities including Xcel Energy, who have installed a 20-50kW unit in South Dakota adjacent to an 11MW wind farm. NGK is using its ceramic expertise in the field of fuel cells, and recently developed a new SOFC that they claim is one of the most efficient in the world. This product is currently undergoing testing.

Saft Batteries

Bagnolet, France
www.saftbatteries.com
Euronext Paris: Saft
Market cap: €716m
52-week range: €14.83-36.99

Saft Groupe SA makes industrial batteries, including rechargeable nickel and lithium-based batteries for trains, subways and trams. It also makes high performance batteries for the electronics, defence and space industries. It is developing a project with Conergy and solar manufacturer Tenesol to integrate large-scale li-ion batteries into PV systems, and is also working with ABB on large-scale grid stabilisation batteries; the first demonstration plant will be installed by EDF Energy in the UK.

Saft has entered into a joint venture with Johnson Controls to develop batteries for EVs and PHEVs, and has won $95.5m in stimulus funding to build a li-ion factory in Florida and $150m in federal funding to build a new battery factory in Michigan. Johnson Controls-Saft has built a manufacturing facility in Narsac, France, which they claim is the world's first dedicated production facility for li-ion batteries for electric vehicles. It already produces batteries for the Mercedes S400 hybrid car and the BMW 7 Series ActiveHybrid and started production for the BMW HEV in 2010. The company has also won a contract with Ford for the supply of the complete battery system for Ford's first mass-produced plug-in vehicle, which is scheduled for launch in 2012, and with Azure Dynamics for the five year supply of li-ion batteries for hybrid commercial vehicles. The company is also a supplier to Ford's new Transit Connect BEV and is working with Volkswagen and Jaguar Land Rover on EVs. With approximately 4000 employees worldwide, Saft is present in 18 countries.

Sirius Exploration

Berkeley, UK
www.siriusexploration.com
AIM: SXX
Market cap: £30m
52-week range: 1.00-15.75p

Sirius Exploration was incorporated on 30 October 2003 as a private company. It subsequently re-registered as a public company under the name of Sirius Exploration Plc on 22 March 2005. It originally had a broad exploration remit but since 2008 its focus has become highly defined on the salt and potash mining markets. Today, the company has major interests in properties overlying three significant recognised salt deposits. Firstly, a 6000 acre area over the Williston Basin in North Dakota; secondly, a 600km² area in Australia overlying the Boree Salt Member in Queensland; thirdly, 1250km² in the Kimberley region of Western Australia that reaches over the Canning Basin.

In addition, Sirius has acquired the IP and the issued share capital of three research and development companies focused on innovative new technologies for using its properties after mining has terminated for power storage. These centre on either storing or sequestering carbon dioxide in the salt caverns or salt beds created through solution mining, or establishing conventional Compressed Air Energy Storage facilities – and potentially new carbon dioxide-based CAES facilities – on its properties for storing electricity. Sirius continues for the present to maintain its historic copper and gold interests in Macedonia and an iron ore interest in China through its equity position in a CIC Mining Resources Ltd vehicle.

Valence Technology Inc

Austin, Texas, USA
www.valence.com
NASDAQ: VLNC
Market cap: $105m
52-week range: $0.74-2.50

Founded in 1989, Valence Technology has been at the forefront of energy storage for 20 years and was the first manufacturer to use lithium phosphate technology. Its third generation li-ion batteries, U-Charge, launched in 2010. This new long-life lithium phosphate technology utilises a phosphate-based cathode material and is specifically designed for EVs and PHEVs. Valence has agreements to provide batteries to leading companies including Siemens, PVI, EVI, Brammo, Oxygen and S&C Electric Company. The company is also working on applications such as UPS for commercial and utilities applications. Valence has manufacturing facilities in Nevada, China and Northern Ireland and is planning a new li-ion production plant in Texas which will be capable of producing over 600,000 battery packs per annum. Valence is a supplier to the Tanfield Group for their Smith Edison and Smith Newton EVs.

ZBB Energy Corporation

Menomonee Falls, Wisconsin, USA
www.zbbenergy.com
Amex: ZBB
Market cap: $14.5m
52-week range: $0.71-2.00

Founded in 1998, ZBB is based in Wisconsin and Perth, Western Australia. The company makes batteries which are said to offer two to three times the energy density of present lead-acid batteries. Its technology is based on the reaction between zinc and bromide. ZBB's products include the ZESS 50 (50kWh) and the ZESS 500 (500kWh), which consists of ten 50kWh modules, a power conversion system and system control package. The ZESS 500 has been tested successfully with the California utility Pacific Gas and Electric and the company has made sales in the USA, Canada, Ireland, Africa and Australia (including a $2.6m project with the Australian government). ZBB has an agreement with Eaton Corp to expand sales growth in the utility, renewable energy and critical power markets. In January 2010 the company gained $14million in ARRA tax credits towards the building of a new $49 million manufacturing facility in Wisconsin.

Smart grids

ABB

Zurich, Switzerland
www.abb.com
NYSE: ABB
Market cap: $42,252m
52-week range: $10.88-22.01

ABB is the world's largest supplier of electrical products and services to wind turbine manufacturers, with a portfolio ranging from generators to compact substations to grid connections.

In smart grids, the company is a global leader in flexible AC transmission systems as well as high voltage direct transmission (HVDC) lines. ABB have pioneered the development of HVDC on projects such as the 580km-long NordNed linking the electricity grids of Norway and the Netherlands.

The company is the world's leading supplier of power systems for the marine industry, including high-performance diesel engine turbochargers. More than 50% of the world's tankers, container ships, diesel power stations and mining vehicles are fitted with ABB turbochargers.

Other power products include energy-saving building controls, solar inverters, instrumentation, low-voltage products, drives, motors and industrial robots. The ABB Group of companies operates in around 100 countries and employs about 120,000 people.

Badger Meter

Milwaukee, Wisconsin, USA
www.badgermeter.com
NYSE: BMI
Market cap: $588m
52-week range: $29.89-44.90

Badger Meter, founded in 1905, is a manufacturer of liquid flow measurement and control technologies serving markets worldwide. The company's products are used in a range of applications, including water, oil and chemicals. Its water applications include the sale of water meters and related technologies and services used by water utilities. Badger's products are also used for irrigation, water reclamation and industrial process applications. Specialty applications include metering a range of fluids in industries, such as food and beverage; pharmaceutical production; petroleum; heating, ventilating and air conditioning (HVAC); and measuring and dispensing automotive fluids.

Badger Meter has a reputation as an innovator in the development of flow measurement metering, from their original frost-proof meters to today's technologically advanced automated meter reading (AMR) systems and advanced meter infrastructure (AMI) technologies.

The company markets two main metering systems that interface with communications networks: these are their Orion radio-frequency automatic meter reading system and Galaxy fixed-network meter reading systems. Badger meters equipped with data transmitters can interface with leading meter reading technologies offered by other companies, including mobile, fixed-base, power-line carrier, Wi-Fi and virtually every other available means of sending the signal from the meter to the utility for billing.

Badger has expanded its offerings in specialist metering services with the acquisition in April 2010 of Cox Instruments of Scottsdale, Arizona, and its subsidiary Flow Dynamics. Cox Instruments and Flow Dynamics manufacture high performance flow meters that are used in applications such as aerospace, custody transfer and flow measurement calibration test stands.

Bglobal plc

Darwen, UK
www.bglobalplc.com
LSE: BGBL
Market cap: £36.5m
52-week range: 8.00-57.75p

Founded in 2004, Bglobal has quickly grown to become a market leader in smart metering in Britain. The company offers a complete service which includes installation, collecting and analysing data, and management tools.

Clients include British Gas, Gazprom, Scottish and Southern, npower and BizzEnergy. Floated in 2007, Bglobal had installed its 50,000th business meter by 2008. By the end of 2009 Bglobal was installing 4000 meters per month. The company is now rolling out Smart1, which they say is a "revolutionary new design of smart meter" built specifically for SME and residential customers. Bglobal is the exclusive supplier of Smart1 in the UK and claim that its innovative features will give them a lead over the competition.

Composite Technology Corporation

Irvine, California, USA
www.compositetechcorp.com / www.ctccable.com
NASDAQ: CPTC
Market cap: $75m
52-week range: $0.15-0.75

The Composite Technology Corporation manufactures high performance energy efficient electrical transmission conductors through its subsidiary, CTC Cable Corporation. CTC also developed a wind turbine business, known as DeWind, which it sold to Daewoo Shipbuilding & Marine Engineering of Korea for $48m in 2009.

The company's main product now is ACCC (aluminium carbon composite core) conductor cable, which offers significant efficiency advantages over conventional cable. It utilises a high-strength, lightweight composite core wrapped with trapezoidal-shaped aluminum strands. This offers greater performance and capacity compared to conventional conductors of the same diameter and weight. The company says that their cable has the potential to revolutionise electrical grids by offering twice the power of traditional aluminium cables, with 25% stronger materials and improved reliability. To date they have sold around 8000km of ACCC on five continents.

Comverge

East Hanover, New Jersey, USA
www.comverge.com
NASDAQ
Ticker: COMV
Market cap: $232m
52-week range: $4.05-13.87

Comverge products and solutions cover a wide range of demand response and advanced metering applications. Comverge has over 500 clients and over 4.5m devices deployed throughout North America, with a growing number of consumers participating in Comverge programmes via utilities. In smart metering the company has partnered with Itron, Elster, Digi International and White-Rodgers. Comverge's PowerPortal in-home displays as well as its digital control units and programmable thermostats have all gained ZigBee Smart Energy certification. Comverge is a long-standing member of the ZigBee Alliance.

Echelon

San Jose, California, USA
www.echelon.com
NYSE: ELON
Market cap: $334m
52-week range: $5.13-15.38

Incorporated in 1988, Echelon is a market leader in control networks and smart metering. The company's LonWorks control networks are used around the world in the Louvre, the New York City subway system and the Rhoponghi Hills in Tokyo.

The company's Pyxos embedded control networking platform puts the power of control networks inside machines, adding functionality and allowing the creation of items such as smart uniforms, smart carpeting and smart furniture.

Echelon's Networked Energy Services (NES) infrastructure consists of a family of integrated, advanced electronic electricity meters accessed via a web-based operating system. Besides being an open, automated meter-reading system, NES can be used for additional energy and operational needs and services such as pre-paid energy, energy quality monitoring and reporting, and outage and theft detection. Echelon's technology is used by utilities in Austria, Denmark, Finland, Germany, Italy, the Netherlands, Russia, Sweden, Switzerland, the US and other countries.

In 2009 Echelon announced a tie-up with Eaton Corporation to integrate the latter's home automation products into the NES System. The agreement will focus on utilities and electricity providers in Europe, the Middle East and Africa. Echelon also signed agreements in 2009 with Duke Energy in the US – a $15.8m contract for smart metering that could expand to $150m if rolled out across all of Duke Energy's customers – and with Spanish company Telvent, to install 500,000 meters in Finland.

EnerNOC

Boston, Massachusetts, USA
www.enernoc.com
NASDAQ
Ticker: ENOC
Market cap: $685.60m
52-week range: $9.9-37.00

EnerNOC, which stands for Energy Network Operations Center, is a leading smart grid company providing demand response, energy efficiency, energy procurement, and emissions tracking and trading services. It was floated in May 2007.

The company uses its Network Operations Center to remotely manage and reduce electricity on demand. EnerNOC's demand response network has expanded to include over 5500 customer sites throughout North America.

The company offers an audit service for commercial and industrial customers which is designed to monitor building operations for energy efficiency. EnerNOC also offers a carbon accounting system to measure, manage and report GHG emissions, and help reduction efforts.

ESCO Technologies

St. Louis, Missouri, USA
www.escotechnologies.com
NYSE: ESE
Market cap: $841m
52-week range: $29.90-46.87

Originally a subsidiary of Emerson Electric, ESCO has since grown organically and through a series of acquisitions and mergers. It is a technology-driven business with around 60% of revenues derived from utility communications. It has over 400 clients for its Aclara products, which encompass AMI for gas, water and electricity, demand-response solutions, and other integrated smart grid solutions. Its Doble products offer solutions for diagnosing and monitoring grid assets such as transmission sub-stations. Other divisions are focused on shielding and testing for electronic, magnetic and acoustic media, and filtration systems for fluid flow products.

General Cable

Highland Heights, Kentucky, USA
www.generalcable.com
NYSE: BGC
Market cap: $1257m
52-week range: $12.77-42.73

General Cable is a global leader in copper, aluminum and fibre optic wire and cables. With one of the most diversified product lines in the industry, the company offers customers a single source for all types of wire and cable.

The company and its 13,000 associates conduct business in 46 manufacturing locations in 23 countries, with sales representation around the globe. As one of the premier wire and cable companies in the world, General Cable is well positioned to take advantage of upgrades to electricity networks and the expansion of fibre optics globally. The company has recently invested significantly in new products such as submarine energy cable for the offshore wind power and deep-water oil and gas markets, submarine repeatered fibre optic communications cables and extra-high voltage energy cable.

ITC Holdings Corp

Detroit, Michigan, USA
www.itc-holdings.com
NYSE: ITC
Market cap: $2753m
52-week range: $32.26-54.67

ITC Holdings Corp is the largest independent electric transmission company in the US. The company operates approximately 15,000 miles of overhead and underground transmission lines. ITC is proposing a major upgrade of the grid in order to integrate renewables into the network through a project called the Green Power Express. This would be a broad network of 765kV transmission facilities that has been designed to efficiently move up to 12GW of renewable energy in wind-rich areas to major Midwest load centres. The lines would traverse portions of North Dakota, South Dakota, Minnesota, Iowa, Wisconsin, Illinois and Indiana, and will ultimately include approximately 3000 miles of extra high-voltage facilities. Project cost is estimated at between $10 and $12bn.

Itron

Liberty Lake, Washington, USA
www.itron.com
NASDAQ: ITRI
Market cap: $2505m
52-week range: $40.10-72.50

Itron is a market leader in smart grid supplies to the global energy and water industries, providing intelligent metering, data collection and software solutions. The company is the world's leading provider of solid-state meters and data collection systems – it claims 8000 utility companies worldwide use its technology, including AMR and AMI technology.

Itron's smart meters include RF wireless networking and automated meter reading, data management and related software options. In August 2009 Itron unveiled a new automated manufacturing process for meters in order to handle unprecedented production demand for their meters.

The company has strategic alliances with a wide range of organisations (including Google, Logica, IBM, Motorola, HP and Microsoft) to collaborate on software, telecoms, hardware and management issues.

One of Itron's biggest smart grid projects to date has been the $480m contract to supply metering as part of Southern California Edison's $1.6bn Smart Connect programme. Itron began deploying its OpenWay AMI units in September 2009 and plans to ship more than 4 million meters by the end of 2012.

National Grid

London, UK
www.nationalgrid.com
LSE: NG
Market cap: £15,767m
52-week range: 511.00-685.50p

National Grid owns the high-voltage electricity transmission network in England and Wales and operates the system across Great Britain. It also owns and operates the high pressure gas transmission system in Britain, distributing gas to 11m homes and businesses. In the US, National Grid distributes electricity to nearly 5m customers in Massachusetts, New Hampshire, New York and Rhode Island. It is the largest power producer in New York State, with 4GW of electricity generation. It is also the largest distributor of natural gas in the north-eastern US, delivering gas to 3.4m customers in the same states. National Grid also has a number of related businesses such as Liquefied Natural Gas (LNG) importation and storage, land remediation and metering.

National Grid launched its climate change strategy in 2006 with a bold statement of support for a post-Kyoto framework linking carbon trading mechanisms around the world and for regulatory measures to be aligned with public policy (in both the UK and the US) to incentivise energy savings and not energy use. In a radical move, the company has called for a decoupling of energy usage from profits: 'volume drivers' need to be removed from energy regulation in order to decouple energy use from the revenue an energy company receives, they say. The company would also like to see regulation and tax mechanisms being used to incentivise the reduction and leakage of GHGs not covered by cap and trade schemes.

National Grid is currently investing £22bn on its own networks, partly funded by a recent £3.2bn rights issue. Measures taken by the company to mitigate climate change include increasing their own consumption of renewables; investigating new and alternative technologies to help it reduce its impact on climate change; starting a pilot project to capture the energy used to move gas around its gas networks; and investigating CHP.

National Grid says that it is helping individuals to become more energy efficient; reduce their energy usage; and switch to lower carbon-intensity fuels, such as from oil to gas.

The company presented a report to the UK government in 2009 on how biodegradable waste streams such as sewage, food and wood could be turned into biogas and injected into the gas distribution system: the company states that half of Britain's homes could be heated by this renewable gas.

It is also involved in plans for an underwater grid in the North Sea (see the European super grid feature on p.136.

Nexans

Paris, France
www.nexans.co.uk
EPA: NEX
Market cap: €1853.06m
52-week range: €31.20-66.82

Nexans SA is a worldwide leader in the cable industry. The company operates in four main areas. In infrastructure it provides cables for power production, transmission and distribution as well as integrated solutions for telecom operators and airports. For industry, the company offers a complete portfolio of cables for market segments as diverse as the automotive, rolling stock and aerospace industries, shipbuilding, nuclear power, oil, gas and petrochemicals, material handling and automation. In the buildings sector, Nexans supplies cables and network solutions for structures of all types, from small residences to public and office buildings and big industrial complexes. In information technology, the company provides copper and fibre-optic cabling for resource-intensive applications such as data centres and local area networks.

The company has developed a significant presence in offshore wind infrastructure, having supplied components for several UK and Belgian wind farms including a €100m contract to supply high voltage submarine cables for the London Array. It supplies medium-voltage cables to collect the power from the turbines, high-voltage cables to transport it back to land and fibre optic data cables for controlling the installations. Nexans says that its share of the offshore market has tripled over the past four years and it expects this segment to expand further in coming years.

The company is also positioning itself in smart grid developments with sales of high capacity overhead tables and bi-directional cables to allow integration of renewables into the grid.

Power-One

Camarillo, California, USA
www.power-one.com
NASDAQ: PWER
Market cap: $366m
52-week range: $0.33-4.81

Power-One is a designer and manufacturer of power conversion and power management products, primarily for communications and server/storage infrastructure equipment, industrial applications, high-end consumer and industrial appliances, and renewable energy markets. The company's products are used to convert, process and manage electrical energy, in both AC and DC form. In the renewable energy market, Power-One sells inverters for roof-top solar applications. Power-One has manufacturing and R&D operations in Asia, Europe and the Americas.

PowerSecure

Wake Forest, North Carolina, USA
www.powersecure.com
NASDAQ: POWR
Market cap: $128m
52-week range: $3.15-10.25

Founded in 1991, PowerSecure offers a range of services and products in the field of energy and smart grid infrastructure for electric utilities and their commercial, institutional and industrial customers, including demand-response networks. A significant portion of their business involves designing, building and installing high quality transmission and distribution networks – in other words, they make the grid hardware as well as the software. They also provide energy services to the oil and natural gas industry through their Southern Flow and WaterSecure business units, and legal and regulatory consulting services for power utilities.

Additionally, PowerSecure has a commercial lighting division which designs and installs LED products. Their EnergyLite team provides consultancy in auditing, designing and installing cost-effective lighting, whilst the EfficientLights division manufactures the LED lighting fixtures.

Prysmian

Milan, Italy
www.prysmian.com
MIB: PRY
Market cap: €2,845M
52 week range: 7.82 - 16.07

Originally part of the Pirelli group, Prysmian became an independent company in 2005 and floated on the Milan exchange in 2007. Today it is a leading player in high-technology cables and systems for energy and telecommunications, with subsidiaries in 39 countries, 56 plants in 24 countries, seven R&D centres and 12,000 employees.

Prysmian operates two separate divisions: energy cables and systems (comprising submarine and underground cables), and telecom cables and systems (optical cables and fibres, and copper cables for video, data and voice transmission).

The company is a global leader in submarine energy cables and has completed more than 30 submarine power links worldwide in recent years. It has projects under development in Italy, Bahrian, Spain, Qatar and the USA and in late 2009 was awarded a contract of €300 million to develop the new Sicily-Italian mainland connection, one of the largest projects of its kind in the world. Prysmian has also stepped up its involvement in offshore wind, and as well as projects currently being built in the UK such as a transmission link for the Greater Gabbard and Thanet wind farms, the company has also won contracts for the Ormonde and Walney offshore wind farms.

The group has also made recent acquisitions in Russia and India to bolster its offering on high voltage underground cables globally.

In March 2010 Prysmian successfully placed a €400 million bond issue.

Quanta Services

Houston, Texas, USA
www.quantaservices.com
NYSE: PWR.N
Market cap: $3695m
52-week range: $15.84-25.80

Quanta Services is a leading provider of specialised contracting services for the electric power, telecommunications, broadband cable and gas pipeline industries. The company provides a comprehensive range of services, including the design, installation, maintenance and repair of virtually every type of network infrastructure. Additionally, Quanta provides point-to-point fibre optic telecommunications infrastructure and leasing in select markets and offers related design, procurement, construction and maintenance services. The company has more than 13,000 employees with major offices in 40 states and field and support offices in all 50 states and Canada.

Quanta has worked with wind for more than a decade and has recently moved significantly into solar, providing complete engineering, design, procurement, project management and construction for utility-scale and large commercial solar generation facilities.

RuggedCom

Woodbridge, Canada
www.ruggedcom.com
TSE: RCM
Market cap: CAD$255m
52-week range: CAD$17.06-30.50

RuggedCom is a leading provider of communications networking solutions designed for critical applications in harsh environments. Their technologies include Ethernet switches, network routers, wireless devices, serial servers, media converters, software (proprietary embedded software and application software) and professional services. The company's products are designed for use in harsh environments such as those found in electrical power substations, oil refineries, military applications, roadside traffic control cabinets, and metals and minerals processing. The company is a leading supplier to electric utilities for products such as their RuggedSwitch substation hardened Ethernet switches, which allow reliable substation local area networks (LANs) for intra-substation communications used in applications including power system protection and control. In addition, their RuggedRouter appliances provide a secure method for implementing inter-substation communications across the grid.

Spice

Leeds, UK
www.spiceplc.com
LSE: SPI
Market cap: £190m
52-week range: 33.50-91.75p

Spice is a leading provider of support services and works in partnership with a large number of commercial, public and utility organisations. The company was admitted to AIM in August 2004 and to the LSE in July 2008. Spice has two divisions: the supply side, offering billing and energy services and the distribution operation which includes the electricity, gas, facilities, telecoms and water businesses. On the supply side the company's divisions include Revenue Assurance Services (which recovers previously unbilled revenue); Inenco (one of the country's leading utility and energy consultancies); Energy 2000 (another market leader within the energy and utility management field); Saturn Energy Ltd (a leading energy brokerage supplying gas and electricity contracts, mainly to the SME market); and the NIFES Consulting Group (energy consultancy, engineering and property appraisal). The distribution side encompasses the Freedom Group (engineering services for the utility industry); the Facilities Services Group; the Team Telecom Group; H2O Water Services; and the Liberty gas group.

Spice is well placed to benefit from smart meter roll-outs since it runs a training centre for meter engineers – it is estimated some 9000 will need to be trained by 2015 if Britain is to install meters for all households.

Zenergy Power

London, UK
www.zenergypower.com
LSE: Zen
Market cap: £64m
52-week range: 121.00-150.50p

Zenergy Power is a developer of high-temperature superconducting (HTS) wire, which is used in energy-intensive industrial applications, power distribution and renewables.

Its first commercial product, launched in 2008, is an induction heater for metals processing. These devices are capable of reducing energy usage by 50% and increasing productivity by 25% in metal and alloy processing. Their second commercial product is an HTS fault current limiter (FCL), with units sold to two American utilities.

Zenergy is also working on the use of HTS coils for hydro and wind power in partnership with power conversion specialists Converteam SAS. They recently installed the world's first superconducting electricity generator at E.on's hydropower dam in Bavaria, Germany.

The company is working on the development of a lightweight 10MW direct-drive wind generator specifically for the offshore market. They hope that the weight savings achieved through the use of superconductors could lead to a 25% reduction in the overall cost of offshore wind energy. It is also working on electric ships, and has received funding under the EU's Electric Ships programme to develop HTS motors and generators for marine systems.

Low-cost production techniques for the mass manufacture of its second generation (2G) superconducting wire are currently being refined. The aim is to provide its own low-cost supply of the wire. Zenergy has operating subsidiaries in Germany, USA and Australia.

Hydrogen & fuel cells

Acta

Pisa, Italy
www.acta-nanotech.com
AIM: ACTA
Market cap: £5.66m
52-week range: 3.00-25.88p

Acta is developing a range of catalysts geared towards the renewable energy, automotive, battery and industrial markets. The company's catalyst technologies are capable of working with a wide variety of fuels including ethanol, hydrogen, glycerol, methanol, butanol and ammonia. Acta's catalysts are undergoing tests in applications such as ammonia treatment and zinc-air batteries, as well as fuel cell and other applications. Acta has developed a new electrolyser that contains no precious metals and is capable of safely producing clean, dry, low-cost pressurised hydrogen. The system is designed for domestic or light industrial applications and the company says that has the potential to enable the commercial launch of various small to mid-sized fuel cell applications (such as fuel cell bikes, outboard motors, and other personal mobility and light transport applications).

AFC Energy

Cranleigh, UK
www.afcenergy.com
AIM: AFC
Market cap: £21.75m
52-week range: 0.25-17.49p

AFC's target market is large chlorine manufacturers and other industries who produce waste hydrogen. The company has designed an alkaline fuel cell, which they say has a 60% efficiency rate at turning waste hydrogen into electricity. The system doesn't use expensive catalysts such as platinum and can therefore be manufactured at lower cost – AFC estimates this to be around one-tenth that of the cost of competitors' products.

The company has successfully produced electricity from this system at Akzo Nobel's Bitterfield chlorine plant in Germany and has since signed an agreement with European chemicals major INEOS ChlorVinyls to develop a project at its Runcorn Site manufacturing complex in Cheshire. Acta is now working on a much bigger, 50kW, system, which it expects to be ready for field trials in early 2011. The company is also working with energy-from-waste firm Waste2Tricity, which plans to use the technology for plasma gasification of coal reserves in Scotland, and WSP Group plc.

Ballard Power Systems

Burnaby, British Columbia, Canada
www.ballard.com
NASDAQ: BLDP
Market cap: $189m
52-week range: $0.85-3.25

Ballard Power Systems is a world leader in PEM fuel cells, which are used in a variety of applications. Ballard spun out its vehicle technologies in 2008 to create the Automotive Fuel Cell Cooperation Corp (AFCC) (now owned 50% by Daimler, 30% by Ford and 20% by Ballard). AFCC has thus become a key Ballard customer.

In the stationary power supply market, Ballard supplies fuel cells for back-up power in the wireless telecom market. It also supplies fuel cells to Plug Power (fuel cell stacks), Raymond (lift trucks), IdaTech (back-up power), Baxi Innotech (residential micro-CHP), Dantherm Power (back-up power), H2 Logic (hydrogen vehicles), and FutureE Fuel Cell Solutions (back-up power).

Ballard is a member of a consortium working on the BC Transit fuel cell bus fleet (the first of which went into service in October 2009), the largest single deployment of fuel cell buses worldwide.

Ceramic Fuel Cells

Melbourne, Australia
www.cfcl.com.au
LON: CFU
Market cap: £87.539m
52-week range: £7.35-17.50

Ceramic Fuel Cells is developing micro-CHP units with leading appliance partners and utility customers in Germany, France, the UK and Japan. It has two main systems, one of which is a micro-CHP unit which produces power and heat, and the second of which is a natural gas-to-electricity unit called BlueGen. The company's Gennex fuel cell stacks are used in its BlueGen units, which can be installed either as a stand-alone power generator or coupled with a hot water tank as a co-generation system to provide power and hot water. Each BlueGen can produce up to 17,000kWh hours of electricity per year – more than twice the amount needed to power the average home (the surplus can be sold back to the grid). At present, the BlueGen units are about the size of a dishwasher and the company admits that they need to be made smaller and cheaper before they can expect mass market take-up.

Ceramic Fuel Cells opened a new plant in Germany in October 2009 with the capacity to produce 10,000 of its Gennex fuel cell stacks a year.

Ceres Power

Crawley, UK
www.cerespower.com
LON: CWR
Market cap: £117m
52-week range: 80.00-240.75p

Founded in 2001 as a spin-off from Imperial College London, Ceres Power is a developer of SOFC units for micro-CHP. Its 1kW wall-mountable CHP units have the same natural gas, water and electricity connections as existing boilers and are small enough to fit in a standard kitchen. The units produce electricity to meet most of a typical home's power requirements as well as producing the heat needed for central heating and hot water.

The firm has signed a development programme with British Gas for the delivery of 37,000 units over a four-year-period from 2011, and another deal with Calor Gas to deliver units suitable for the more than 2m homes and businesses in Britain that aren't connected to mains gas. Ceres has built a new plant in Horsham, Sussex, with a capacity of 1m fuel cells a year, but has contracted the manufacturing of the completed CHP units to the Dutch company Daalderop BV. Ceres also has a contract with EDF Energy Networks to develop a hybrid fuel cell and battery storage appliance and are selling CHP units to Bord Gáis Éireann for the Irish market. Ceres raised £31.4m through a share placing in 2009.

FuelCell Energy

Danbury, Connecticut, USA
www.fuelcellenergy.com
NASDAQ: FCEL
Market cap: $225m
52-week range: $1.98-5.47

FuelCell Energy's stationary DMFC units are generating power at over 60 installations worldwide; they operate on a variety of fuels including biogas, methanol, diesel, coal gas, coal mine methane and propane. The company has a product line offering systems from 300kW to 2.8MW, scalable up to 50MW. The company says that it has approximately 65MW of power plants installed or in backlog in Europe, Asia, and the US. Of this, over 30MW were ordered by POSCO Power, the company's manufacturing and distribution partner for South Korea. California is the company's next largest market.

Hydrogenics

Ontario, Canada
www.hydrogenics.com
NASDAQ: HYGS
Market cap: $21m
52-week range: $0.21-0.75

Hydrogenics Corporation makes electrolysis technology and fuel cells based on PEM technology. The company has supplied fuel cell systems for vehicles including buses, commercial fleets, utility vehicles and electric lift trucks. Hydrogenics has also supplied fuel cell systems for freestanding electrical power plants and UPS systems, and hydrogen storage and power systems for optimising solar and wind power.

IdaTech

Bend, Oregon, USA
www.idatech.com
LON: IDA
Market cap: £38.8m
52-week range: 73.00-99.00p

Founded in 1996, IdaTech designs, develops, and manufactures extended run back-up power fuel cell products for telecommunications and other UPS applications. IdaTech's PEM fuel cells can be fuelled either directly by hydrogen or by generating hydrogen on-site and on demand from HydroPlus (a methanol and water liquid fuel), using IdaTech's proprietary fuel reformer. The company offers 250W, 3kW and 5kW fuel cell products that provide solutions for applications requiring 100W to 15kW of back-up power generation. IdaTech is working with a number of partners including Ballard Power Systems.

Intelligent Energy

Loughborough, UK
www.Intelligent-energy.com
Pink Sheets: IENG
Market cap: N/A
52-week range: N/A

Intelligent Energy is a leading UK player in fuel cells. The company has formed a joint venture with Scottish & Southern Energy to commercialise micro-CHP systems. It has also developed fuel cell motorbikes and scooters with Suzuki Motor Corporation, and hybrid delivery vehicles with PSA Peugeot Citroen. It has also provided the fuel cell engine to Boeing to power the world's first manned fuel cell aircraft and supplied Airbus with a multifunctional fuel cell system for potential use in commercial airliners. The company leads a programme aimed at fielding a fleet of fuel cell taxis in London for 2012.

ITM Power

Sheffield, UK
www.itm-power.com
LON: ITM
Market cap: £18.48m
52-week range: £0.00-38.00

ITM Power is developing a range of electrolyser products based on PEM technology. The company is planning a demonstration of their 2-10kW system in a zero carbon home currently being built in South Tyneside. The company is also working on a dual-fuel Ford Focus which runs on both petrol and hydrogen. Unlike cars powered by fuel cells, which use hydrogen gas to create electricity and drive electric motors, the car burns hydrogen directly in a conventional engine. ITM underwent significant re-structuring in 2009 in order to cut costs.

Plug Power

Latham, New York, USA
www.plugpower.com
NASDAQ: PLUG
Market cap: $70.39m
52-week range: $0.49-1.35

Floated on NASDAQ in 1999, Plug Power was one of the first companies to market with commercially viable fuel cell products: to date, it has installed around 1000 low-temperature PEM systems for forklift trucks (marketed as GenDrive). It also makes mini-CHP systems for residential use (known as GenSys and GenCore). The company received over $6m in awards from the US Department of Energy to further refine its GenSys units in 2009 and is hoping to be profitable by 2012.

Proton Power Systems

London, UK
www.protonpowersystems.com
AIM: PPS
Market cap: £4.68m
52-week range: £1.00-9.00

Proton is a developer of PEM fuel cells, mostly targeting industrial applications. In 2009 Proton unveiled the world's first passenger bus using their triple-hybrid fuel cell system, which uses a combination of fuel cells, batteries and ultracapacitors. At the heart of the system is Proton's 50kW unit – the same fuel cell powers the Alsterwasser, a ferry on Hamburg's Alster river. Proton is also working with the US military on various military and civilian applications. In 2010 Proton announced a collaboration with Smith Electric Vehicles, part of the Tanfield group, to jointly develop a battery-powered commercial vehicle which would use fuel cells as a range extender.

Protonex

Southborough, Massachusetts, USA
www.protonex.com
LON: PTX
Market cap: £19.5m
52-week range: 25.75-38.00p

Protonex is a leading provider of PEM and SOFC technologies designed for military, commercial and consumer applications. These applications include portable emergency power, unmanned aerial vehicles, marine power and robotics. Protonex has its headquarters in Southborough, Massachusetts, and a development facility in Broomfield, Colorado.

SFC Smart Fuel Cell

Brunnthal, Munich, Germany
www.sfc.com
ETR: F3C
Market cap: € 44.6m
52-week range: € 5.20-9.19

SFC Smart Fuel Cell is a market leader in DMFC technologies. Its units, marketed under the EFOY brand name, generate energy for mobile homes, yachts, vacation cabins, observation stations, metering and early warning devices, EVs and more. The company won the 2009 Technology Innovation Award (a prize presented by the *Wall Street Journal*) for its JENNY fuel cell: this is a portable power supply for soldiers. It reduces their battery-load weight by up to 80% while providing energy for equipment such as night-vision goggles, laptops, communication and global positioning system (GPS) devices and sensors; the fuel cell provides enough power for a 72-hour mission. SFC is based in Brunnthal, Germany, and has a US sales and technical service office in Atlanta.

Green transport

Azure Dynamics

Detriot, Michigan, USA
www.azuredynamics.com
TSX: AZD
Market cap: C$85.5m
52-week range: C$0.04-0.35

Azure makes electric and hybrid electric drive technology for buses, delivery vans, and other utility vehicles. The company has over 20 years of experience and their technology powers over 4,000 vehicles worldwide. The company has offices in Detroit and Toronto with manufacturing facilities in Vancouver and Boston. The company has developed partnerships with car and truck makers such as Ford, Collins Bus Company and others. It is supplying the drivetrain for Ford's new Transit Connect BEV. The company stands a good chance of being the supplier for future BEVs planned by Ford, such as the Ford Focus.

Azure also make hybrid buses, using its own drivetrain and controls on an adapted bus chassis and body. It is designed for low speed, frequent stop routes.

Its third vehicle product is the Leep Freeze system for refrigerated vehicles, which draws energy from the vehicle's primary engine and delivers it to a freezer system. This system saves fuel, reduces emissions, and is much quieter. In October 2009 Azure received a record order from the Schwan Food Company for 248 of these units.

Clean Air Power

High Wycombe, UK
www.cleanairpower.com
AIM: CAP
Market cap: £13.5m
52-week range: 17.41-42.00p

Clean Air Power has pioneered a Dual-Fuel system which allows diesel engines to operate on up to 90% natural gas, delivering cost savings and lower emissions. Clean Air Power's Dual-Fuel technology has been incorporated on around 1600 vehicles operated by around 50 customers around the world.

Clean Air Power offers to versions of its technology. Its Genesis Dual-Fuel is a retro-fit product applied to exisiting engines (allowing a 50% substitution of diesel). It is also developing original equipment manufacturer (OEM) integrated engine technology which allows a substitution rate of up to 90%. Clean Air Power has an engineering facility in Leyland, Lancashire, and a manufacturing and R&D centre in San Diego, California.

The company raised £10.6m from its admission to AIM in February 2006 and in 2008 the company agreed another financing package to provide up to a further £5m. Investors include Endeavor Capital Partners, EnerTech Capital Partners, and Royal Bank of Canada.

Clean Power Technologies

Newhaven, UK
www.cleanpowertech.co.uk
OTCBB: CPWE
Market cap: $11.92m
52-week range: $0.08-0.61

Clean Power Technologies has developed a Clean Energy Separation and Recovery (CESAR) system, which takes waste heat from the exhaust of a conventional engine and uses it to generate power through a heat recovery system. The company's main focus is on refrigerated trailers where the power is used for auxiliary cooling motors. The first commercialisation for refrigerated trailers is targeted for the summer of 2011.

The second main application is for landfill gas plants, where the CESAR system will increase the net output of a generator by 8% without consuming any additional fuel. Field trials are taking place with Renewable Power Systems & NewEnCo on various landfill sites.

The company moved into manufacturing and installation in 2009. Backers include the Quercus Trust.

Eco City Vehicles

London, UK
www.ecocityvehicles.com
AIM: ECV
Market cap: £19.63m
52-week range: 2.00-7.13p

Eco City Vehicles is an established distributor to the London taxi market. The company is now planning to distribute EVs and is importing hybrid 3.5 ton Mitsubishi trucks which have been converted by the Italian company Veicoli Ecologici Metropolitani to run on electric propulsion, backed up by an on-board LPG generator. Eco City has an option to manufacture and convert the vehicles in the UK. In February 2010 the company launched an all-electric prototype of their existing taxi, the Mercedes Vito. Called the eVito taxi, the vehicle was developed by a consortium of companies including Mercedes Benz UK and Zytec Automotive. The electric taxi is powered by Zytek's 70kW electric powertrain and expected to have a range of around 120 miles.

ECOtality

Scottsdale, Arizona, USA
www.ecotality.com
OTCBB: ETLE
Market cap: $33.5m
52-week range: $1.44-27.60

ECOtality's main business is providing charging infrastructure for electric vehicles but it also has interests in many other green areas including fuel cells, solar, and power storage.

The company's chief subsidiary is the Electric Transportation Engineering Corporation (eTec). Founded in 1989, eTec has worked on every EV initiative in North America since the 1990s. Their primary product is the Minit-Charger advanced battery system which can give a fast charge in 15 minutes. These are used mostly for PHEVs, BEVs, forklift trucks, and airport ground handling vehicles.

Through eTec, the company is leading on one of the world's largest trials of electric vehicle charging infrastructure, with support from a $100m grant from the US Department of Energy. The company will install around 12,500 Level 2 (220V) charging systems and 250 Level 3 (fast-charge) systems during 2010 ready for the launch of the Nissan Leaf. The locations chosen are Phoenix, Tucson, San Diego, Portland, Eugene, Corvallis, Seattle, Nashville, Knoxville and Chattanooga. This will be the largest deployment of EVs and charging infrastructure in the world to date. Nissan and eTec will work with over 40 government and industry partners to collect and analyse data from the project, which will look at how the cars are used in different climates, whether the charging infrastructure is effective, and conduct trials of various revenue systems for commercial and public charging. The intention is to have around 12,500 normal charging systems and 250 fast-charge systems up and running in time for the launch of the Leaf.

Another ECOtality subsidiary, the Innergy Power Corporation based in San Diego, makes solar PV modules and rechargeable batteries. Its durable, rugged solar modules are manufactured using fibreglass-reinforced panels and are designed for outdoor environments such as off-grid lighting, mobile communications, signalling devices and surveillance cameras.

ECOtality is also the parent company of the Fuel Cell Store which develops, manufacturers, and sells a wide range of fuel cell products including fuel cell stacks, systems, component parts and educational materials.

Enova Systems

Torrance, California, USA
www.enovasystems.com
NYSE: ENA
Market cap: $26.32m
52-week range: $0.12-2.42

Enova Systems is a leading supplier of power management and conversion systems for EVs, PHEVs, and FCVs. Customers for its HybridPower system include Smith Electric Vehicles, Isuze, Th!nk, Ford, Hyundai, Mack Truck and WrightBus. In February 2010 Enova Systems was awarded a contract with the US government's General Services Administration to provide a number of vehicles for government agencies and the armed forces. The company will supply the Enova Ze, which is powered by a 120kW all-electric drive system and is currently the only zero emissions step van available.

Johnson Controls

Milwaukee, Wisconsin , USA
www.johnsoncontrols.com
NYSE: JCI
Market cap: $21,445.77m
52-week range: $17.55-35.77

Johnson Controls operates in three primary businesses: building efficiency, automotive parts and power solutions. The building efficiency business is engaged in designing, producing, marketing and installing integrated heating, ventilating and air conditioning systems, building management systems, controls, security and mechanical equipment. The company invented the first electric room thermostat back in 1885, and can justifiably claim to have a long-standing commitment to sustainability solutions. It is currently involved in more than 500 renewable energy projects including solar, wind and geothermal technologies. Its second largest division is in automotive interiors, principally providing components including seating systems, instrument panels and cockpits, door systems, overhead systems, and car electronics and electronic energy-management. Its third division, power solutions, is a leading supplier of lead acid batteries for virtually every type of passenger car, light truck or utility vehicle as well as the leading independent supplier of hybrid battery systems through a joint venture with Saft. In March 2010, the company acquired National Energy Services (NES), a lighting services company. As well as being a leading player in energy-efficient building retrofits and on-site renewable energy applications, Johnson Controls plays an active part in the Climate Group and participates in the Global Reporting Initiative and the Carbon Disclosure Project.

Li-ion Motors

Las Vegas, Nevada, USA
www.Li-ionMotors.com
OTCBB: LMCO
Market cap: $12m
52-week range: $0.20-2.00

The company was founded in 2000 as EV Innovations; it completed a 1 for 2 reverse split and name change from EV Innovations (OTCBB:EVII) to Li-ion Motors Corporation (OTCBB:LMCO) in February 2010. The company converts vehicles (everything from scooters, bicycles, mopeds, motorcycles, cars and trucks) to lithium-power. It has a fully owned subsidiary in Bangalore, India. Its main models include the Inizio (a 170 mph supercar that does zero to 60 in 4.5 seconds and travels up to 200 miles on a single charge), the Wave (80mph, 170 mile charge), the LiV Wise (75 mph, 120 mile range), the LivDash (an electric version of Mercedes' Smart Car; 80 mph, 120 mile range) and Liv Flash (an electric version of BMW's Mini; 80 mph, 120 mile range). The company also makes electric scooters, a 4WD work vehicle, and is currently developing an electric truck.

OriginOil

Los Angeles, California, USA
www.originoil.com
NASDAQ: OOIL
Market cap: $53m
52-week range: $0.22-0.48

OriginOil has developed a system using quantum fracturing whereby water, carbon dioxide and other nutrients are fractured at very high pressure to create a slurry which is then channelled to the algae culture awaiting it in a lower-pressure growth vessel. The company has designed a live extraction system, designed to 'milk' algae oil without destroying algae cultures, and a bioreactor prototype specifically designed for waste water applications.

The company unveiled its first pilot system in January 2010. OirginOil has a partnership with Desmet Ballestra, an international pioneer in oil and fats technologies, for commercialising its technology, and is also working with other partners including London-based StrategicFit, who are refining the algae productivity model. It has a co-operative R&D agreement with the Department of Energy's Idaho National Laboratory and a partnership with the Research Institute of Tsukuba Bio-Tech, an affiliate of Japan's Science and Technology Agency, to develop algae for fuel applications.

PetroAlgae

Melbourne, Florida, USA
www.petroalgae.com
OTCBB: PALG
Market cap: $186m
52-week range: $2.00-40.00

Founded in 2006, PetroAlgae has developed a system for growing various strains of micro-algae which produce clean fuels and, an important by-product, high-quality proteins suitable for human and animal food. Its bioreactor and harvesting technology uses proprietary methods of controlling nutrients and light exposure to produce high yields of biomass and protein extracts. The company has a working prototype at its Fellsmere farm in Florida and is now starting to scale up and commercialise this system.

The company's strategy is to select the best micro-organism for each specific location (indigenous to the region) and apply their processes to scale from a micro-organism to a high output-producing micro-crop. The company has an MOU with IndianOil with the goal of a commercial production facility in the near future.

PetroAlgae announced its first commercial revenues in January 2010 with the sale of a licence for development of PetroAlgae projects in Egypt and Morocco.

Quantum Technologies

Irvine, California, USA
www.qtww.com
NASDAQ: QTWW
Market cap: $118m
52-week range: $0.58-1.77

Quantum Fuel Systems Technologies Worldwide is involved in the development and production of propulsion systems, energy storage technologies, and alternative fuel vehicles.

The company works across a wide range of technologies and provides services which include powertrain engineering, system integration, manufacturing and assembly of packaged fuel systems and battery control systems for vehicles and other applications including fuel cells, hybrids, plug-in electric hybrids, alternative fuels, and hydrogen refuelling stations and systems. It also designs, engineers and manufactures hybrid and fuel cell vehicles.

The company's portfolio of technologies include advanced lithium-ion battery systems, electronic controls, hybrid electric drive and control systems, hydrogen storage and metering systems, and other alternative fuel technologies.

Quantum's most high profile role is as a co-founder of Fisker Automotive, a JV with automobile designer Henrik Fisker. All Fisker models will feature Quantum's proprietary high-performance PHEV architecture known as Q-Drive. Fisker's first vehicle is the Fisker Karma, with production expected to reach 15,000 vehicles annually by 2011.

Quantum's clients include Volvo-Eicher, GM, Ford, Department of Energy, other government agencies, and the military. Quantum also makes solar panels in Germany.

Ricardo

Shoreham-by-Sea, UK
www.ricardo.com
LON: RCDO
Market cap: £145m
52-week range: 282.00-314.75p

Ricardo is best known as a business-to-business services company within the automotive market. However, it is now also developing expertise in energy services.

Ricardo has technical centres in the US, Europe and Asia and is a world leader in hybrid and EV technologies. The company is also researching the fuel efficiency of ICE technology, and flex-fuel and second-generation biofuel technologies. Ricardo has also developed a new EV charging station in conjunction with PEP Stations LLC in North America.

The company is increasingly active in related markets such as renewable energy, power generation and transportation and infrastructure planning. Ricardo is developing capabilities in wind turbines, wave and tidal generators, CAES systems, micro-CHP systems, fuel cells and hydrogen, flywheels and batteries.

Tanfield Group

Washington, UK
www.tanfieldgroup.com
LON: TAN
Market cap: £18m
52-week range: 23.00-91.25p

The Tanfield Group's operations are split broadly into two divisions: Powered Access and Zero Emission Vehicles.

The company's powered access brands, UpRight and Snorkel, service different geographical markets, but manufacture a common portfolio of electric and diesel-powered aerial lifts. This division has been loss making due to a drop off in demand for powered access equipment.

Tanfield is the world's largest manufacturer of commercial electric vehicles, sold under the Smith Electric Vehicles brand. These vehicles are used by organisations such as the Royal Mail, Sainsbury's, BSkyB, Parcelforce, DHL, TNT, Scottish & Southern Energy, British Telecom and Balfour Beatty. Sainsbury's was an early adopter and has used electric vans in its online shopping delivery fleet since 2006.

The company is currently expanding into Asia and Europe. It is one of four producers of low carbon vans to be selected for the Government's Low Carbon Vehicle Procurement Programme, and is the largest supplier of electric vans into the programme. Tanfield is also part of two consortia that both won funding for Technology Strategy Board programmes. These programmes will see the company deliver 16 electric passenger vehicles and develop new, high-efficiency vehicle ancillary systems.

In 2009, Tanfield established an associate company in North America, Smith Electric Vehicles US Corp. The company has delivered Smith Newton electric trucks to major companies including Coca-Cola Enterprises, Frito-Lay, AT&T and Staples, along with the utilities Pacific Gas & Electric and Kansas City Power & Light. SEV US Corporation has won $10m in funding from the US Department of Energy to subsidise private sector procurement for up to 100 electric vehicles, which includes the first fleet of Ford Transit Connect BEV electric light vans.

In early 2010 Tanfield signed an MoU with Proton Power Systems to collaborate on building a battery-powered commercial vehicle equipped with a Proton Power fuel cell system as a range extender.

Despite these promising signs, the company is unfortunately saddled with a loss-making division specialising in powered access platforms which has led to a downturn in its share price over the medium term.

UQM Technologies

Frederick, Colorado, USA
www.uqm.com
NYSE: UQM
Market cap: $173m
52-week range: $1.25-7.45

UQM Technologies makes high efficiency electric motors, generators and power electronic controllers for the automotive, aerospace, military and industrial markets. A major emphasis is on propulsion systems for EV, HEV, PHEV, and FCV programmes.

Historically, the company has made electric propulsion systems for vehicles ranging from wheelchairs to passenger automobiles to large trucks, tractors, construction equipment and military vehicles. Recently the company has switched focus on to EVs. UQM has also supplied propulsion motors for buses operated by the Flint Michigan Mass Transportation Authority which have demonstrated savings of 15-20% over the hybrid motors they replaced, and 40% over a standard diesel-powered vehicle.

Recent contracts include components for 36 hybrid buses in Denver, Colorado and units to power 20,000 of Coda's new EV sedan. In January 2010 the company was awarded a $45.1m in ARRA funding.

ZAP

Santa Rosa, California, USA
www.zapworld.com
OTCBB: ZAAP
Market cap: $39m
52-week range: $0.09-0.49

ZAP ('zero air pollution') was founded in 1994 as an electric bicycle kit manufacturer. Since then it has grown to become a leading distributor of low-carbon vehicles and launched its first own-manufactured vehicle, the four-passenger XEBRA, in 2006. Since then it has launched the Xebra truck, the Zaptruck, the Zapvan Shuttle, and various electric scooters (including the Zapino, the Zappy, and Zappy Pro) as well as electric all-terrain vehicles (the ZAP Dude).

ZAP's latest vehicle is the Alias, a high performance EV powered by an array of large-format lithium batteries, which can top 85 miles per hour and travel over 100 miles on a charge. The drive system uses a compact, high-efficiency, air-cooled, AC-induction motor and carries an expected list price of around $35,000.

In January 2010 ZAP announced an agreement to produce electric sport utility vehicles, cars and other electric vehicles with the Chinese auto maker Zhejiang Jonway Automobile. ZAP and Jonway partnered on the production of the five-door Jonway A380 SUV, integrating the latest AC propulsion and lithium battery system technologies to produce a high performance mid-range EV. Jonway currently manufactures several thousand units per month of its A380 compact SUV in three- and five-door models and is expanding its product line with new model sedans and other automobiles.

ZENN Motor Company

Toronto, Canada
www.zenncars.com
TSX: ZNN
Market cap: $95m
52-week range: $1.80-6.50

The Canadian company ZENN ('zero emission no noise') was one of the first to mass produce a low speed, short range electric car. The three-door hatchback, which could reach 25mph and had a range of 50 miles, was designed for urban commuters and applications such as golf resorts. Launched in 2006, it ceased production in April 2010. Although ZENN was an innovator in EVs the car simply wasn't considered robust or fast enough to compete with the new generation of EVs – especially since it was excluded from an Ontario EV car rebate programme in 2009 on the grounds of it being unsafe for highway use.

ZENN is now focusing on the commercialisation of its ZENNergy drivetrain, which is to be powered by EEStor's ultracapacitors. The company intends to become a key supplier and partner with industry leading.

OEMs and Tier 1 companies. The company owns 10.7% of EEStor and has exclusive rights to use the technology in vehicles with a curb weight of up to 1400kg.

Green buildings

Accsys Technologies

London, UK
www.accsysplc.com
LON: AXS
Market cap: £1m
52-week range: 0.41-1.32p

Accsys Technologies has developed a process that enables softwoods and non-durable hardwoods to be modified to resemble hardwood in terms of performance. Their Accoya wood can be used in all external applications (it has even been used to line canals in the Netherlands) and has a lifespan of 60 years. Accsys has licensed the technology in China and the Middle East and has developed a sales network in North America.

The company's manufacturing facility at Arnhem in the Netherlands has recently been upgraded to provide more capacity. It is also planning to expand into the production of acetylised wood fibre-based panels and is working with Medite (Europe) Ltd to commercialise this technology. The first samples of MDF (medium-density fibreboard) using this method were produced in September 2009.

Advanced Environmental Recycling Technologies

Springdale, Arkansas, USA
www.aertinc.com
NASDAQ: AERT
Market cap: $16m
52-week range: $0.12-0.75

Advanced Environmental Recycling Technologies recycles polyethylene plastic into building materials. Its products include commercial and residential decking planks and accessories, such as balusters and handrails (MoistureShield and Weyerhaeuser ChoiceDek), exterior door components, and exterior housing trim (MoistureShield).

Axion International Holdings

New Providence, New Jersey, USA
www.axionintl.com
OTCBB: AXIH
Market cap: $42m
52-week range: $0.60-3.35

Axion manufactures structural building components made from recycled plastics, railroad crossties, bridge infrastructure, marine pilings and bulk heading. Axion's high-load thermoplastic structures are more durable and have a substantially greater useful life than wood, steel and concrete, with minimal long-term maintenance costs.

The company has won several contracts from the US Army for plastic bridges, including a contract for two bridges at Fort Eustis in Virginia which are used by freight traffic with a load rating of 130 tons. Axion has previously built bridges for the US Army in North Carolina which are used as tank crossings.

It claims that its plastic railroad ties have environmental advantages over creosote-treated wood ties. The company estimates that the market for replacing ties on America's 140,490 miles of rail track represents potential sales of $1bn.

BluGlass Ltd

Silverwater, Australia
www.bluglass.com.au
ASX: BLG
Market cap: AU$32.5m
52-week range: AU$0.15-0.38

Founded in 2005, BluGlass has invented a new process using Remote Plasma Chemical Vapour Deposition (RPCVD) to grow semiconductor materials such as gallium nitride (GaN) and indium gallium nitride (InGaN). Their process would mean cheaper solar cells and LEDs.

BluGlass is exploring the potential of high efficiency nitride-based solar cells for the CPV market and has received AU$4.96m in Australian government funding.

The BluGlass IP portfolio includes 12 patents accepted or granted in territories including Australia, USA, China and Japan. The company, which floated on the ASX in August 2006, is currently strengthening its IP portfolio, developing partnerships, and refining the technology.

Carmanah Technologies

Victoria, Canada
www.carmanah.com
TSE: CMH
Market cap: C$31.9m
52-week range: C$0.55-1.08

Carmanah is a developer of solar-powered LED devices, including marine lanterns. Other solar-powered LED devices are used in the aviation, traffic, telecom, construction and mining industries. The company is also expanding into solar-powered LEDs for public lighting, such as car parks and street lighting. The company is working with PTL Solar, based in the UAE, to jointly produce outdoor lighting based on this LED/solar combination for the Middle Eastern and African markets.

Carmanah is also one of the largest installers of commercial grid-tied PV in Canada. Major projects have included a 100kW system at Exhibition Place in Toronto and a 108kW system at the Jean Canfield building in Charlottetown, Prince Edward Island. As one of the Government of Canada's greenest buildings, the facility is a showcase for sustainable technologies.

Cree

Durham, North Carolina, USA
www.cree.com
NASDAQ: CREE
Market cap: $6908m
52-week range: $17.88-65.21

Founded in 1987, Cree introduced its first blue LED in 1989. Cree's products are used in general illumination, backlighting, electronic signs and signals, variable-speed motors, and wireless communications.

The company runs an LED City programme (which promotes LED lighting in municipal and local government bodies) and an LED University programme (which does the same thing at university campuses).

Cree has its headquarters in Durham, North Carolina, and facilities in California, Malaysia, Hong Kong and China. The company currently employs 3172 people. It is expanding its North Carolina manufacturing capacity and building a chip-production facility in China to increase production.

Recent high-profile contracts include a deal to retrofit 650 WalMart stores and installations at important buildings including the US Federal Reserve, the Pentagon, and the National Air and Space Museum.

Eaga

Newcastle, UK
www.eaga.com
LON: EAGA
Market cap: £389m
52-week range: $113.50-160.10

Eaga is Britain's largest residential energy efficiency provider. The company was established in Newcastle in 1990 and currently employs over 4500 people. It is an employee-owned partnership, run along similar lines to John Lewis. It is hoping to make major inroads into the installation of renewable and micro-generation technologies following the introduction of the new FITs in 2010.

Eaga works in co-operation with central and local government, all six major UK energy suppliers, local authorities, and social housing providers. The company installs and maintains insulation and central heating and is currently expanding into micro-generation devices. It has installed energy efficiency measures into 5m homes and holds the contract to deliver the £1.5bn Warm Front programme in England. Their estimates are that out of Britain's 6m social housing units, about 1m are suitable for solar panels.

Since 2005 Eaga has expanded through the acquisition of Millford (insulation installers), Everwarm (Scotland's largest provider of domestic insulation services), Iguana (boiler installation), HEAT (boiler installations in Northern Ireland), JD Heating (central heating installations in the social housing market) and R G Francis (heating installation and repairs).

Eaga is currently working towards becoming a carbon neutral organisation and is engaged in developing products which will enable other businesses to benefit from their expertise in this area.

Eaton

Cleveland, Ohio, USA
www.eaton.com
NYSE: ETN
Market cap: $11,209m
52-week range: $30.02-70.15

Eaton's businesses comprise five distinct segments: electrical, hydraulics, aerospace, truck and automotive.

Eaton has a significant presence in green building controls and technologies. It is a global leader in electrical components and systems for power distribution and the world's second-largest supplier of UPS systems. The company offers a range of products and services geared towards energy efficiency in buildings.

Their green portfolio also includes hydraulic and electrical systems for wind turbines and hydropower installations. The company is working with Ocean Power Technologies on their PowerBuoy technology. They also have an emerging presence in solar power through the installation of solar inverters and battery storage systems.

Eaton is also involved in green transport, particularly the development of electric and hydraulic power systems for commercial vehicles; it is the world's only manufacturer to offer a full range of hybrid systems for truck and bus applications. These include hybrid electric, plug-in hybrid electric and hybrid hydraulic power systems.

Eaton has approximately 70,000 employees and sells products to customers in more than 150 countries.

Johnson Controls

See entry under green transport directory.

Kingspan Group

KingsCourt, Ireland
www.kingspan.com
LON: KGP
Market cap: €980m
52-week range: €2.05-7.31

Kingspan is Europe's largest manufacturer of insulation panels and flooring, with manufacturing and distribution operations throughout Europe, the Far East and the United States. The company employs over 5500 people worldwide.

High performance insulation products for roofs, walls and floors, and HVAC ductwork are among their products. The company also manufactures a comprehensive range of structural systems and is a market leader in providing waste and surface water management and conservation solutions for sustainable drainage, rainwater harvesting and off-mains effluent treatment systems.

Kingspan has moved into low carbon technologies such as solar thermal (vacuum tube or flat plate), air-source heat pumps, and thin-film PV systems. It is also marketing a new product called EnergiPanel, which is a solar air heating system designed for roof and wall applications to supplement heating systems. The system, which can reduce heating costs by as much as 20%, has been used on Asda's new £42m 'eco-depot' distribution centre in Oxfordshire. The firm is planning to add heat pumps to the system to help store heat overnight and further increase energy efficiency.

Lighting Science Group

Satellite Beach, Florida, USA
www.lsgc.com
PINK: LSCG
Market cap: $22.5m
52-week range: $0.15-1.90

Lighting Science Group makes retrofit LED lamps that look like traditional bulbs, as well LED luminaires for a range of indoor and outdoor applications. The group expanded into Europe with the acquisition of Dutch rival Lighting Partner BV in 2008. This has allowed Lighting Science to integrate its LED modules into around 500 consumer lighting products.

LSG is currently focused on five core markets: 'architainment' installations; retail; public infrastructure such as street lighting; commercial and industrial applications; and the gaming market.

LSG has an agreement with NASA's John F. Kennedy Space Center to develop LED light fixtures for space exploration. The company hopes that this deal will give them an opportunity to explore LED lighting's impact on human factors, such as circadian rhythms, which will also have terrestrial applications.

Lime Energy

Chicago, Illinois, USA
www.lime-energy.com
NASDAQ: LIME
Market cap: $121m
52-week range: $3.01-8.94

Lime Energy specialises in energy efficient lighting upgrades, mechanical and electrical retrofit and upgrade services, water conservation, weatherisation and renewable project development and implementation. The company works across a variety of facilities ranging from high-rise office buildings to manufacturing plants, retail sites, mixed use complexes and large, government sites. It has performed nearly 1bn square feet of energy efficient building upgrades across America.

Since its formation in 1977, the company has grown organically and by acquisitions, the most recent of which was the takeover of Applied Energy Management in 2008.

Lime claims to be the only company offering the full range of energy efficiency services on a national scale. Recent big wins have included a doubling of their existing contract with the New York Power Authority (NYPA) to provide up to $20m in energy efficiency services and a projected $27m contract with National Grid to provide energy efficiency upgrades for small businesses.

Nanoco Group

Manchester, UK
www.nanocotechnologies.com
LON: NANO
Market Cap: £199.74m
52-week range: 81.00-111.50p

Nanoco is a leading nanotechnology company involved in the development and manufacture of fluorescent semi-conducting nanoparticles called quantum dots. Nanoco was founded in 2001 by Professor Paul O'Brien and Dr Nigel Pickett in order to advance quantum dot technology that was previously developed at the University of Manchester and Imperial College, London. Since 2001, Nanoco has raised £4.1m of private equity funds. The company began trading on the AIM market of the London Stock Exchange in May 2009.

Nanoco is unique in the nanomaterials market in having the capacity to manufacture large quantities of quantum dots. Their molecular seeding process for the bespoke manufacture of these nanoparticles on a commercial scale is protected by worldwide patents. Additionally, the company is the only manufacturer currently able to supply production quantities of these nanoparticles without using a regulated heavy metal.

The first applications are expected to be in liquid crystal display (LCD) TVs, where quantum dots can offer dramatically reduced energy consumption. Nanoco has several development agreements in place with major manufacturers. Other significant areas which the company is exploring include the use of quantum dots in CIGS cells for solar PV and biological imaging. Nanoco's quantum dots can be combined into a wide range of materials including liquids, polymers and glass. The company currently operates facilities in the UK and Japan.

Nexxus Lighting

Charlotte, North Carolina, USA
www.nexxuslighting.com
NASDAQ: NEXS
Market cap: $26m
52-week range: $2.66-7.22

Founded in 1991, the company first moved into LED systems in 2000 and since then has made various acquisitions including Advanced Lighting System and the Lumificient Corporation. Other wholly-owned subsidiaries include SV Lighting (a world leader in solid-state LED and fibre-optic lighting).

The company says that its LED lamps provide 80% energy savings and last over 50,000 hours. The lamps feature new high colour rendering and white colours which are close to incandescent 'warm whites'. Its flagship product is the Array range, which it says are easier and cheaper to manufacture than conventional LEDs.

Nexxus has a partnership with QD Vision to develop quantum dot technologies. Quantum dot/LED lamps exploit the unique light emitting properties of quantum dots to deliver huge reductions in power consumption and dramatic colour quality improvements. The lights integrate a quantum dot optic with cool white LEDs to produce colour-rich, warm white light at the high efficiency of 65 lumens per watt. The brightness of these lights is equivalent to 75-watt incandescent light bulbs, but they use only a quarter of the energy. Nexxus raised $15.9m through a common stock offering in December 2009.

NIBE Industrier AB

Markaryd, Sweden
www.nibe.com
SSE: NIBE B
Market cap: Kr6,809.20m
52-week range: Kr47.30-82.25

This Swedish company has three main divisions. NIBE Element is a leading European manufacturer of components and systems for electric heating applications (such as heating cables, toaster elements and so forth). The energy systems division is Scandinavia's biggest manufacturer of domestic heating products and a leading name in northern Europe, supplying ground source and air source heat pumps, domestic boilers and water heaters. NIBE is also the market leader in Sweden – and one of the leading manufacturers in the rest of Europe – for wood-burning stoves.

Rockwool Group

Hedehusene, Denmark
www.rockwool.com
LI: 0M0A
Market cap: DKK10.43bn
52-week range: DKK338-678

Founded in 1909, the Rockwool Group is the world's leading producer of stone wool. The company began production of stone wool in 1935 and now operates 23 factories and has a world-wide network of sales offices, distributors and partners employing 8500 people in 35 countries. Rockwool International A/S was floated on the Copenhagen Stock Exchange in 1995.

Stone wool can be used for many other purposes apart from just insulation, and Rockwool has developed numerous other products including partitions for walls, floors and ceilings, acoustic products, and water-absorbing mineral wool for horticultural uses.

Rockwool recently opened a new factory in Toronto, Ontario, which will double its production capacity in North America – an area it regards as important in the growth of insulation products.

SIG

Sheffield, UK
www.sigplc.com
LON: SHI
Market cap: £652m
52-week range: 82.25-173.00p

Founded in 1957, SIG is the largest supplier of insulation products in Europe. The company holds leading market positions in several countries and trades from 800 locations, with 12,000 employees.

The company's main business is insulation products but it also supplies partitioning systems, other interior products, roofing materials, and other products for infrastructure and civil engineering.

SIG maintains that trading remains "extremely challenging", with both public and private sector work facing reductions. However, sales of insulation and related products in the UK performed better than SIG's other UK divisions, strongly influenced by the CERT (Carbon Emissions Reduction Target) scheme.

Superglass

Stirling, UK
www.superglass.co.uk
AIM: SPGH
Market cap: £17m
52-week range: 25.00-43.00p

Superglass Insulation is the only independent manufacturer of mineral wool insulation in the UK. The company, which supplies a full range of thermal and acoustic mineral wool products for the construction industry, has formulated a glass fibre that uses over 80% of recycled material in the form of reclaimed glass, and claims that it operates a higher recycling level than any other mineral wool producer. Superglass has also made significant investments in machinery which enable it to recycle a high percentage of water during the manufacturing process.

The company has benefited from a £1.3m CERT-funded Superdad scheme, in conjunction with Scottish and Southern Energy, which was launched in September 2009. This was the first of this kind of initiative, whereby DIY customers can obtain discounted Superglass insulation through the independent builder's merchant sector; the company says that early indications suggest that the scheme is working well. Superglass is also hoping to benefit from the extension of the CERT programme to 2012 and the introduction of the Community Energy Saving Programme (CESP).

Trex

Winchester, Virginia, USA
www.trex.com
NYSE: TREX
Market cap: $272m
52-week range: $5.11-21.22

Trex Company is America's largest manufacturer of wood-alternative decking, railing and fencing products. The company uses 300m pounds of used polyethylene and an equal amount of hardwood sawdust each year, as well as recycling over 1.3bn plastic bags. Its decking, railing and fencing products are used primarily for residential and commercial buildings. Trex products are stocked in more than 5500 retail locations across the United States and Canada.

Universal Display Corporation

Ewing, New Jersey, USA
www.universaldisplay.com
NASDAQ: PANL
Market cap: $405m
52-week range: $5.04-14.26

Universal Display Corporation (UDC) is a world leader in the development of innovative OLED technology for use in flat panel displays, lighting and organic electronics. Universal Display has more than 30 licensing agreements globally with leading manufacturers such as Chi Mei EL, DuPont Displays, Konica Minolta, LG Display, Samsung SMD, Seiko Epson, Sony, Tohoku Pioneer and Toyota Industries.

As well as technology licensing, the company also engages in material sales of its high-performance proprietary phosphorescent (PHOLED) materials to its development and manufacturing customers.

The company was awarded two grants from the US Department of Energy's Solid State Lighting Programme in 2009 to demonstrate further advances in the performance of white OLEDs, including the development of a very high efficiency white PHOLED lighting device which would exceed 102 lumens per watt.

VPhase

Chester, UK
www.vphaseplc.com
AIM: VPHA
Market cap: £22m
52-week range: 3.00-9.00p

VPhase's flagship product is the VX1, aimed at the residential user. The technology is based on creating a small anti-phase voltage similar to that used by noise-cancelling headphones. For example if the incoming voltage is measured at 243V, the VPhase technology will apply an opposite voltage of 23V, stabilising the voltage at an energy-efficient 220V.

VPhase has made significant progress towards full commercialisation in 2009, achieving CE certification and getting their first device on the market.

The VX1 is also currently being tested by Scottish and Southern Energy in a number of customers' homes, with funding from the UK Government's Carbon Emissions Reduction Target (CERT) scheme. VPhase also has an agreement with British Gas and is in talk with other potential customers, including house builders, housing associations, local councils and other utility companies.

The company, which raised £3.5m from backers including Allianz and BlackRock in 2008, is also developing products which will be available for North American 120V markets. In addition, VPhase technology can be embedded into high energy consumption products, such as air conditioning units. VPhase is a subsidiary of the Energetix Group (LON: EGX).

Vu1

Seattle, USA
www.vu1.com
OTCBB: VUOC.OB
Market cap: $41m
52-week range: $0.36-1.41

Founded in 2004, Vu1 is developing a novel design for an energy efficient light bulb using their patented electron stimulated luminescence (ESL) process. This technology uses accelerated electrons to stimulate phosphor to create light, making the surface of the bulb 'glow'. The company says that ESL creates the same light quality as an incandescent, but is more energy efficient and is also mercury-free. Its initial designs have a lifespan of 6000 hours. The company began investing in high-volume manufacturing capability in 2007 and gave the first public demonstration of ESL technology in 2009. The bulb, which screws into any standard Edisonian-style light socket, is intended as a fully functional replacement for existing R-30 reflector bulbs.

WaterFurnace Renewable Energy Inc

Fort Wayne, Indiana, USA
www.waterfurnace.com
TSE: WFI
Market cap: C$304m
52-week range: C$22.07-28.50

Founded in 1983, WaterFurnace Renewable Energy listed on the Toronto stock exchange in 1993. The company offers three basic systems: all-in-one systems are built to heat through the winter months, and provide cooling all summer; hydronic geothermal systems are designed for heating and cooling water in applications such as radiant floor heating, domestic hot water and snow/ice melt; and split geothermal systems can be used to provide comfort for the entire home, or individual zones (such as the second storey on a large home).

Waste & energy resources

Alkane Energy

Nottingham, UK
www.alkane.co.uk
AIM: ALK
Market cap: £15m
52-week range: 12.50-25.50p

Alkane Energy captures CBM for electricity generation and industrial heating. The company currently has seven CBM plants operating in the UK with installed capacity of 17MW. It has a further 6MW of plant commissioned and another 14MW under construction. Once projects currently under construction are commissioned, Alkane plans to have 50MW of generating capacity from these sources in the medium term. Alkane also has an agreement with TEG to jointly develop AD facilities which will use food waste and various crops to produce methane for electricity generation.

Covanta

Fairfield, New Jersey, USA
www.covantaholding.com
NYSE: CVA
Market cap: $2718m
52-week range: $12.47-19.69

Covanta Holding Corporation has two subsidiaries: Covanta Energy Corporation – a provider of EFW facilities – and NAICC (insurance products). Covanta Energy operates ten different types of EFW technologies, including biomass and biogas facilities in the US. In other countries, Covanta owns and operates a coal plant in the Philippines and China, a liquid fuel plant in India and a natural gas plant in Bangladesh.

In 2009 Covanta bought six EFW businesses and one transfer station from Veolia Environmental Services North America for $450m. The EFW facilities collectively process approximately 3m tons of waste each year. Covanta's portfolio now includes operation of 44 EFW facilities that process approximately 19m tons of waste annually.

Covanta is also developing a $500m EFW project on Vancouver Island, British Columbia. Scheduled for completion in 2012, the plant will process 500,000 to 750,000 tons of waste a year into RDF and produce 90MW of power. The company is also constructing a €350m EFW facility in Dublin which will process up to 600,000 tonnes of waste per year.

Environmental Power Corporation

Tarrytown, New York, USA
www.environmentalpower.com
NASDAQ: EPG
Market cap: $15m
52-week range: $0.14-0.82

Environmental Power Corporation is a small-scale developer of AD facilities. Its main operating arm is Microgy, which owns the North American licence to AD technology provided by Danish Biogas Technology A/S. The company is currently operating or developing facilities in Texas, Nebraska and California. EPC has also entered into an agreement with Cargill to investigate installing AD facilities amongst Cargill's vast network of farmers and agricultural partners in North America.

IGas

London, UK
www.islandgas.com
AIM: IGAS
Market cap: £53m
52-week range: 40.00-91.00p

Founded in 2003, IGas Energy Plc was set up to produce and market CBM. The company has licences across north Wales and England covering an area of approximately 1,656km². It has managed to produce gas from its pilot production site at Doe Green in Warrington, Cheshire, and to sell electricity from it – initial production rates indicate that the company should exceed its threshold for commerciality, they say. It is currently developing a second production site at Keele University Science Park and planning has been granted for a full production site at Ellesmere Port, Cheshire. The group has submitted planning applications for a further four production sites in north-west England. A potential problem is that the horizontal drilling technique is expensive and in other countries has mostly been applied to young coal beds rather than the old coal found in Britain. IGas are making bold claims about their potential generating capacity – the industry is watching closely to see if CBM can be made profitable.

Mercury Recycling

Manchester, UK
www.mercuryrecycling.co.uk
LSE: MRG
Market cap: £3.57m
52-week range: 8.50-23.98p

Mercury Recycling operates a lamp recycling plant in Manchester, which has the capacity to recycle 40m lamps per annum, making it the largest dedicated lamp recycling facility in the UK. In 2008 the company bought a second recycling unit in Perth, Scotland. Mercury expanded its services in 2009 to include batteries and general electrical products. It is also carrying out a feasibility study into the automated recycling of mercury bearing flat panel displays, LCD TVs and computer screens and plasma displays. This is partly in response to a fall in lamp sales (and hence a fall in the need for recycling them) during the recession. However, the company estimates that 130m lamps will need to be recycled in 2010. Mercury is also looking into the opportunities which will arise when new energy efficient lamps need to be recycled.

Republic Services

Phoenix, Arizona, USA
www.republicservices.com
NYSE: RSG
Market cap: $10,441m
52-week range: $15.05-29.82

Republic Services provides waste services through 400 collection companies in 40 US states and Puerto Rico. The company owns or operates 242 transfer stations, 213 solid waste landfills and 78 recycling facilities. The company has 35,000 full-time employees.

Republic Services merged with Allied Waste Industries in December 2008 to create the second-largest waste-hauler in the US.

The company is currently experimenting with covering landfill sites with thin-film PV panels. Its first pilot project in Texas began producing energy in March 2009. The company's research suggests that as much as 2350 acres of its 213 landfill sites could be covered with solar energy covers.

Shanks Group plc

Buckinghamshire, UK
www.shanksplc.co.uk
LSE: SKS
Market cap: £476m
52-week range: 45.50-136.20p

Shanks has operations in the UK, Belgium, the Netherlands and Canada. The company has 4500 employees and operates 104 waste management centres, of which 65 have recycling/recovery facilities. It has nine landfill sites and handles around 8m tonnes of waste per annum, with around 5.6m tonnes of materials recovered.

Shanks has a portfolio of EFW technologies ranging from AD to biological treatment and incineration. The company says that it is committed to further development of sustainable waste management and EFW infrastructure, and has commissioned new composting, AD, waste-water treatment, CHP, and recycling facilities at various locations in Europe and Canada. Shanks was the first company in the UK to build an MBT plant, which has been operational since 2006. The company has recently entered into a strategic partnership with Wheelabrator Technologies Inc (WTI), a subsidiary of Waste Management Inc, to offer more comprehensive EFW solutions. Shanks' Orgaworld business, which treats organic waste, has a contract to handle waste from Marks & Spencer shops up until 2012.

Shanks' most recent PFI success (its fourth to date in the UK), was a 25-year PPP waste disposal contract with Cumbria County Council, reached in June 2009. The 220,000 tonne per annum contract is worth an estimated £720m and will allow Shanks to develop two 75,000 tonne per annum MBT facilities.

Suez Environnement

Paris, France
www.suez-environnement.com
EPA: SEV
Market cap: €7977m
52-week range: €9.70-17.53

One of Europe's top waste management companies, Suez Environnement has 65,400 employees. The company operates 1107 waste treatment and reuse/recovery/recycling sites including 278 sorting centres, 14 open landfills, 106 composting plants, 126 hazardous waste platforms, 47 non-hazardous waste incineration sites, 8 hazardous waste incineration sites, 9 medical waste treatment sites, 305 transfer stations, and 85 recovery facilities for Waste Electrical and Electronic Equipment (WEE). The company collects waste from over 50m people and has more than 500,000 industrial and commercial clients. It deals with around 40m tons of waste annually.

The company has a wide-ranging brief covering waste and remediation of all kinds. In water, the company supplies 76m people with drinking water and deals with waste water from 44m. It operates more than 10,000 water treatment plants in 70 countries, 1535 waste-water treatment sites and 150,000 km of drinking water distribution networks.

Suez Environnement is a world leader in reverse-osmosis desalination. In 2009 the company won the contract for the world's largest public-private desalination partnership in Melbourne, Australia (worth €1.2bn over 30 years) and also unveiled the largest desalination plant in Europe in Barcelona. Other recent major contracts include the Disi Amman water conveyance project in Jordan ($200m over 25 years), the extension of the West Basin contract in California won by United Water for water reuse and the water concession contract of Yuelai in China ($800m over 40 years).

In waste water treatment, the company has recently launched its 'Green Cube' campaign, which focuses on energy recovery and biomass conversion to transform waste water treatment plants into environmental platforms and energy sources.

TEG Group

Preston, UK
www.theteggroup.plc.uk
LSE: TEG
Market cap: £21m
52-week range: 33.50-58.75p

TEG Environmental specialises in IVC and has two operating subsidiaries: TEG Environmental and the Natural Organic Fertiliser Company (NOFCO). TEG Environmental builds the IVC plants which convert biodegradable products into high quality compost and then NOFCO markets the compost. TEG is in a unique position as regards commercial-scale composting.

TEG's Silo Cage IVC technology is claimed to be one of the leading methods for the treatment of green and organic waste in the UK, producing marketable compost in around two weeks. The company has four of its own compost plants (in Norfolk, Perth, Preston and Todmorden).

TEG's compost machines are a key part of a huge waste management contract in Manchester. The company is providing four composting plants which will generate £38m in revenues once they are completed.

The company is looking to expand into complementary waste management processes. It has formed a collaboration with Munich-based UTS Biogastechnik to incorporate AD technology alongside IVC processing. The company is also working with Alkane Energy to generate electricity from the methane created in the AD process.

Veolia Environnement

Paris, France
www.veolia.com/en
EPA:VIE
Market Cap: € 10,195.76M
52 week range: € 19.89 - 27.10

The original enterprise, the Compagnie Générale des Eaux (CGE), was founded in 1853 with a contract to supply water to Lyon. Just seven years later, the company was awarded a 50-year concession to supply water to Paris. By the time of its centennial in 1953, the company was supplying eight million people with water in France over a 10,000km network. It was also branching out into new services, such as municipal waste collection.

The company changed its name to Veolia Environnement in 2003 and its four main divisions (water, environmental services, energy and transportation) were brought together under this umbrella in 2005. Today the Veolia group has operations in 42 countries.

The company's water services division includes the management of water and wastewater services for municipal and industrial clients and design/build of technological solutions and the public works. It provides drinking water and wastewater services to 163 million people.

The environmental services division manages municipal and industrial waste processes and covers the entire waste cycle, including urban cleaning services, soil and site remediation, collection, sorting, transfer, treatment and recycling/recovery. Veolia claims to be the biggest company globaly in waste management, with 819,000 industrial and tertiary clients in 33 countries.

The energy services division covers heating and cooling networks, industrial utilities, integrated building management services, climate control and power equipment installations, and public lighting. It manages some 5.8 million housing units.

The transportation division manages urban, regional and national public transit systems under public-private partnerships. The company claims to be the biggest European operator of ground passenger transportation services, with 27,223 road vehicles, 3,259 rail cars and 55 boats under management.

Waste Management

Houston, Texas, USA
www.wm.com
NYSE: WM
Market cap: $16,158m
52-week range: $22.10-35.00

Waste Management is the leading provider of waste and environmental services in North America. The company serves nearly 20m customers through a network of 367 collection operations, 355 transfer stations, 273 active landfill disposal sites, 16 EFW plants, 104 recycling plants and 111 landfill gas projects.

Amongst many environmental initiatives, the company has converted 425 vehicles from diesel fuel to natural gas, providing them with one of the nation's largest fleets of trucks powered by natural gas. In conjunction with Linde, the company has developed a system to convert landfill gas into vehicle fuel. The $15m installation, at the Altamont Landfill in California, can produce up to 13,000 gallons a day of liquefied natural gas.

Through its subsidiary WM Recycle America, Waste Management is North America's largest recycler with 104 facilities. Through its subsidiary Wheelabrator Technologies, the company operates EFW facilities generating up to 836MW of electricity.

Waste Management's 'Think Green' initiative is designed to place profit-from-waste at the top of its agenda. It has also partnered with communities, government and industries to redevelop closed landfill sites into recreational facilities such as parks, athletic fields, campgrounds and golf courses. Their landfills provide more than 21,000 acres of protected land for wildlife (49 landfills are certified by the Wildlife Habitat Council). Waste Management's environmental initiatives have drawn recognition from organisations such as the US Environmental Protection Agency and the US Department of Energy.

GREEN FUNDS 2

Allianz RCM Global EcoTrends Fund

Fund type: OEIC (open-ended investment company)
Launch date: 14 February 2008
Fund size: $103m
Expense ratio: 1.67%
Minimum direct investment: £500 lump sum or £50 monthly
Manager: Bozena Jankowska
www.globalecotrends.co.uk

Allianz RCM Global EcoTrends Fund is a global portfolio of companies worldwide that directly or indirectly have exposure to or get benefits from trends in the eco-energy, pollution control or clean water sectors. Benchmarked to the FTSE ET50 (environmental technology) Index, the fund is composed of the 50 largest pure-play environmental technology companies from around the world. The fund seeks to identify stocks with attractive growth characteristics, including a strong balance sheet, sustainable and visible earnings growth, strong market positioning and growth at a fair price. The fund manager has access to the proprietary global research and environmental investment expertise of RCM, a company of Allianz Global Investors.

Manager's comment

"Allianz RCM Global EcoTrends is the UK's only dedicated environmental technology OEIC. Its mandate is not constrained by ethical, green or sustainability screening and it enjoys a full international remit – EcoTrends opportunities are found across the globe. A maximum of 20% can be invested in emerging markets to balance potential risk and the fund is diversified across the entire environmental technology sector, not just climate change stocks. The fund has the flexibility to invest up to 30% outside the areas of eco energy, pollution control and clean water, and has transparent risk control systems to provide accountability with respect to performance metrics."

BlackRock New Energy Investment Trust

Fund type: investment trust
Launch date: 1 April 1988
Fund size: £315m
Annual charges: 1.75%
Minimum investment: £500 lump sum or £50 monthly
Manager: Robin Batchelor/Poppy Allonby
www.blackrock.co.uk

The fund invests at least 70% of its total assets in new energy companies, including those engaged in alternative energy and energy technologies including renewable energy, alternative fuels, automotive and on-site power generation, materials technology, energy storage and enabling energy technologies. Rising energy demand over the longer term is likely to cause energy prices to rise: when this trend is set against the continuing cost improvements within the new energy sector, the cost competitiveness of alternative technologies becomes increasingly favourable.

Manager's comment

"The stimulus packages for new energy technologies by the US (approximately $118bn) and China (approximately $218bn) have furthered our belief that this is, and will continue to be, an area of growth as this funding is released through 2010/2011. Within the renewables sector, we currently favour wind as it is a high-growth, cost-competitive, low carbon and scalable option (and one of the top choices for utilities looking to increase their production capacity). We are also positioned to take advantage of the areas targeted in stimulus package investment, such as upgrading the power grid in the US and China."

CIS Sustainable Leaders Trust

Fund type: unit trust
Launch date: May 1990
Fund size: £244m
Initial charge: 5%
Annual charge: 1.5%
Manager: Mike Fox
www.co-operativeinvestments.co.uk

The CIS Sustainable Leaders Trust aims to provide capital growth from a diverse portfolio of equities, mainly in the UK. Investment is limited to companies that are likely to benefit from measures to improve the environment, human health and safety, and quality of life. In addition, investment may be made in companies considered to be beneficiaries of changing attitudes towards a cleaner and safer environment, including those seen to be making above-average efforts to minimise environmental damage caused by their activities. Areas of avoidance constitute animal testing, countries where human rights are disregarded, items with military applications, tobacco and nuclear power.

Manager's comment

"The fund is managed in a way that combines principles with performance. The ethical considerations taken into account and the Co-operative Insurance's responsible investment approach work together to help achieve this goal."

CIS Sustainable World Trust

Fund type: unit trust
Launch date: 30 October 2009
Fund size: £74m
Initial charge: 5%
Annual charge: 1.5%
Manager: Mike Fox
www.co-operativeinvestments.co.uk

The fund invests in a mix of assets including UK equities, overseas equities, UK corporate bonds and cash. In order to qualify for investment, the majority of companies need to be involved wholly or in part in the manufacture of products, industrial processes or the provision of services associated with improving the environment and the enhancement of human health and safety, and quality of life. The fund has both positive and negative inclusion criteria. A best in sector approach is additionally used by the fund. The fund also applies the Co-operative Investments' Ethical Engagement policy to its investment decisions.

Manager's comment

"Fundamentally, the fund looks to deliver long-term capital growth by picking equities, fixed interest and alternative assets that fit within the core sustainable themes that are integral within the fund. Not being constrained to just the UK allows the fund to invest overseas and look for the most attractive undervalued securities on a global basis."

First State Asia Pacific Sustainability Fund

Fund type: OEIC
Launch date: 19 December 2005
Fund size: £101m
Initial charge: 4%
Annual charge: 1.55%
Minimum investment: £1000 lump sum, £50 monthly
Manager: David Gait/Angus Tulloch
www.firststate.co.uk

The fund aims to achieve long-term capital growth through investing in equities in the Asia-Pacific region (excluding Japan, including Australasia). The investment process takes account of sustainability themes and issues, and requires positive engagement with companies in respect of these themes. The fund has significant holdings in companies with exposure to clean energy and energy efficiency. The managers believe that developing countries will be unable to follow the development path pursued by industrialised nations in the past and they expect significant investment opportunities to result from this.

Manager's comment

"We believe that environmental, social and governance issues are becoming increasingly important drivers of long-term shareholder value in the Asia-Pacific region. As a result, our fund adopts an explicit positive screening approach when constructing the portfolio. We target companies that are sustainability leaders and whose business models are well positioned to benefit directly from new opportunities in the following six areas: renewable and cleaner energy; energy efficiency; waste and pollution management; water management; environmentally aware consumer products and services; and broad sustainable development. Over the long term, successful companies with good quality management teams will anticipate the environmental, human rights, social and governance risks they face and manage them accordingly. Encouragingly, there are already a growing number of clean technology and alternative energy companies listed on regional stock markets."

F&C Global Climate Change Opportunities

Fund type: SICAV (*société d'investissement à capital variable*)
Launch date: February 2008
Fund size: €38m
Initial charge: 5%
Annual charge: 1.5%
Minimum investment: €2500
Manager: Sophie Horsfall/Terry Coles
www.fandc.com

The fund invests at least two-thirds of its total assets in companies that have substantial activities that fall within technologies or strategies including: alternative energy, energy efficiency, sustainable mobility, waste, advanced materials, forestry and agriculture, water, acclimatisation and support services. The investment themes represent a holistic approach to the problems posed by climate change, addressing the development of alternative energy industries, identifying the broader technologies, support systems and advanced material that will underpin emissions reductions. As society responds to the threat of climate change, new opportunities will present themselves to companies worldwide, irrespective of size, sector and geographic location. Innovative companies able to recognise and create value from these opportunities will provide investors with significant potential for profit.

Manager's comment

"The fund focuses on companies that are leading advances in key areas that we believe lie at the heart of the climate change issue. We select stocks without any negative screening or regional benchmark restrictions. We look at the long-term adaptation effects that will be prompted by climate change, ranging from necessary infrastructure investments to acclimatisation measures in areas such as agriculture and health. We believe that investors wish to outperform broader equity markets while gaining exposure to positive themes, and therefore the benchmark is the unscreened MSCI World Index."

Guinness Alternative Energy Fund

Fund type: OEIC
Launch date: 19 December 2007
Fund size: $2.5m
Annual charges: 1.9%
Minimum direct investment: £5000
Managers: Tim Guinness, Edward Guinness and Matthew Page
www.guinnessfunds.com

The fund is focused on providing long-term capital appreciation by investing in the alternative energy and energy efficiency sectors. To be considered for investment, companies must have at least 50% of their business in the alternative energy or energy technologies sector and have a market capitalisation of more than US$100m. The fund's holdings are concentrated in the solar, wind, hydro, geothermal, efficiency and biomass sectors, spread across Europe, the Americas and Asia. The fund is split into around 30 equally weighted positions – this is an unusual structure that provides risk management and return benefits to the fund. Currently, Guinness has approximately US$60m in its alternative energy strategy, split between its US sister mutual fund, the Guinness Atkinson Alternative Energy Fund ($64.5m) and the Guinness Alternative Energy Fund (US$2.5m).

Manager's comment

"In the long run, the main drivers for this fund's performance are expected to be rising costs of fossil fuels as reserves decline, underpinned by political and public support to address energy security and climate change concerns. The investment process uses a quantitative tool to rank the universe on a weekly basis, which is used alongside top-down subsector based research and allocation to identify specific stocks to research in depth."

Henderson Industries of the Future

Fund type: OEIC
Launch date: February 1995
Fund size: £77m
Initial charge: 5%
Annual charges: 1.5%
Minimum investment: £1000 lump sum, £50 regular saving
Manager: Tim Dieppe
www.henderson.com/sri

The fund aims to achieve long-term capital appreciation by investing globally in companies that enable an environmentally sustainable and socially responsible economy. The fund actively seeks out companies whose goods, services and technology provide profitable solutions to the world's sustainability challenges. It revolves around ten themes under the rubric *industries of the future*, and these encompass five environmental themes (cleaner energy; efficiency; environmental services; sustainable transport; and water management) and five social themes (health; knowledge; quality of life; safety; and social property and finance). Whilst the emphasis is on seeking out sustainability solution providers, the fund also applies ethical, social, environmental and governance filters in selecting companies and avoids those involved in controversial areas such as tobacco, arms manufacturing and nuclear power, as well as those with irresponsible business practices. The Henderson SRI team has a long and established track record in integrating sustainability, corporate responsibility and ethical factors into asset management, and has been managing SRI funds since 1977.

Manager's comment

"Sustainability is shaping markets: legislation increasingly rewards sustainable practice, technological improvements are cutting costs, and increased environmental and ethical awareness is driving demand for sustainable living. Consequently, those *industries of the future* companies seen to be providing solutions to the problems of today and tomorrow are ideally positioned to benefit from strong growth opportunities. By investing in a diverse range of sustainability themes, the fund spreads the risk of investment across many different companies and sectors, and is thus able to respond to changing economic conditions. The themes we use may change from time-to-time to reflect new research findings and new investment opportunities."

HSBC Global Climate Change Fund

Fund type: Luxembourg-based SICAV
Launch date: November 2007
Fund size: $43.15m
Initial charge: 5.54%
Annual charge: 1.5%
Minimum investment: $5000
Manager: François Dossou
www.assetmanagement.hsbc.com

The fund invests in companies from around the world that are thought to be well placed to benefit from developing solutions to meet the challenges presented by climate change. It aims for long-term capital growth through selecting around 50-70 stocks from the HSBC Global Climate Change Benchmark Index using an active, quantitative process. The fund invests in companies developing activities related to climate change such as alternative energies, water, waste and pollution, energy efficiency, low carbon players and industry transformers.

Manager's comment

"Given that it will take many decades to arrest global warming, HSBC sees climate change as one of the most significant investment themes for the foreseeable future. Companies that are considered best placed to benefit from addressing, combating and developing solutions to the challenges presented by climate change, such as alternative energies and energy efficiency, water, waste and pollution, as well as low carbon players, will continue to benefit from a growing awareness of these issues and the increase in supportive legislation."

Impax Asian Environmental Markets

Fund type: investment trust
Launch date: October 2009
Fund size: £105m
Charges: 1%
Minimum investment: n/a
Manager: Bruce Jenkyn-Jones
www.impax.co.uk

Impax Asian Environmental Markets is a fund listed on the London Stock Exchange. The fund's objective is to enable shareholders to benefit from the expected superior, long-term capital growth of companies active in the environmental sector that are based in the Asia-Pacific region. In managing the fund, Impax will draw on its strong relationship with Ajia Partners, the Asian specialist investment manager based in Hong Kong. The fund manager, Bruce Jenkyn-Jones, is Managing Director at Impax and one of the architects of Impax's listed equity business.

Manager's comment

"We believe that there is a compelling case for investing in Asian environmental stocks. There are many exciting, undervalued companies in the region that are supplying local environmental markets as well as international demand."

Impax Environmental Leaders Fund

Fund type: OEIC
Launch date: March 2008
Fund size: £5.6m
Initial charge: 5%
Annual charge: 1.5%
Minimum investment: £1000
Manager: Bruce Jenkyn-Jones and Simon Gottelier
www.impax.co.uk

The Environmental Leaders Fund invests worldwide, primarily in the stocks of companies that operate in the environmental sector including, without limitation, the stocks of companies that are at the forefront of developing products or services to solve the world's most pressing environmental problems. The fund focuses on three key environmental subsectors: alternative energy and energy efficiency; water treatment and pollution control; and waste technologies and resource management.

Manager's comment

"We launched the Environmental Leaders fund to target the larger, potentially leading companies which have moved into this market recently. Compared to the Environmental Markets fund, they tend to be a lot more liquid and are not pure-play companies. There is less risk, and they tend to have lower tracking errors, but they are still targeted exclusively on the environment and with the same objective of getting share price appreciation from the opportunities in this sector."

Impax Environmental Markets

Fund type: investment trust
Launch date: February 2002
Fund value: £368m
Annual charges: 1%
Minimum investment: n/a
Manager: Bruce Jenkyn-Jones
www.impax.co.uk

The fund's purpose is to enable investors to benefit from the rapid and sustained growth anticipated by Impax in the markets for cleaner or more efficient delivery of basic services of energy, water and waste. Investments are made predominantly in quoted companies which provide, utilise, implement or advise upon technology-based systems, products or services in environmental markets, particularly those of alternative energy and energy efficiency, water treatment and pollution control, and waste technology and resource management. The fund's top ten holdings list illustrates the continued preference for a diversified portfolio, with all sectors (energy, water and waste) and geographical regions (North America, Europe and Asia) represented.

Manager's comment

"We believe that the universe of companies developing and promoting new technologies to address the world's environmental problems is one of the most exciting, dynamic and fastest-growing segments of the global economy. For example, fuel cell technologies offer of more efficient, stable and reliable energy supply for the world's automotive and power industries. Biomass, superconductors, flywheels, photovoltaics, hydrogen technologies and wind turbines are influencing electricity supply across the globe. There are also exciting developments in long-lasting batteries, water purification, reverse vending machines and digestion technologies that will offer compelling value propositions to consumers. As the sector grows and attracts more interest from investors, increased levels of capital are expected to facilitate even faster growth of these companies."

IM WHEB Sustainability Fund

Fund type: OEIC
Launch date: June 2009
Fund size: £14m
Initial charge: 5%
Annual charge: 1.5%
Minimum investment: £3000 lump sum, £50 regular saving
Managers: Nicola Donnelly and Clare Brook
www.whebam.com

The fund's goal is long-term capital growth by investing globally in the most compelling growth themes of the 21st century, which the managers believe are solutions to the problems of climate change, water and an ageing population. Companies need to have at least 30% and rising of their revenues derived from one or more of these themes to be included in the portfolio. Both fund managers have long pedigrees in environmental investment themes. Clare Brook managed Jupiter's Ecology Fund from 1990-1994, which she ran alongside Jupiter's International Green Investment Trust before managing sustainable funds at NPI, Henderson and Morley. Nicola Donnelly has managed sustainable and other funds for over a decade at CIS, UBS and JP Morgan.

Managers' comment

"Investment in renewables is rapidly gathering pace: we see enormous potential in the short to medium term for the wind and photovoltaic sectors, and longer term for concentrated solar power, tidal power and other alternative technologies. The global population is increasing and water usage per capita is growing. Meanwhile, changing weather patterns mean that potable water is increasingly scarce in many parts of the world. We will invest in companies providing solutions to this problem in the form of metering, purification, conservation and supply. The developed world's population is ageing fast; according to the UN's latest population forecast, the median age for all countries is due to rise from 29 now to 38 by 2050. We see this ageing population as fuelling a huge increase for demand in healthcare products and services."

Jupiter Ecology Fund

Fund type: unit trust
Launch date: 1 April 2008
Fund size: £311m
Expense ratio: 1.50%.
Minimum direct investment: £500
Manager: Charlie Thomas
www.jupiteronline.co.uk/PI/Our_Products/Green_Funds/SRI_Funds/J3.htm

The fund's policy is to invest worldwide in companies which demonstrate a positive commitment to the long-term protection of the environment. The fund has rigorous ethical exclusions on the companies that can be invested in, while actively focusing on six green investment themes: clean energy; water management; green transport; waste management; sustainable living; and environmental services. To assist the manager in stock selection, Jupiter's Socially Responsible Investment and Governance team assesses each company's financial prospects and their ethical and environmental performance. Only once they meet these criteria will the manager consider investing. The focus is on companies with proven technology, strong balance sheets and robust business models. Manager Charlie Thomas joined the Jupiter SRI team in 2000 and has been the lead fund manager of both the Jupiter Ecology Fund and Jupiter Green Investment Trust since September 2003.

Manager's comment

"We remain optimistic about the outlook for green investment. The Copenhagen Accord announced at the end of the UN Climate Change Conference in Copenhagen crystallised the policy momentum we had seen at the regional level in the preceding months. We believe the most important initiatives have been taking place at this level and will continue to do so in the immediate future. Our investment thesis is further supported by the approximate $500bn that was pledged by governments around the world for green projects following the financial crisis, of which only around $60bn had been spent by the end of 2009. We are mindful, however, that the fall out from the economic recession, with persistently high unemployment in the West and the growing risk of downgrades for sovereign debt, could lead to some market turbulence in the near term."

Schroders Global Climate Change Fund

Launch date: 28 September 2007
Fund type: OEIC
Fund size: £24.1m
Annual charges: 1.5%
Minimum direct investment: £1000
Managers: Simon Webber and Matthew Franklin
www.schroders.co.uk

The difference that companies can make in addressing the problems of climate change offers a compelling long-term opportunity for today's investors. The fund invests in a wide range of companies, as climate change impacts on virtually every area of the investment universe. Examples are companies that provide renewable energy solutions with solar power, wind power, biofuel, as well as companies that develop low energy light bulbs, hybrid-powered cars, and insulation for commercial and residential use. The fund also seeks opportunities in the agriculture industry, with climate change making it vitally important to improve crop production. These are all long-term investment themes that can benefit investors today.

Manager's comment

"The Schroders' Global Climate Change strategy seeks to generate long-term out-performance through a fundamental, benchmark unconstrained approach to investing in companies benefiting from efforts to accommodate the impact of climate change. The team maintain a proprietary database of companies where the effects of climate change have a significant impact on the long-term investment case. We employ a bottom-up approach, using holding level stock contribution to overall risk as a way of constructing a portfolio that combines efficiently large and small cap stocks.

"We believe that the impact on companies globally of efforts to tackle climate change will become one of the most compelling investment themes over the next 20 years. Climate change will have large financial consequences for most companies, and the policy implications are already broad and far reaching. The competitive landscape is changing, with implications for sales, margins, earnings and valuations. There will be significant variations in the impact on earnings, both intra-country and intra-sector. These impacts are poorly understood, creating an attractive investment opportunity today."

GREEN INDICES & ETFS

3

There are a growing number of specialised indices tracking the performance of companies in environmental technologies. Indices are used extensively by a range of investors such as researchers, fund managers, brokers and so forth for analysis, the measurement of performance, asset allocation, portfolio hedging and so forth. For individual investors they can be useful for researching specific sectors or companies in particular countries. More pertinently, indices are used for the creation of passively managed funds such as trackers and ETFs.

London

FTSE Responsible Investment Indices

www.ftse.com/Indices/

- The **FTSE4Good Index Series** has been designed to measure the performance of companies that meet globally recognised corporate responsibility standards.

- The **FTSE Environmental Technology Index Series** measures the performance of companies from around the world whose core business is in the development and deployment of environmental technologies, including renewable and alternative energy, energy efficiency, water technology, and waste and pollution control. The index requires companies to have at least 50% of their business derived from environmental markets and technologies.

- The **FTSE Environmental Opportunities Index Series** measures the performance of companies around the world that have significant involvement in environmental business activities, including renewable and alternative energy, energy efficiency, water technology, and waste and pollution control. The index requires companies to have at least 20% of their business derived from environmental markets.

- The **FTSE Environmental Markets Index Series** comprises the **FTSE Environmental Technology Index Series** and the **FTSE Environmental Opportunities Index Series**.

- **FTSE4Good Environmental Leaders Europe 40 Index** is designed to identify European companies with leading environmental practices. These are the companies that are doing more to manage their environmental risks and impacts whilst reducing their environmental footprint. The index is constructed by taking all

European companies in the **FTSE4Good Index Series** that have obtained the best practice environmental rating of five, ranking them by full market capitalisation and then selecting the top 40 to be included in the index.

HSBC Global Climate Change Benchmark Index

Developed by CIBM's Global Research team, this is a global reference index that has been designed to track the stock market performance of key companies that are best placed to profit from the challenges presented by climate change.

From this benchmark, HSBC has established four investable climate change indices:

1. **HSBC Climate Change Index**

2. **HSBC Low Carbon Energy Production Index** (including: solar, wind, biofuels and geothermal)

3. **HSBC Energy Efficiency & Energy Management Index** (including: Fuel Efficiency Autos, Energy Efficient Solutions and fuel cells)

4. **HSBC Water, Waste & Pollution Control Index** (including: water recycling, waste technologies and environmental pollution control).

United States

Dow Jones Sustainability Indexes are the first global indexes tracking the financial performance of the leading sustainability driven companies worldwide. Based on the cooperation of Dow Jones Indexes, STOXX Limited and SAM Group they provide asset managers with reliable and objective benchmarks to manage sustainability portfolios. Currently 70 DJSI licences are held by asset managers in 16 countries to manage a variety of financial products including active and passive funds, certificates and segregated accounts. In total, these licensees presently manage close to $6bn based on the DJSI. www.sustainability-index.com

- **Wilderhill New Energy Global Innovation Index (NEX)**: an index of 88 companies listed in 24 exchanges in 19 countries with technologies that focus on the generation and use of cleaner energy, conservation, efficiency and renewable energy. www.nexindex.com

- **S&P Global Clean Energy Index**: an index of 30 companies in ten countries involved with clean energy production, clean energy technology and equipment providers. www2.standardandpoors.com/spf/pdf/index/SP_Global_Clean_Energy_Index_Factsh eet.pdf

- **NASDAQ Clean Edge Green Energy Index (CELS)**: an index of US-listed companies involved in advanced materials, energy intelligence, energy storage and conversion, renewable energy and fuels. www.cleanedge.com/ceindex

- **NASDAQ OMX Clean Edge Global Wind Energy Index**: an index for the global wind energy sector. files.shareholder.com/downloads/NDAQ/0x0x209170/c6188fcb-5aea-489d-8b7b-588593c0ee63/NDAQ_News_2008_6_26_General.pdf

- **ISE Global Wind Energy Index (GWE)**
  www.ise.com/WebForm/options_product_indexDetails.aspx?categoryid=234&header0=true&menu2=true&link2=true&symbol=GWE

- **MAC Global Solar Energy Index (SUNIDX)**: tracks around 25 securities in China, Germany, Norway, Spain, Switzerland and the US. Launched: March 2008. www.macsolarindex.com

- **World Alternative Energy Index (WAEX)**: tracks the world's 20 largest companies operating in the fields of renewable energy, energy efficiency and decentralised energy supply. Operated by Société Générale. Launched: December 2003. www.sgindex.com/services/quotes/details.php?family=4

Germany

ÖkoDAX replicates the performance of the ten biggest companies from the German renewable energy sector. The index universe is linked to the industry group PRIME IG Renewable Energy. All companies from ÖkoDAX are related to the following sub-sectors: solar, wind, water and bioenergy. www.deutsche-boerse.com

South Africa

The Johannesburg Stock Exchange's **Socially Responsible Investment (SRI) Index** was launched in May 2004 in response to the burgeoning global debate around sustainability – particularly in a South African context. www.jse.co.za/about-us/SRI.aspx

Brazil

The Sao Paula stock exchange, Bovespa, launched the **Corporate Sustainability Index (ISE)** in December 2005. ISE is designed to measure the return on a portfolio composed of shares of companies highly committed to social responsibility and corporate sustainability, and also to promote good practices in the Brazilian corporate environment. www.bmfbovespa.com.br/indices/ResumoIndice.aspx?Indice=ISE&Idioma=en-US

Australia

The **ACT Australian Cleantech Index** provides a measure of the performance of the Australian listed stocks in the Cleantech sector. With over 60 companies following under the coverage of the index and with a combined market capitalisation of over $11bn, the index presents a picture of the industry's growth in a single measure. The index is weighted by market capitalisation and is benchmarked against both the S&P/ASX200 and the S&P/ASX Small Ordinaries. www.auscleantech.com.au

Green ETFs

Fund	Launched	Ticker	Tracks	Website
iShares S&P Global Clean Energy	July 2007	LON: INRG	S&P Global Clean Energy Index	www.ishares.co.uk
Lyxor ETF New Energy	March 2008	LON: LNEW	World Alternative Energy Index (WAEX)	www.lyxoretf.co.uk
Invesco PowerShares Global Clean Energy Portfolio	June 2007	LON:PSBW, NYSE: PBD	Wilderhill New Energy Global Innovation Index (NEX)	www.invescopowershares.com/products
Osmosis Climate Solutions Index	February 2010	LON: OCS	Osmosis Climate Solutions Index	www.osmosisim.com
Invesco PowerShares WilderHill Progressive Energy Portfolio	October 2006	NYSE:PUW	WilderHill Progressive Energy Index	www.invescopowershares.com/products
PowerShares Cleantech Portfolio	October 2006	NYSE:PZD	Cleantech Index	www.invescopowershares.com/products
First Trust NASDAQ Green Energy Index Fund	February 2007	NASDAQ:QCLN	NASDAQ Clean Edge Green Energy Index	www.ftportfolios.com

Solar

Fund	Launched	Ticker	Tracks	Website
Claymore/MAC Global Solar Energy Index	March 2008	NYSE: TAN	MAC Global Solar Energy Index (SUNIDX)	www.claymore.com/etf/fund/tan
VanEck Market Vectors Solar Energy	April 2008	NYSE:KWT	Ardour Solar Energy Index (SOLRX)	www.vaneck.com

Wind

Fund	Launched	Ticker	Tracks	Website
Invesco PowerShares Global Wind Energy Portfolio	January 2008	NASDAQ:PWND	NASDAQ OMX Clean Edge Global Wind Energy Index	www.invescopowershares.com/products
First Trust Global Wind Energy	June 2008	NYSE:FAN	ISE Global Wind Energy Index (GWE)	www.ftportfolios.com/Retail/etf/etfsummary.aspx?Ticker=FAN

GREEN PRIVATE EQUITY FIRMS

4

Imperial Innovations

Launch date: 1986
Fund value: £260m
LSE: IVO
www.imperialinnovations.co.uk

Founded in 1986 as a wholly owned subsidiary of Imperial College, Imperial Innovations was one of the first technology transfer offices to be established in Europe. They are now a leading international technology commercialisation company as well as one of the most prolific investors in early stage companies. Their business model combines the activities of technology transfer, company incubation and investment. The company has equity investments in over 80 companies, spread across a range of technologies.

In the energy and environment field these include Ceres Power, Novacem, Quantasol, Evo Electric (see individual directory entries for more detail on these companies) and DUVAS (Differential Ultraviolet Spectrometer System) Technologies Ltd, who have developed a product for rapid air pollution detection and monitoring. In health services, companies include the Acrobot Company, which develops precision surgical systems for minimally invasive orthopaedic surgery; Bioceramic Therapeutics, who are developing smart materials that help the body repair itself; Cell Medica, a transplantation service for virus-specific immune cells; and deltaDOT, who are developing technologies for the separation and analysis of biomolecules. Imperial Innovations has interests in many other companies in IT, software and engineering.

Low Carbon Accelerator

Launch date: October 2006
Fund value: £34m
AIM: LCA
www.lowcarbonaccelerator.com

Low Carbon Accelerator Limited is a closed-end investment company whose objective is to provide shareholders with a return on their investments primarily through significant minority (predominately 25% and above) holdings in a portfolio of unquoted private companies providing low carbon products and services in various sectors, including building, fuels and energy generation. Low Carbon Accelerator is managed by Low Carbon Investors Ltd, whose individual members have over 200 years' aggregate experience in the low carbon sector. This experience is across commercialisation of technology, engineering, energy efficiency, public policy, renewable energy generation, green fuels, fund management, low carbon technology incubation, and managing and implementing projects ranging from £25,000 to £500,000,000 in size. Current holdings include:

- Eco-Solids International, waste-water and sewage sludge treatment technologies

- EnergyMixx, a Swiss holding company investing in renewable energy

- Proven Energy, small scale wind

- Sterling Planet, a US retailer of green power

- RLTec, smart grids; Quantasol

- Lumenenergi, lighting management

- Saddlehorn, community living in Montana

- Vykson, small-scale power generation from low quality landfill gas and other waste fuels

- Vaperma, membrane gas separation systems

Ludgate Environmental Fund

Launch date: August 2007
Fund value: £44m
AIM: LEF
www.ludgateenvironmental.com

Ludgate Environmental Fund Limited aims to deliver capital growth to investors through active investment in a diverse portfolio of holdings in cleantech companies. The fund is a Jersey domiciled closed-end investment company and focuses on the following core areas within the environmental/cleantech sector: waste management and recycling; alternative energy resources; energy efficiency and industrial process advances; emission reduction technologies; and water treatment and management. The fund concentrates mostly on companies in Europe and the UK, although its investments are not geographically restricted.

Principal investments to date include:

- Hydrodec Group PLC (AIM: HYR), specialist oils recycling

- agri.capital, a German biogas company

- Rapid Action Packaging Limited, sustainable food packaging

- New Earth Solutions Group Limited, waste treatment and renewable energy

- Emergya Wind Technologies, wind turbine manufacturing

- STX Services, an Amsterdam-based company specialising in carbon trading

- Renewable Energy Generation (AIM: RWE), UK onshore wind development

- Phoslock Water Solutions Ltd (ASX: PHK), water treatment technology

- Azure Dynamics Corporation (TSX: AZD), electric and hybrid electric drive technology

Oxford Capital

Launch date: 1999
Fund size: £45m
www.oxcp.com

Oxford Capital is a specialist investment manager focused on emerging science and technology. Oxford Capital currently oversees a portfolio of around 30 companies in a range of technology sectors, focusing on three high-growth themes: healthcare, communications and sustainability. It invests across all stages of development, from start-up to IPO and it works with portfolio companies to accelerate them into international markets in Europe, the US, the Middle East and Asia. The company pioneered the use of Enterprise Investment Scheme (EIS) Funds and manages £36m in five Oxford Gateway EIS Funds. Its current fund Oxford Gateway Fund No.5, is open to individuals with a minimum of £25,000 to invest. It also offers the Oxford Gateway Protected IHT Portfolio, which is a lifetime capital growth fund best suited to investors who are looking for a shelter from inheritance tax and for estate planning.

Specialist Energy Group

Launch date: August 2007
Fund value: £3.5m
LON:NVR
www.segroupplc.com

Formerly known as Nviro Cleantech, the company merged with the niche engineering and manufacturing group Southbank plc in January 2010 and the new enlarged group was re-named the Specialist Energy Group. The company has interests in clean fuel technologies, a laser-based air purification device and a microwave-based solution for recycling scrap MDF. It is also developing 'Lab-on-a-Chip', a patented plasma emission detector embedded on a glass microchip.

Triodos Renewable Energy Funds

Launch date: 1996
Fund value: n/a
www.triodos.co.uk

Triodos Renewables plc has been in operation since 1996 and currently owns five wind farms across the UK, with two more due to come on stream in 2010. Once the two new projects (in Wales and East Anglia) start operations, Triodos Renewables will have a combined capacity of 37.7MW. The company recently launched a fifth share issue, with the aim of raising £7m to be invested directly in renewable energy projects (its previous offering in 2008 successfully raised £9.9m). Roughly 97% of Triodos Renewables' asset portfolio is invested in renewable energy-operating projects, with the remaining 3% in early stage developments, joint ventures and investments in new sustainable energy technology. Triodos Renewables is managed by Triodos Bank, Europe's leading ethical bank.

Ventus

Launch date: 2005
Fund value: £50m
www.ventusvct.com

There are three Ventus Funds managed by Climate Change Capital (www.climatechangecapital.com). These are specialist venture capital trusts focused on making investments in the small to medium-sized UK onshore renewable energy sector. Since 2005 the Ventus Funds have invested £50m in over 25 companies, contributing to the delivery of over 1GW of new generating capacity. The company recently issued new shares in Ventus VCT plc, Ventus 2 VCT plc and Ventus 3 VCT plc. The Ventus funds won the Specialist Investment Vehicle of the Year awards in 2009.

RESOURCES IV

D ue to the fast changing nature of the green tech investment sector it is important for investors to keep themselves up to date with news and developments from the sector, as well as using the information in this book. In this part of the book there are lists of websites where you can find additional resources on green finance and investment in general. These include:

- subscription services specialising in cleantech finance

- useful news websites and RSS feeds

- green and ethical banking services

- green microfinance

- green and ethical financial advisors.

Online trading

Online trading platforms

ADVFN: www.advfn.com
Barclays: www.stockbrokers.barclays.co.uk
Fidelity: www.fidelity.co.uk
Hargreaves Lansdown: www.h-l.co.uk
Jarvis Asset Management: www.jarvisim.co.uk
Selftrade: www.selftrade.co.uk
Stocktrade: www.stocktrade.co.uk
TD Waterhouse: www.tdwaterhouse.co.uk
The Share Centre: www.share.co.uk

Fund supermarkets

Fidelity: www.fidelity.co.uk
Funds direct: www.fundsdirect.co.uk
Hargreaves Lansdown: www.h-l.co.uk

Cleantech news sources

Most of the news sources listed below offer RSS feeds, which is probably the best way of keeping up with industry news on your desktop. *Recharge News* and *Renewable Energy*

World both produce printed subscription publications, but offer news by email free. Environmental Finance also offers free weekly emails.

Alternative Energy News: The latest alternative and renewable energy news headlines, syndicated by RSS from a variety of clean energy news sources. You can have separate feeds on energy, biofuels, solar, hydrogen, and so on. www.alternative-energy-news.info

BusinessGreen.com: wide-ranging resource on green business which covers everything from green capital to company news and in-depth analysis. The website also provides companies with information on how to plan and undertake successful green initiatives that both cut costs and enhance the brand values of their organisations. www.businessgreen.com

CleanTechnica: this is another very useful blog with a fresh, up-to-date perspective on the latest trends in cleantech from renewable energy sources to more efficient IT. www.cleantechnica.com

Greentech Media: an online media company providing daily news and market analysis about all aspects of the greentech market. Content is organised via dedicated solar, smart grid and enterprise channels, and includes coverage of other emerging market sectors. With editorial offices in San Francisco, the channel is particularly strong on emerging technologies. Greentech Media also owns GTM Research, which provides market analysis for the energy, environmental, emerging technology, investment banking, information technology and strategic consulting sectors. The company also hosts one-day conferences and two-day summits throughout the year on the greentech market. www.greentechmedia.com

Green Tech: part of the huge CNET news network (owned by CBS), this is another useful site for keeping up to date with global cleantech news stories. news.cnet.com/greentech

Recharge News: top news source for the global renewables industry. Options include a paid subscription to the weekly newspaper which also provides full access to breaking news stories on the website. Alternatively, you can sign-up for a free daily news email. www.rechargenews.com

Renewable Energy World: Founded in 1998 by a group of renewable energy professionals, REW was for a long time the only source of news and information on these sectors. Its network includes RenewableEnergyWorld.com, *Renewable Energy World* magazine, Hydrovision International, *PV World* magazine, and global conferences and expos. www.renewableenergyworld.com

Green business information services

Bloomberg New Energy Finance

Founded in 2004, *New Energy Finance* is the world's leading independent provider of subscription-based news, data and research on clean energy and the carbon markets. It was taken over by Bloomberg in December 2009. New Energy Finance's Insight Services provide deep market analysis to investors in wind, solar, bioenergy, geothermal, carbon capture and storage, energy efficiency, smart grid, nuclear power and traditional energy markets. The company provides dedicated services for each of the major emerging carbon markets: Europe, International (Kyoto), Australia and the US, where it covers the planned regional markets as well as potential federal initiatives, plus the voluntary carbon market. Its Industry Intelligence service provides access to the world's most comprehensive database of investors and investments in clean energy. The New Energy Finance News and Briefing Service is the industry-standard global news service focusing on clean energy investment. The company also undertakes custom research and consultancy and runs high-level networking events.

You can sign-up for free weekly emailed newsletters (*Week in Review* or specialised carbon, water or nuclear headlines). Some research papers and podcasts are also freely accessible. The subscription-only (£1500 per annum) News and Briefing Service includes access to the news archive via a desktop portal, daily news watch (major news stories, market reports and movements in individual clean energy shares) and a monthly briefing which provides an overview of global investment activity and trends. www.newenergymatters.com

Cleantech Investor

Established in 2006, Cleantech Investor is a publisher of finance, investment and business information focused on the fast-growing cleantech space. Their flagship product is *Cleantech* magazine, published six times a year. Features on cleantech themes are combined with news on deals and fundraising in the sector, both on quoted markets and in the private equity/venture capital space. They also publish *Cleantech Infocus*, which offers in-depth industry research with coverage of both quoted and unquoted companies on cleantech industry sectors or themes. In addition, there is *Quoted Cleantech*, which is a monthly electronic newsletter. Subscription to the Cleantech Investor costs £285 per year and includes full access to the website and *Cleantech* magazine (by post and online access). You can also take out a subscription to *Cleantech* magazine only (£95 per year) or to the *Quoted Cleantech* newsletter (£45 per year). www.cleantechinvestor.com

Environmental Finance

Online resource and monthly magazine covering the impact of environmental issues on the lending, insurance, investment and trading decisions affecting industry. The magazine also features a data file of key prices, deals, and indexes, as well as profiles of companies and individuals, the latest people moves, and news and analysis of the biggest environmental stories affecting finance professionals. Free weekly email news service. One year subscription £350; academic/developing countries rate £175. www.environmental-finance.com

Financial information services

Trustnet

Free website with detailed information on the features and benefits of different types of funds. It also provides current and past performance indicators for hundreds of funds. Search under Ethical/Sustainable on the Fund Focuses drop-down menu for facts on green funds. www.trustnet.com

Other useful finance websites

Google finance: www.google.com/ig
The Motley Fool: www.fool.co.uk
Morningstar UK: www.morningstar.co.uk

333

Green and ethical information services

Ethical Investment Research and Information Service (EIRIS)

The Ethical Investment Research and Information Service (www.eiris.org) is an independent, not-for-profit organisation which is a leading global provider of research into corporate environmental, social and governance performance. It has a consumer-oriented website with a funds directory (containing a breakdown of each fund's top holdings, policies, charges, and so forth) and a searchable database of green IFAs. www.yourethicalmoney.org

Ethical Investment Association (EIA)

A branch of UKSIF (see below), the EIA is an association of UK financial advisors dedicated to the promotion of green and ethical investment. It provides a membership directory for green IFAs. www.ethicalinvestment.org.uk

UK Social Investment Forum (UKSIF)

UKSIF promotes sustainable investment and finance and has more than 200 members including financial advisors, asset managers, charities, banks, researchers, pension funds and NGOs. It is responsible for co-ordinating the UK's National Ethical Investment Week (www.neiw.org) and shares a membership directory of green IFAs with the Ethical Investment Association. www.uksif.org

Green and ethical financial advisors

To find an Independent Financial Advisor (IFA) who has some understanding of green and ethical issues there are two main databases, one run by EIRIS and the other shared between the UK Social Investment Forum and the Ethical Investment Association. Members of the UKSIF are required to sign up to a code of conduct and to take part in professional development in the field of green and ethical investment. The EIRIS directory only includes IFAs who meet specific criteria for each financial year (including putting more than £100,000 or more than 40% of their business into ethical funds) or who have passed the UKSIF training course on green and ethical investment. The EIRIS directory is more comprehensive in that it gives IFA's addresses: the UKSIF database only gives a regional breakdown by location such as 'south east' or 'north west', which is not much use if you are looking for an IFA in your home town.

Some of the better known green IFAs are listed below.

Barchester Green

Launched in 1985, Barchester Green is the longest established independent financial advice firm specialising in ethical investment in the UK. In 2008 the business was re-formed as an advisor and employee-owned partnership. Barchester Green is a whole of market, fully independent practice, which means that clients have the choice of paying by commission or by fee. Areas covered include environmental and ethical investments, SIPPS, ISAs, retirement planning, lump sum investment and portfolio management, mortgages, insurance and inheritance tax planning. The company has offices in Bristol, Brighton, Exeter, Salisbury and London. www.barchestergreen.co.uk

Ethical Financial Planning

Established by Andrew Sotiriou, who has been working in financial services for over 24 years, the London-based firm offer a professional service in various areas such as pensions, life assurance, investments and mortgages. The company specialises in ethical investments and provides advice to individuals, charities and companies. www.ethicalfp.ifa-web.co.uk

The Ethical Investors Group

Formed in 1989, Ethical Investors has over 20 years' experience in providing high quality ethical financial advice. As well as helping individuals, charities and businesses with advice, the company is also committed to the development of the ethical financial market and to the development of investments, pensions, ISAs and mortgages which fulfil the financial and ethical needs of clients. Ethical Investors is unusual in that it has a pledge to distribute at least 50% of its own net profit to charities and good causes each year, with the distribution allocated according to clients' votes. Since 1989, the Cheltenham-based company has distributed in excess of £500,000. www.ethicalinvestors.co.uk

The Ethical Partnership

The Ethical Partnership was set up in 1998 as a co-operative and went limited in 2001. The four directors (Jeremy Newbegin, Simon Kirkup, Gregory Braithwaite and Michael Marsden) have accumulated many years of experience in the financial services industry. The group specialises in financial planning linked to ethical and socially responsible investment, and offers both an advisory and execution-only service (through their discretionary portfolio management service). www.the-ethical-partnership.co.uk

The Gaeia Partnership

Brigid Benson, founder of the Gaeia Partnership, is a trailblazer for ethical investment and a past winner of the FT Ethical Investment Advisor of the Year award. The business currently has five partners who can advise on ethical pensions, ethical lump-sum investments, ethical regular savings, green mortgages or general financial advice. They provide services for both individuals and businesses as well as for charities and other organisations. www.gaeia.co.uk

Holden & Partners

Holden & Partners is a wealth management firm who combine financial planning with investment management. The company emphasises personal service; clients include individuals, business owners, trustees and charities, with assets ranging from £100k to £15m. The company is investment focused, with clients' objectives ranging from wealth preservation to the provision of income in retirement. Holden & Partners is at the forefront of the field of climate change investment and publishes an annual *Guide to Climate Change Investment*. www.holden-partners.co.uk

Green and ethical banks

The Co-operative Bank

The Co-operative Bank offers a range of services including high street banking, online banking through its Smile subsidiary (www.smile.co.uk), mortgages, credit cards and loans. Other financial services available from the group include pensions, insurance and unit trusts (see Green Funds). The Co-operative has a long-standing commitment to ethical, environmental and community issues. Its banking division is the only UK clearing bank to publish an ethical policy, which it has been doing since 1992 (since the policy was launched, the Co-op has turned down over £1bn in unsuitable loans). The Co-op has managed retail funds for around 20 years and currently has over £18bn under management: it is the only UK fund manager to also analyse social, ethical, environmental and other company management issues across all its funds (which includes UK Growth, UK Income with Growth, Sustainable Leaders, Sustainable World Trust and Corporate Bond Income Trusts).

The bank also has a pro-active policy to facilitate lending to projects within the renewable energy and carbon reduction sectors. It has a substantial track record in funding a wide range of renewable energy projects, particularly onshore wind, and they have also funded a number of carbon saving schemes deploying state-of-the-art fuel-efficient systems to cut clients' carbon dioxide emissions. As well as having first-hand experience of utilising a number of these technologies to help reduce their own carbon footprint (99% of the group's electricity is from renewable sources), the Co-operative also offers structured funding packages for UK-based renewable energy projects of up to £25m. www.co-operativebank.co.uk

Accounts offered: current, internet, savings, ISAs, student, business, community groups.

Ecology Building Society

Established in 1981, the prime focus of the Ecology Building Society is to promote an ecological approach to the built environment and to foster sustainable communities. Their lending programme covers everything from energy-efficient new residential dwellings to eco-renovations and the promotion of sustainable local building technologies. They also fund small scale ecological industries or businesses (such as recycling, organic farms, local shops) and co-operative living. The society has assets in excess of £60m. www.ecology.co.uk

Accounts offered: Instant, cash ISA, deposit, SIPP deposit.

Triodos Bank

Triodos Bank was established in 1980 in the Netherlands, with a UK office following in 1995, and now has €4.1bn under management. It won Sustainable Bank of the Year at the FT's Sustainable Banking Awards 2009. The bank only finances enterprises creating social, environmental or cultural-added value – ranging from large ethical enterprises to smaller, innovative organisations meeting local needs. Key sectors include organic food and farming, renewable energy, social housing and fair trade. Transparency is a core value: customers are informed about the bank's lending and can target their savings to particular areas of investment.

A range of personal savings accounts is offered and full banking services are available for businesses and charities. One of its most recent products is a Climate Change Bond, which will be used exclusively to finance organisations that actively work against the causes of climate change. The bonds are available for two, three and five years. The bank has also launched a new online tool which offers its customers transparency about the organisations it lends to and invests in; the new 'Know where your money goes' microsite pinpoints every organisation that the bank finances in the UK and Ireland.

The bank's investment arm has pioneered social and environmental investments across the UK and Europe, offering investment opportunities and funds in a range of sustainable business sectors. Triodos has evolved a range of financial services (from loans to venture capital investments) in renewable energy and environmental technologies. It also offers several managed funds (see Private Equity Funds). www.triodos.co.uk

Accounts offered: savings, cash ISAs, climate change bonds, young savers and others.

Green microfinance

There are a number of ways to invest in microfinance, with several organisations working to deliver green energy in developing countries by this means. Microfinance is a method of lending small amounts of money in the developing world to help people out of poverty. It originated with the Grameen Bank ('bank of the villages') which was started in Bangladesh in 1976 by Muhammad Yunus, who later won the Nobel Peace Prize for his work. Since then, microfinance has grown globally and today there are more than 10,000 organisations making small loans (typically under $100) of this type. Critics say that microfinance is not an efficient means of helping poor people, and providing them with loans which benefit the lenders is not a long-term solution. For an understanding of the issues, check the substantial Wikipedia entry (en.wikipedia.org/wiki/Microfinance).

The following organisations provide either microfinance and/or clean and renewable energy services in the developing world:

Acumen Fund: www.acumenfund.org

D.light: www.dlightdesign.com

E+Co: www.eandco.net

Global Exchange for Social Investment (GEXSI): www.gexsi.org

Global Village Energy Partnership (GVEP): www.gvep.org

Grameen Shakti Bank: www.grameen-info.org

Green microfinance: www.greenmicrofinance.org

Solar Electric Light Fund: www.self.org

Additional resources

General

World Energy Council: www.worldenergy.org
World Resources Institute: www.wri.org

Australia

Clean Energy Council of Australian companies: www.cleanenergycouncil.org.au

UK

Centre for Climate Change Economics and Policy: www.cccep.ac.uk
UK Energy Research Centre: www.ukerc.ac.uk

Energy Saving Trust: www.energysavingtrust.org.uk
Energy Technologies Institute: www.energytechnologies.co.uk
Greenpeace climate change solutions: www.greenpeace.org.uk/climate/solutions
Renewable Energy Association: www.r-e-a.net
Renewable Energy Centre: www.therenewableenergycentre.co.uk/wave-and-tidal-power
RenewableUK: www.renewable-manifesto.com
The Carbon Trust: www.carbontrust.co.uk

USA

Business Council for Sustainable Energy: www.bcse.org
Clean Energy 2030 (Google's proposal for reducing US dependency on fossil fuels): knol.google.com/k/jeffery-greenblatt/clean-energy-2030/15x31uzlqeo5n/1#
Earth Policy Institute: www.earth-policy.org
Green Power Partnership: www.epa.gov/greenpower
National Renewable Energy Laboratory: www.nrel.gov
Post Carbon Institute: www.postcarbon.org
Renewable Energy Policy Project: www.repp.org
Rocky Mountain Institute: www.rmi.org
Union of Concerned Scientists: www.ucsusa.org
Worldwatch Institute: www.worldwatch.org

Geothermal power

Alternative Energy News Geothermal Energy: www.alternative-energy-news.info/technology/heating
Geothermal Digest: www.geothermaldigest.net/blog
Geothermal Energy Association (USA): www.geo-energy.org
Geothermal Resource Council (USA): www.geothermal.org
International Geothermal Association: www.geothermal-energy.org

Heat pumps

European Heat Pump Association: www.ehpa.org
Geothermal Exchange Organisation: www.geoexchange.org
International Energy Association (IEA) Heat Pump Centre: www.heatpumpcentre.org
International Ground Source Heat Pump Association: www.igshpa.okstate.edu

Hydrogen and fuel cells

International Partnership for Hydrogen and Fuel Cells in the Economy: www.iphe.net

UK

Fuel Cell Markets: www.fuelcellmarkets.com
Fuel Cell Today: www.fuelcelltoday.com
Fuel Cells UK: www.fuelcellsuk.org
UK Hydrogen Association: www.ukha.org

USA

American Hydrogen Association: www.clean-air.org
Fuel Cells 2000: www.fuelcells.org

Hydrogen Energy Centre: www.hydrogenenergycenter.org
National Hydrogen Association: www.hydrogenassociation.org
National Fuel Cell Research Center: www.nfcrc.uci.edu/2/default.aspx
US Fuel Cell Council: www.usfcc.com

Canada

National Research Council of Canada Institute for Fuel Cell Innovation:
www.nrc-cnrc.gc.ca/ifci-iipc

Australia

Fuel Cell Institute of Australia: www.fuelcells.org.au

Germany

German Hydrogen and Fuel Cell Association (DWV): www.dwv-info.de

Marine and tidal

European Marine Energy Centre: www.emec.org.uk
Foundation for Ocean Renewables: www.foroceanrenewable.typepad.com

Power storage

Electricity Storage Association: www.electricitystorage.org/about.htm
Global Energy Network Institute (GENI): www.geni.org
Smartmeters.com: www.smartmeters.com
UK Energy Retail Association smart meters campaign:
www.energy-retail.org.uk/smartmeters.html

Europe

EU smart grids programme: www.smartgrids.eu

USA

Alliance to Save Energy: www.ase.org
American Council for an Energy-Efficient Economy: www.aceee.org
Demand Response and Smart Grid Coalition: www.drsgcoalition.org
Electric Power Research Institute's Intelligrid:
my.epri.com/portal/server.pt?open=512&objID=386&mode=2
Global Energy Network Institute: www.geni.org
GridWise Alliance: www.gridwise.org

Australia

Smart Grid Australia: www.smartgridaustralia.com.au/index.php?page=about

Solar power

Concentrator Photovoltaics Consortium: www.cpvconsortium.org
CSP Today: social.csptoday.com/index.php

European Photovoltaic Industry Association (EPIA): www.epia.org
Solar Buzz: www.solarbuzz.com
Solar Energy Industries Association: www.seia.org
SolarPlaza: www.solarplaza.com

Wind Power

American Wind Energy Association: www.awea.org
British Wind Energy Association: www.bwea.com
European Wind Energy Association: www.ewea.org
Global Wind Energy Council: www.gwec.net
Wind Power Works: www.windpowerworks.net

Waste management

Campaign for Real Recycling: www.realrecycling.org.uk
Letsrecycle.com: www.letsrecycle.com
Recycling & Waste World: www.recyclingwasteworld.co.uk
Waste Resources Action Programme (WRAP): www.wrap.org.uk

Magazines and newsletters

Environmental News Network: www.enn.com
Green Energy News: www.green-energy-news.com
Greenjobs: www.greenjobs.com/public/index.aspx
International Sustainable Energy Review: www.internationalsustainableenergy.com
New Energy Focus: www.newenergyfocus.com
Renewable Energy World: www.renewableenergyworld.com/rea/home
Windpower Monthly: www.windpower-monthly.com

Research and consultancy

Frost & Sullivan: www.frost.com/prod/servlet/frost-home.pag
iSuppli: www.isuppli.com
Kleiner Perkins Caufield & Byers: www.kpcb.com
Photon Consulting: www.photonconsulting.com
Prometheus Institute: www.prometheus.org
NanoMarkets: www.nanomarkets.net

REFERENCES

[1] Will Oulton (ed.), *Investment Opportunities for a Low Carbon World* (GMB Publishing 2009), p.xxi.

[2] *Quoted Cleantech* newsletter, www.cleantechinvestor.com/portal/qc-editors-message/5063-emqcjan10.html [subscription required] (January 2010).

[3] James Murray, '2010 – The beginning of the end for green businesses', *BusinessGreen*, www.businessgreen.com/business-green/comment/2255496/2010-beginning-green-businesses (31 December 2009).

[4] Carl Krosinsky and Nick Robins (eds), *Sustainable Investing: The Art of Long-Term Performance* (Earthscan Publications Ltd, 2008), p.4.

[5] Damian Kahya, 'Copenhagen Fails Green Investors', *BBC News* (22 December 2009).

[6] Renewables Global Status Report 2009 Update, www.ren21.net/pdf/RE_GSR_2009_Update.pdf (2009).

[7] 'Clean Energy Shares Recover Ground in 2009', Bloomberg New Energy Finance press release (6 January 2010).

[8] Robin Pagnamenta, 'Watchdog warns of $500bn annual cost of delaying action on climate change', *The Times* (11 November 2009).

[9] Jill Insley, 'Co-op fund sees world of opportunity', *Observer* (27 July 2009).

[10] Holden & Partners 3rd annual Climate Change Investment Guide, www.holden-partners.co.uk (September 2009).

[11] Sarah Pennells, *Green Money: How to Save and Invest Ethically* (A&C Black, 2009), p.13.

[12] Holden & Partners 3rd annual *Climate Change Investment Guide*, www.holden-partners.co.uk (December 2009).

[13] Ron Pernick and Clint Wilder, *The Cleantech Revolution* (Collins Business, 2008), p.xvii.

[14] Matthew J. Kiernan, *Investing in a Sustainable World: Why Green is the New Color of Money on Wall Street* (Amacom 2009), p.222.

[15] Jim Slater, *The Zulu Principle* (Harriman House, 2008), p.33.

[16] Travis Bradford, *Solar Revolution: The Economic Transformation of the Global Energy Industry* (MIT Press, 2006), p.20.

[17] George Johnson, 'Plugging into the Sun', *National Geographic* (September 2009, vol. 216, no. 3).

[18] Richard Asplund, *Profiting from Clean Energy* (John Wiley, 2008), p.123.

[19] 'The United States PV Market: Project Economics, Policy, Demand, and Strategy Through 2013', *GTM Research*, www.gtmresearch.com/report/the-united-states-pv-market-project-economics-policy-demand-and-strategy (December 2009).

[20] Karl-Erik Stromsta, 'Algeria to build $100m solar factory as Desertec beckons', www.rechargenews.com/energy/solar/article199732.ece (23 November 2009).

[21] 'Desertec attracts heavyweight support, but also serious concerns', *New Energy Finance* (vol. v, issue 29, September 2009), p.15.

[22] Joseph Berwind, *Investing in Solar Stocks* (McGraw Hill, 2009), p.259.

[23] Ashley Seager, 'Solar Future Brightens as oil soars by', *Guardian* (16 June 2008).

[24] 'Solar Could supply 12% of EU Electricity by 2020', *Renewable Energy World* (5 September 2008).

[25] Matthias Fawer, 'Solar Energy – Technologies and Markets', Bank Sarasin in *Investment Opportunities for a Low Carbon World* (GMB Publishing, 2009), p.29.

[26] Zachary Shahan, 'Thin-Film Solar Panels to Double their Share of the Market by 2013?', Cleantechnica.com (12 November 2009).

[27] Glen Allen, 'NanoMarkets predicts that thin-film solar cell industry will produce more than 26 gigawatts by 2015', *Renewable Energy World* (7 July 2008).

[28] Ucilia Wang, 'Sharp Guns for US Thin-Film Market', Greentech Media (14 October 2008).

[29] 'The parabolic trough power plants Andasol 1 to 3', Solar Millennium report. www.solarmillennium.de/upload/Download/Technologie/eng/Andasol1-3engl.pdf (December 2008)

[30] Emma Ritch, 'Cleantech Group picks winners and losers in concentrated solar thermal', www.cleantech.com (30 October 2008).

[31] 'The Global Concentrated Solar Power industry report 2010-2011', Csp Today and Altran, (23 November 2009).

[32] 'With Spain at the Epicenter, Global Concentrated Solar Power Industry to Reach 25GW by 2020', *Emerging Energy Research*, www.emerging-energy.com (28 April 2009).

[33] Siemens press release, 'Siemens to decisively strengthen its position in the growth market solar thermal power', www.siemens.com/press/en/pressrelease/?press=/en/pressrelease/2009/renewable_energy/ere20091013.htm (15 October 2009).

[34] Ben Backwell, 'Bright Outlook for CSP', *Recharge News* (29 May 2009).

[35] Vinod Khosla, 'Scalable Electric Power from Solar Energy', Breaking the Climate Deadlock Briefing Paper (The Climate Group, 2008), p.7.

[36] Mark Chediak and Alex Morales, 'Areva Says Solar Thermal Market May Increase 30-Fold by 2020', Bloomberg (9 February 2010.)

[37] Nancy Hartsoch, 'Concentrator PV: Harvesting More, Spending Less', *Renewable Energy World* (8 September 2009). www.renewableenergyworld.com/rea/news/article/2009/09/concentrator-pv-harvesting-more-spending-less

[38] Garrett Hering, 'Concentrating PV: Window Closing for CPV start-ups,' *Photon International* (August 2009).

[39] Hartsoch, 'Concentrator PV'.

[40] 'CPV: New Applications and Emerging Markets', 2010 Technology and Market Analysis, GTM Research www.gtmresearch.com/report/cpv-technology-and-market-analysis-2009 (November 2009).

[41] Jennifer Runyon, 'Researchers Explore Hybrid Concentrated Solar Energy System', *Renewable Energy World*, www.renewableenergyworld.com/rea//news/article/2008/11/researchers-explore-hybrid-concentrated-solar-energy-system-53981 (3 November 2008).

[42] Ron Pernick and Clint Wilder, *The Cleantech Revolution* (Collins Business, 2008), p.75.

[43] James Kanter, 'A Record for Wind in Ireland', greeninc.blogs.nytimes.com/2009/08/11/a-record-for-wind-in-ireland (11 August 2009).

[44] 'Spanish wind power capacity reaches 18 GW in 2009', www.rechargenews.com/energy/wind/article202124.ece (7 January 2010).

[45] Jeff Siegel, *Investing in Renewable Energy: Making Money on Green Chip Stocks*, (Angel Publishing, 2008), p.56.

[46] 'Indian Wind Energy Outlook 2009', Global Wind Energy Council (GWEC) and Indian Wind Turbine Manufacturers Association (IWTMA), www.gwec.net/index.php?id=30&no_cache=1&tx_ttnews[pointer]=3&tx_ttnews[tt_news]=223&tx_ttnews[backPid]=97&cHash=d4289f26ae (9 September 2009).

[47] Sarah Azau and Chris Rose, 'Looking into the Future: Wind Energy in 2020 and beyond' , *Wind Directions*, vol. 28, no. 6, www.ewea.org (December 2009), p.18.

[48] James Kanter, 'A Record for Wind in Ireland', greeninc.blogs.nytimes.com/2009/08/11/a-record-for-wind-in-ireland (11 August 2009).

[49] 'U.S. Wind Energy Breaks All Records, Installs nearly 10,000MW in 2009', www.awea.org/newsroom/releases/01-26-10_AWEA_Q4_and_Year-End_Report_Release.html (26 January 2010).

[50] 'DOE to help fund large wind turbine drivetrain test facility', Recharge News www.rechargenews.com/energy/wind/article199801.ece (November 2009)

[51] 'The International Offshore Wind Market to 2020', ODS-Petrodata, www.ods-petrodata.com/renewables (September 2009).

[52] 'Capturing the massive wind resource in Europe's seas', Wind Power Works case studies, www.windpowerworks.net/12_case_studies/burbo_bank_united_kingdom.html

[53] *Wind Directions*, vol. 28, no. 6, www.ewea.org (December 2009).

[54] 'European offshore wind power market grew 54% in 2009', www.ewea.org/index.php?id=60&no_cache=1&tx_ttnews[tt_news]=1784&tx_ttnews[backPid]=259&cHash=7b7ca63b59 (January 2010).

[55] Terry Macalister, 'Renewable energy? It's an offshore thing', *Guardian*, (5 October 2009) www.guardian.co.uk/business/2009/oct/05/wind-farms-north-sea

[56] 'European governments feel the heat on offshore wind', *New Energy Finance* (22 September 2009).

[57] David Biello, 'China's Big push for renewable energy', *Scientific American* (4 August 2008).

[58] 'Global Wind Energy Outlook 2008', Global Wind Energy Council, p. 9. www.gwec.net/index.php?id=92

[59] Rikki Stancich, 'Offshore wind turbine technology: Harnessing the Saudi Arabia of wind', Wind Energy Update, social.windenergyupdate.com/qa/offshore-wind-turbine-technology-harnessing-saudi-arabia-wind (13 October 2009)

[60] 'Location location, location: Domestic small-scale wind field trial report', Energy Saving Trust, www.energysavingtrust.org.uk/Global-Data/Publications/Location-location-location-The-Energy-Saving-Trust-s-field-trial-report-on-domestic-wind-turbines (9 July 2009).

[61] *Small Wind Systems UK Market Report 2009*, www.bwea.com/pdf/small/BWEA%20SWS%20UK%20Market%20Report%202009.pdf (22 April 2009).

[62] AWEA Small Wind Turbine Global Market Study, www.awea.org/smallwind/pdf/09_AWEA_Small_Wind_Global_Market_Study.pdf (5 May 2009).

[63] Will Oulton (ed.), *Investment Opportunities for a Low Carbon World* (GMB Publishing, 2009), p.48.

[64] 'The World Wave and Tidal Market Report 2009-2013', Douglas Westwood www.dw-1.com (2009).

[65] 'Forecasting the Future of Ocean Power', GTM Research, www.gtmresearch.com/report/forecasting-the-future-of-ocean-power (6 October 2008).

[66] Carbon Trust. www.carbontrust.co.uk

[67] Alasdair Cameron, 'An Update on Marine Renewable Energy in Britain', *Renewable Energy World* (12 January 2010).

[68] Jack Uldrich, *Green Investing* (Adams Media, 2008).

[69] Chris Goodall, *Ten Technologies to Save the Planet* (Profile Books, 2008).

[70] Jeff Siegel, *Investing in Renewable Energy – Making Money on Green Chip Stocks* (John Wiley, 2008).

[71] 'The Future of Geothermal Energy: Impact of Enhanced Geothermal Systems on the United States in the 21st Century', geothermal.inel.gov (MIT, 2006).

[72] Peter Fairley, 'Using CO2 to Extract Geothermal Energy: Carbon dioxide captured from power plants could make geothermal energy more practical', www.technologyreview.com/energy/23953, (16 November 2009).

[73] 'Hot Prospect – Geothermal Electricity Set for Rift Valley Lift-Off in 2009 Poznan', www.unep.org/Documents.Multilingual/Default.asp?DocumentID=553&ArticleID=60 17&l=en, (9 December 2008).

[74] Dan Jennejohn, 'U.S. Geothermal Power Production and Development Update', Geothermal Energy Association www.geo-nergy.org/GEA_January_Update_Special_Edition_Final.pdf, (January 2010).

[75] DOE press release: 'Department of Energy Awards $338 Million to Accelerate Domestic Geothermal Energy', www.energy.gov/8233.htm, (29 October 2009).

[76] 'Hot Prospect – Geothermal Electricity Set for Rift Valley Lift-Off in 2009 Poznan', www.unep.org/Documents.Multilingual/Default.asp?DocumentID=553&ArticleID=60 17&l=en,(9 December 2008).

[77] John Rubino, *Clean Money: Picking Winners in the Green-tech Boom* (John Wiley, 2009), p.70.

[78] 'Alternative Power: Ranking Battery Companies on the Lux Innovation Grid', *CNET News* news.cnet.com/8301-11128_3-10308058-54.html?tag=mncol (12 August 2009).

[79] 'Alliance Formed to Manufacture Advanced Automotive Batteries in the U.S', National Alliance for Advanced Transportation Batteries press release, naatbatt.org/news/alliance-formed-to-manufacture-advanced-automotive-batteries-in-the-us, (18 December 2008).

[80] In Focus: Battery Technology. www.cleantechninvestor.co.uk, (July 2009).

[81] Richard Apslund, *Profiting from Clean Energy* (John Wiley, 2008), p.251.

[82] Premium Power, www.premiumpower.com/company.php

[83] 'Bridging the Gap with Supercapacitors: a Tale of Two Markets', www.luxresearchinc.com

[84] 'What Is the Cheapest Energy Storage Idea of Them All?', Greentech Media, www.greentechmedia.com/articles/read/what-is-the-cheapest-energy-storage-of-them-all, (5 June 2009).

[85] 'Compressed Air Energy Storage State-of-Science', Electric Power Research Institute my.epri.com/portal/server.pt?Abstract_id=000000000001020444 (27 October 2009)

[86] David L. Chandler, 'Liquid battery big enough for the electric grid?', *MIT News*, web.mit.edu/newsoffice/2009/liquid-battery.html, (19 November 2009).

[87] John Rubino, *Clean Money: Picking Winners in the Green-Tech Boom* (John Wiley 2009), p.130.

[88] 'Cisco Outlines Strategy for Highly Secure, "Smart Grid" Infrastructure', newsroom.cisco.com/dlls/2009/prod_051809.html, (18 May 2009).

[89] www.marketresearch.com/vendors/viewVendor.asp?VendorID=2702

[90] 'Smart Grid: China Leads Top Ten Countries in Smart Grid Federal Stimulus Investments', Zpryme Reports, www.prurgent.com/2010-01-27/pressrelease75088.htm, (27 January 2010).

[91] 'Global Smart-Meter Installations to Reach 250 Million Units', Environmental Leader, www.environmentalleader.com/2009/11/02/global-smart-meter-installations-to-reach-250-million-units, (2 November 2009).

[92] Report summary of 'Smart Metering in Western Europe – 6th Edition', Berg Insight, www.berginsight.com/ReportPDF/ProductSheet/bi-sm6-ps.pdf, (1 June 2009)

[93] 'Taiwan set to make grand entrance into smart metering', www.smartmeters.com/the-news/660-taiwan-set-to-make-grand-entrance-into-smart-metering.html, (15 October 2009).

[94] US Department of Energy, Office of Electricity Delivery and Energy Reliability, www.oe.energy.gov/hts.htm

[95] Stephen Kennett, 'Will it ever take off? Hydrogen fuel cell technology', Building www.building.co.uk/story.asp?sectioncode=331&storycode=3138420 (17 April 2009).

[96] 'Carbon Trust launches UK Bid for breakthrough in fuel cell technology', press release, www.carbontrust.co.uk/news/news/press-centre/2009/Pages/carbon-trust-launches-uk-bid.aspx (9 October 2009).

[97] Andrew Hore, 'AIM cleantech recovery lags wider market', quoted *Cleantech* (10 January 2010).

[98] 'Carbon Trust Launches UK Bid for breakthrough in fuel cell technology', Press release, www.carbontrust.co.uk/news/news/press-centre/2009/Pages/carbon-trust-launches-uk-bid.aspx (9 October 2009).

[99] Jack Uldrich, *Green Investing: A Guide to Making Money through Environment-Friendly Stocks* (Adams Media, 2008), p.199.

[100] Margot Hornblower, 'Geoffrey Ballard: In a Hurry to Prove the "Pistonheads" Wrong', *Time* Magazine (8 March 1999).

[101] 'Joint Press Release of Linde, Daimler, EnBW, NOW, OMV, Shell, Total and Vattenfall: Initiative "H2 Mobility" – Major companies sign up to hydrogen infrastructure built-up plan in Germany', www.pr-inside.com/joint-press-release-of-linde-daimler-r1474350.htm (10 September 2009).

[102] 'Honda, GM Stick to Fuel-Cell Plans as Obama Guts Hydrogen Funds', Alan Ohnsman and Tina Seeley. www.bloomberg.com/apps/news?pid=newsarchive&sid=abc.hrgl1DPQ (11 May 2009).

[103] Gerard Wynn, 'Sweet dreams are made of geo-engineering', Reuters www.reuters.com/article/GCA-GreenBusiness/idUSTRE58202P20090903?pageNumber=1&virtualBrandChannel=10522 (3 September 2009).

[104] Tim Chapman, 'EV Investment Accelerates', Cleantech Infocus Electric Vehicles, www.cleantechinvestor.com/portal/cleantech-infoucs-publications/1094-infocev/3501-evdec09.html, (December 2009), p17.

[105] Jeff Asplund, *Profiting from Clean Energy* (John Wiley, 2008), p.249.

[106] 'Cleantech Infocus: Electric Vehicles', *Cleantech Investor* (December 2009).

[107] John Rubino, *Clean Money: Picking Winners in the Green-Tech Boom* (John Wiley, 2009), p.81.

[108] Sebastian Blanco, 'Green Car Summit: all hands (almost) on deck for electric vehicles', green.autoblog.com/2010/01/26/green-car-summit-all-hands-almost-on-deck-for-electric-vehicl (26 January 2010).

[109] 'Biofuels 2010: Spotting the Next Wave', www.gtmresearch.com/report/biofuels-2010-spotting-the-next-wave (7 December 2009).

[110] Danny Fortson, 'Buildings face carbon clean-up', *The Sunday Times* (3 May 2009).

[111] 'Green Building Council to launch training programmes', BusinessGreen, www.businessgreen.com (28 August 2009).

[112] 'New Study: Green Building to Support Nearly 8 Million U.S. Jobs Over Next 4 Years', US Green Building Council, www.usgbc.org/Docs/News/Green%20building,%20green%20jobs%20and%20the%20economy%20-%20Booz%20Allen%20report%20GS.pdf (11 November 2009).

[113] John Rubino, *Clean Money: Picking Winners in the Green-Tech Boom* (John Wiley, 2009), p.156.

[114] 'Transforming the Market: Energy Efficiency in Buildings World Council for Business Development', www.wbcsd.org/DocRoot/HtQXNjP1wUMPVlnQDmDx/91719_EEBReport_WEB.pdf (21 April 2009).

[115] Tim Mullaney and Mariko Yasu, 'Panasonic Will Invest $1 Billion in "Green Home" Plan', Bloomberg, www.bloomberg.com/apps/news?pid=20601101&sid=ajhto3eO4fpM (2 December 2009).

[116] Jon Mainwaring, 'Energy Efficiency Solutions' *Cleantech Investor*, Volume 3, issue 4 (July 2009), p.26.

[117] Will Oulton (ed.), *Investment Opportunities for a Low Carbon World* (GMB Publishing, 2009), p.111.

[118] 'Facts About The Solid State Lighting Industry', Next Generation Lighting Industry Alliance, www.nglia.org/documents/NGLIA%20Fact%20Sheet%20August%202009.pdf (20 August 2009)

[119] David Stevenson, 'The Great Light Hope for green energy', *MoneyWeek* (11 December 2009).

[120] 'High-Brightness LED Market Review and Forecast – 2009', Strategies Unlimited su.pennnet.com/press_display.cfm?ARTICLE_ID=369132 (14 September 2009).

[121] 'LED and OLED technologies open up new growth markets', Osram press release, www.osram.com/osram_com/News/Business_Financial_Press/2009/091221_PM_Led.jsp (21 December 2009).

[122] John Rubino, *Clean Money: Picking Winners in the Green-Tech Boom* (John Wiley, 2009), p.184.

[123] 'Private equity-backed waste energy company to build Scottish biogas plant', www.newenergyworldnetwork.com/renewable-energy-news/by_technology/biofuel_biomass/private-equity-backed-waste-energy-company-to-build-scottish-biogas-plant.html, (27 January 2009)

[124] Matthew Kiernan, *Investing in a Sustainable World* (AMACOM, 2009), p.116.

INDEX

Directory entries in **bold**.